CO 1 60 98452 E

CW00758540

A Victorian Wanderer

The Life of Thomas Arnold the Younger

Thomas Arnold the younger, 1870s

A Victorian Wanderer

The Life of Thomas Arnold the Younger

BERNARD BERGONZI

OXFORD
UNIVERSITY PRESS

OXFORD
UNIVERSITY PRESS

Great Clarendon Street, Oxford OX2 6DP

Oxford University Press is a department of the University of Oxford.
It furthers the University's objective of excellence in research, scholarship,
and education by publishing worldwide in

Oxford New York

Auckland Bangkok Buenos Aires Cape Town Chennai
Dar es Salaam Delhi Hong Kong Istanbul Karachi Kolkata
Kuala Lumpur Madrid Melbourne Mexico City Mumbai Nairobi
São Paulo Shanghai Taipei Tokyo Toronto

Oxford is a registered trade mark of Oxford University Press
in the UK and in certain other countries

Published in the United States
by Oxford University Press Inc., New York

© Bernard Bergonzi 2003

The moral rights of the author have been asserted
Database right Oxford University Press (maker)

First published 2003

All rights reserved. No part of this publication may be reproduced,
stored in a retrieval system, or transmitted, in any form or by any means,
without the prior permission in writing of Oxford University Press,
or as expressly permitted by law, or under terms agreed with the appropriate
reprographics rights organization. Enquiries concerning reproduction
outside the scope of the above should be sent to the Rights Department,
Oxford University Press, at the address above

You must not circulate this book in any other binding or cover
and you must impose this same condition on any acquirer

British Library Cataloguing in Publication Data
Data available

Library of Congress Cataloging in Publication Data
Data available

ISBN 0–19–925741–8

1 3 5 7 9 10 8 6 4 2

Typeset by Regent Typesetting, London
Printed in Great Britain
on acid-free paper by
Biddles Ltd,
Guildford and King's Lynn

DURHAM COUNTY COUNCIL Cultural Services	
C016098452	
BfS	24 Jun 2003
B ARNOLDT	

For Anne

In each land the sun does visit
We are gay whate'er betide;
To give space for wand'ring is it
That the world was made so wide.

From Thomas Carlyle's translation of Goethe's
Wilhelm Meisters Wanderjahre

I think I shall bless God through all eternity for having brought me
to your doors last Monday, and for the charity with which you received a wanderer for whom there was so little excuse . . .

Thomas Arnold the Younger to John Henry Newman,
20 October 1876

Contents

List of Illustrations

List of Abbreviations

See the Bibliography for further details

BC, followed by box number	Thomas Arnold papers, Balliol College
BP	Benison family papers
JHN	*Letters and Diaries of John Henry Newman*
L	*Letters of Thomas Arnold the Younger*
MA	*Letters of Matthew Arnold*
MW	Mrs Humphry Ward, *A Writer's Recollections*
NZL	*New Zealand Letters of Thomas Arnold the Younger*
TA	Thomas Arnold, *Passages in a Wandering Life*

Introduction

The subject of this book can be conveniently identified as Matthew Arnold's Catholic younger brother. Readers who know of the Arnolds as one of the famous professional families of Victorian England will be aware that Matthew had brothers; several in fact. Rather fewer are likely to have known that one of them became a Catholic under the influence of John Henry Newman, like many of his contemporaries in the middle decades of the nineteenth century. Tom Arnold, though, wore his Catholicism with a difference; after some years he reverted to Anglicanism (though never moving very far from Catholic beliefs), then finally returned to the Catholic Church. Each of these shifts was the product of a spiritual crisis which involved physical displacement and a family upset.

Tom Arnold was the brother of one famous man and the son of another, the elder Thomas Arnold, the redoubtable headmaster of Rugby. One of his daughters became the best-selling novelist Mrs Humphry Ward, and another married Thomas Huxley's son and was the mother of Julian and Aldous Huxley. Tom Arnold knew many of the famous people of the day. They included the elderly Wordsworth, and Arthur Hugh Clough, who was his closest friend. Among the Catholics, he had a close but sometimes difficult relationship with Newman, and he contributed to Lord Acton's liberal Catholic magazines. When he lived in Oxford in the 1870s he was familiar with such ornaments of the academic scene as Benjamin Jowett, Mark Pattison, and Lewis Carroll. In his later career, as a professor in Dublin, he was a colleague of Gerard Manley Hopkins, and in the last year of his life he read and approved an undergraduate essay by James Joyce.

Tom Arnold thought of himself as a wanderer in both spiritual and physical terms, and he identified with Goethe's Wilhelm Meister. His physical movements across the globe gave his life a different shape from that of most Victorian intellectuals. After a distinguished undergraduate career at Oxford and a year or two of unsatisfying work in the Colonial Office in London, he took himself off to New Zealand, where he failed in his original unrealistic ambition of becoming a farmer and turned to teaching. In 1850 he crossed the Tasman Sea to Tasmania, or Van

Diemen's Land, as it was then known, and embarked on a successful career as director of education and inspector of schools. The colony had been largely settled by convicts and the ugly practice of transportation was in its final phase when Arnold arrived.

His conversion to Catholicism forced his return to England, and the rest of his life was divided between Dublin, Birmingham, Oxford, London, and Dublin again; the Arnold family home in the Lake District provided a place of repose to which he returned when he could. Tom and Matthew were always close, but Tom lacked the intellectual distinction and sense of the way the world was going which gave his brother a special place in the life of the time; nevertheless, he was a clever man with wide interests. He wrote extensively on literature, history, and religion; he was one of the first professors of English in the British Isles and a pioneer Anglo-Saxon scholar who translated and edited *Beowulf.* But if I have found his life worth writing it was not simply because of the people and places he knew, nor of what he wrote or did, but because he was a fascinating personality in his own right. With the Celtic good looks that came from his mother's family, his stammer, his earnestness, his constant lack of funds, and the vacillating habits that were an exasperation to his family and friends (though when he did make his mind up he did so very firmly), Tom Arnold has some of the qualities of a character in a Victorian novel; not a central figure, but one of those lesser characters whom one would like to see more of.

He was affected by many of the issues of his age but his response to them was individual and unexpected. His personal life was intense and sometimes painful. In Van Diemen's Land he married Julia Sorell, a beautiful and hot-tempered member of a distinguished but louche local family. It was a love-match and remained so, but it was subjected to frequent crises by Julia's hatred of Catholicism, which drove them to live apart in the end. After her death from cancer in 1888, Tom married Josephine Benison, whom he had known as a friend for many years; she was a Catholic convert from an Irish Ascendancy family who seems to have long been in love with him.

One difficulty in writing about Tom Arnold is in knowing how to refer to him. I dislike the assumed intimacy which causes a biographer habitually to call a subject by his or her Christian name, but to refer to 'Arnold' throughout is likely to cause confusion with Matthew, and occasionally with some other member of the family. And much of my discussion deals with him in the context of his family, where he was always 'Tom'. In the event I have adopted a rather unsatisfactory compromise, by referring to him as 'Tom' when he is among people who would have addressed him in that way, and 'Arnold' in other contexts, as when he was dealing with Acton and Newman and other professional acquaintances, where there is no likelihood of him being confused with Matthew. But I fear I have not been altogether consistent.

Acknowledging indebtedness is a pleasure in the present context. Formal acknowledgements are set out below, but I want to say now how much this book owes to published collections of letters. There are the volumes of Tom Arnold's letters, edited in an exemplary fashion by the late James Bertram; and magnificent editions of the two eminent Victorians with whom he was intimate: John Henry Newman's *Letters and Diaries* in many volumes, edited by the late C. S. Dessain and others; and the *Letters of Matthew Arnold*, edited by Cecil Y. Lang, which appeared in six volumes between 1996 and 2001, admirably timed for my purposes. I should like to express particular thanks to Matthew Arnold's descendant and literary trustee, Frederick Whitridge, who has enthusiastically supported this project and has kindly permitted me to print an unpublished letter from Matthew to Tom in an appendix.

The Thomas Arnold papers at Balliol College, Oxford, have been a rich source, and I am grateful to the Master and Fellows of the College and to Tom Arnold's great-granddaughter, Mrs Janet Davies, for permission to quote from them. I have drawn considerably on the papers of the Benison family, now in the possession of Mrs Harriet Bennett. They include both sides of the correspondence over many years between Tom Arnold and Josephine Benison, which is informative about his personal life and beliefs. My discovery of the Benison papers makes a story in itself, rather like one of Henry James's tales of literary life (though with a more positive outcome than they tend to have). James Bertram referred to them in his edition of Tom Arnold's *Letters* in 1980; he had seen them but was not able to include any in his edition. My attempts to find their present whereabouts proved unavailing until quite by chance John Fuller told me where they were; he had examined them in the course of writing a study of an older member of the Arnold family, though they were of no use for his purposes. I wrote to their owner, Mrs Susan Ward (no relation to Tom's daughter and son-in-law) and received a cordial response, inviting me to call at her house in Suffolk and examine them. I agreed to do so in due course; then a month or so later I had a phone call from her daughter, Mrs Bennett, to say that her mother had suddenly died. This was distressing and disconcerting news, but Mrs Bennett assured me that once her personal and domestic affairs were in order she would be happy to continue the co-operation that Mrs Ward had started. And so it has proved; Mrs Bennett kindly let me have the papers on a long loan, and has given me permission to quote from letters and reproduce photographs. I am deeply grateful to all three people.

I first became aware of Tom Arnold in the 1970s, when I was writing a short biography of his professorial colleague Gerard Hopkins; my brief remarks there repeated some of the misinformation which has commonly circulated about him. I learned a lot more from John Sutherland's excellent biography of his daughter, *Mrs Humphry Ward: Eminent Victorian, Pre-eminent Edwardian*, published in 1990. This book left me with the conflicting feelings that Tom Arnold was a very interesting man and at the same time that Professor Sutherland was unjustifiably hostile to him (as he has subsequently admitted to me). I have made considerable use of his study, whilst contesting his judgements and correcting some factual errors, and I thank him for the warm support he gave me when I began work on Tom Arnold.

Special thanks are due to my wife, Anne, for (as well as all the other things) attentively reading and annotating the first draft of the book. She helped me to see more clearly what I was trying to say in places, and to remove some, at least, of the infelicities.

Among other people whose help I want to acknowledge, I am particularly indebted to Rusty MacLean, librarian of Rugby School, for the long loan of books by and about the Arnolds. I am grateful too to Ben Bergonzi, Lucy Bergonzi, Penelope Bulloch, Jeff Cowton, Martyn Forrest, Roland Hill, Colin Johnston, Frank Kermode, Peter Larkin, Edward Larrissy, Roger Lonsdale, Kate Manning, Christine Mason, the Revd B. A. Orford, Joanne and Mike Shattock, and Alan Tadiello. And among institutions: Bath and North East Somerset Archives, Bodleian Library, Brotherton Library, Leeds, Cambridge University Library, University College Dublin, Pusey House, Oxford, Inter-Library Loan Service, National Portrait Gallery, Queen Victoria Museum and Art Gallery, Launceston, Tasmania, Rugby School, Tasmania Department of Education, Tasmanian Museum and Art Gallery, Warwick University Library, and Wordsworth Trust.

My thanks are due to the following for permission to quote from copyright works.

To the University of Virginia Press for quotations from *The Letters of*

Matthew Arnold, ed. Cecil Y. Lang (Charlottesville and London, 1996–2001)

To Auckland University Press for quotations from *New Zealand Letters of Thomas Arnold the Younger* (Auckland and Oxford, 1966), and *Letters of Thomas Arnold the Younger* (Auckland and Oxford, 1980), both ed. James Bertram.

To the Fathers of the Birmingham Oratory for quotations from *Letters and Diaries of John Henry Newman*, ed. C. S. Dessain *et al.*, Vols. 16–29 (London and Oxford, 1965–76).

To the University of Leeds for quotations from J. E. Axon's PhD thesis on Tom Arnold, 'The Life of Thomas Arnold the Younger'.

Finally, I want to thank Sophie Goldsworthy and Frances Whistler of Oxford University Press.

CHAPTER 1

Family and Childhood

Tom Arnold was born on 30 November 1823, eleven months after his brother Matthew. Their father, the elder Thomas, was an energetic, active, ambitious young schoolmaster; he had married in 1820 and his first child, Jane, was born the following year. He had already embarked on his life's work as a teacher, though this description understates his intense commitment to the idea of education. His father, William Arnold, had risen from modest beginnings in public service to become Collector of Customs on the Isle of Wight, to which in time were added the further posts of collector of dues for Trinity House, and superintendent of postal services. Thomas was born in 1795, the youngest of seven children, and had a happy childhood on the island. He watched with fascination the many ships that the Napoleonic wars brought into the port of Cowes; his father started to give him lessons in history and geography, but, alas, he died of a heart-attack before Thomas was 6. His mother, Martha, who had been appointed postmistress after her husband's death, continued the lessons, helped by her sister, Susan Delafield. When he was 8 years old Thomas left home to become a boarder at Lord Weymouth's Grammar School in Warminster. He was an intellectually precocious child, with a passion for learning, but shy and inclined to put off strangers by his seemingly aloof manner. After a few years it was decided that he needed to attend a more advanced and demanding school and he was sent to Winchester in 1807.

Winchester was a famous and ancient establishment, but by the early nineteenth century it had fallen into the state of intellectual and moral decline that characterized English public schools, and which Thomas Arnold, in his later career, resolved to change. Formal instruction was a matter of sustained drilling in classical texts and authors. No-one made it their business to be concerned with the boys' individual welfare. Food was often inadequate, bullying was rife, and despite frequent recourse to corporal punishment by the headmaster, the boys remained unruly and barbarous. Thomas was tough enough to survive the prevalent brutality, and seems not to have been actually unhappy at school. He irritated his fellow-students, though, by enjoying study, and irritated his teachers by his forceful opinions, rating the Greek historians far above Cicero. He was deeply religious, but soon after he arrived at the school his devotion was tested when boots were thrown at him as he knelt to say his prayers in the dormitory. George Arthur, in *Tom Brown's Schooldays*, received much the same treatment.

At the early age of 16 Arnold went up to Oxford. He was disappointed not to get a scholarship to New College, Winchester's sister college, but he was successful at Corpus Christi. This was a small college with a good academic reputation, and took teaching more seriously than was the general practice in the university. Arnold enjoyed Oxford; he made friends and at the same time studied hard, and in 1814 he was rewarded with a First in Classics, otherwise *literae humaniores*. He had long assumed that he would become a clergyman, and it was customary for young men intended for the Church to try to stay on in Oxford for a few years in a fellowship and start their theological training. Arnold applied to Oriel, where there were two fellowships on offer, to be awarded by competitive examination. The examiners were not at first impressed by his papers, but they were won round by Richard Whately, a fellow of the college, a forceful, rather eccentric, clergyman, who was an expert on logic and subsequently Archbishop of Dublin for many years. Whately insisted that despite a certain lack of polish Arnold's papers showed intellectual distinction. The other examiners were eventually persuaded—or perhaps bullied—into agreeing, and Arnold was awarded a fellowship. He went on to justify Whately by winning successively the Chancellor's prize for the Latin essay and the prize for the English essay. Thomas Arnold was a fellow of Oriel from 1815 to 1819, one of a succession of remarkable men who frequented its common room. They included, over the years, his ecclesiastical opponent John Henry Newman, his pupil Arthur Hugh Clough, and his son Matthew.

During his years at Oriel Arnold supplemented his small stipend by taking pupils, and studied theology in preparation for his ordination. He had no doubt that he wanted to be a clergyman, but he was weighed down by a growing difficulty. His Christian belief was firm, but the Anglican Church's formulation of it in the Thirty-nine Articles was proving hard to swallow. This was so for many eminent men of the age. Arnold's future student and biographer, Arthur Stanley, was afflicted with exquisite doubts about assenting to the clauses in the Articles that referred to eternal damnation. Eventually he managed it, and went on to a successful academic and ecclesiastical career, ending as Dean of Westminster. Arthur Clough, though he had accepted the Articles on matriculating and graduating and on taking up his Oriel fellowship, found himself unable to do so again in order to renew his fellowship, and left Oxford. Benjamin Jowett regarded the Articles as mere verbal formulas, which he had no difficulty in accepting. Arnold allowed himself to be persuaded by his senior Oriel colleagues, Whately and Edward Hawkins, that his difficulties were unfounded; the Bishop of Oxford told him so too, so he was ordained as Deacon in 1818. But his difficulties returned. Hawkins, a shrewd judge of men, who eventually became Provost of the college, told Arnold that though his problems with the Thirty-nine Articles had no justification, he was increasingly doubtful whether Arnold had the right qualities to become a clergyman. Education, rather than the Church, was, he believed, Arnold's true path in life. In saying this he was telling Arnold what he was already coming to believe: teaching mattered more to him than a conventional clerical career.

Circumstances were propitious. Arnold's sister Frances had married his Oxford friend John Buckland, who was also drawn to teaching and had started a small preparatory school. Buckland wanted to expand it, and suggested to Arnold that they embark on a joint enterprise. The idea was that they should run a school in two sections: Buckland teaching the younger boys, and Arnold the older. Eventually they found a suitable property: two adjacent houses at Laleham, near Staines in rural Middlesex, close to the Thames. Arnold took the larger house, a rather severe Georgian building which would provide a home not only for himself but for his mother, his aunt Susan, and his permanently bed-ridden invalid sister, Susanna. The school was launched in 1819. The following year Arnold married Mary Penrose, the sister of his Oxford friend Trevenen Penrose. The Penroses were of Cornish extraction, and the Celtic element showed in different ways in Arnold's sons: in Tom's appearance; and in Matthew's literary interests.

Mary was four years older than Arnold; a contemporary painting shows a very pretty woman with a delicate air. She was tough enough to survive the frequent pregnancies that marriage brought, though she was inclined to believe that she would not survive the next one. But Mary Arnold lived for many years after her husband's early death, loved and revered as the matriarchal head of the family. The Arnolds had three more children during their years at Laleham: Mary, Edward, and William.

Thomas Arnold had nicknames for all his children. The first three, Jane, Matthew, and Tom, were 'K', 'Crab', and 'Prawn'; Mary, Edward, and William were 'Bacco', 'Didu', and 'Widu'. In a large, rapidly growing family it is not easy to discern clearly the characters of the individual children. But the difference in size and power of the crustaceans denoting Matthew and Tom reflects something of their respective characters. Tom was usually ready to defer to the forceful Matthew, who was reported to have given him a bloody nose on more than one occasion.

The school at Laleham was a success and aroused interest and attracted pupils; after a few years Arnold and Buckland amicably dissolved their partnership and Arnold remained in sole charge, which was the way he preferred things. He took over the second house for his mother, aunt, and invalid sister. His teaching was marked by a great concern for the individual welfare of the boys he taught, and by an intense though doctrinally unspecific Christian faith. He liked to get to know the boys and join them in their games as well as their studies. Scholastic achievement was taken seriously, but it was not given the highest priority. To a remarkable extent he won the loyalty and affection of his pupils. Word of the quality of his work spread, and Arnold was urged to apply for a mastership at his old school, Winchester; it was a post that might have led in time to the headship, but he declined firmly. In the words of his biographer Norman Wymer, 'he knew that if his ideas were to triumph he must be in sole control, whereas at Winchester he would enjoy no such over-riding powers but, on the contrary, would be thwarted at every turn by tradition and prejudice'.[1]

In October 1827 there came another invitation which it was harder for Arnold to dismiss out of hand. He loved his work at Laleham, but despite the success of the school he was under financial pressure, with a growing family and several dependent relations. Rugby School was not as venerable as Winchester; it was a sixteenth-century foundation which had started well but had fallen on bad times, like so many old schools. The headmaster was retiring after twenty-one years, and Edward Hawkins wrote urging Arnold to let his name be put forward for the post. Arnold declined, but in a way which was less than absolute. Once more, the essential question concerned his need for full personal control. In practice this meant freedom to expel pupils who were disruptive or otherwise unsuitable, a measure which Arnold found essential if the school were to be reformed. He anticipated that it would not be acceptable to the trustees, who would not want to reduce the numbers, being likely to prefer quantity to quality. But Hawkins and Whately kept up the pressure, and eventually Arnold agreed to let his name go forward for consideration. Even so, he was only one contender out of a large and well-qualified field and had to be considered an outsider. His Oriel backers, though, were skilled campaigners; Whately had single-handedly got Arnold his fellowship, and now Hawkins wrote to the Rugby trustees to say that if Arnold were elected he would change the face of education all through the public schools of England.

Oriel triumphed, and in December 1827, at the age of 32, Arnold was appointed headmaster. Early in the New Year he and his wife visited Rugby and inspected the school. The school buildings and the headmaster's house were fairly new, dating from the beginning of the century; they would be substantially added to during the coming decades. Arnold was assured by the outgoing headmaster that his lack of ordination would not be any barrier in the post. Indeed, as a deacon he was entitled and accustomed to preach, and had already published a volume of sermons. Nevertheless, Arnold reflected that it would be desirable for the headmaster to be in full priestly orders. As his biographer put it:

Since any reforms he introduced would be founded upon the Christian teachings, he felt that, at least, he should be as well qualified as the assistant master who then held the post of chaplain. Unless he was ordained, he would have to bow to the dictates of one who, though his junior in all other respects, was his superior in the religious field. He wondered whether such a position might not prove intolerable.[2]

He soon decided that it would; authority had to be clear and unimpeded. Arnold consulted the Bishop of London, and found that the difficulties over the Thirty-nine Articles which had hampered his earlier religious progress had somehow dissolved. He was ordained by the bishop in June 1828, and then reinforced his clerical authority by taking the degree of Bachelor of Divinity at Oxford. Among those who questioned him at the oral examination was Newman, then a young don and not yet a Tractarian. Arnold did not know who he was and did not remember him; but Newman remembered him. This qualification was shortly followed by the Doctorate of Divinity; these degrees appear to have been awarded as a formality.

The Arnolds moved into the headmaster's house in August. The move meant much more than a change of location and an improvement in professional prospects. Arnold had mounted a platform, and, as it soon appeared, entered an arena. But the claims of the family were always insistent. Not long after the move to Rugby young Tom Arnold enters the story for the first time, though in such a way that he was in imminent danger of leaving it for good. When he was 4 years old he succumbed to what was described as 'a derangement of the liver', which, it was thought, would either kill him or leave him mentally disturbed. Mrs Arnold and the governess took it in turns to sit by the child's bedside during the night. Arnold meanwhile struggled to teach the sixth form. He was no poet but he liked to write verse and he produced a prayer for his son:

> Spare us in Thy mercy, Lord!
> Lawful the prayer—for Thou has procured
> That earnest, unrepining word—
> Spare us the blow, if such Thy will—
> But if the bitter cup must fill—
> Teach us to drink and thank Thee still.[3]

In a strange mood of self-defence against fate Arnold even lost hope for his son, and wrote to his invalid sister, 'I might have loved him, had he lived, too dearly—you know how deeply I do love him now.'[4] But Tom recovered and was none the worse for his ordeal, though he was henceforth accounted 'delicate'. In 1832 he and some of his younger siblings caught and survived measles. His father, uninhibited by latter-day anxieties about unfairness, openly regarded Tom as his favourite son. On his eighth birthday the boy reflected wistfully, 'I think that the eight years I have now lived will be the happiest of my life.'[5] His father was deeply moved by the words, and once more turned to verse, with Wordsworthian echoes:

> Is it that aught prophetic stirred
> Thy spirit to that ominous word,
>   Foredating in thy childish mind
> The fortune of thy Life's career -
> That nought of brighter bliss shall cheer
>   What still remains behind?
>
> Or is thy Life so full of bliss
> That come what may, more blessed than this
>   Thou canst not be again?
> And fear'st thou, standing on the shore,
> What storms disturb with wild uproar
>   The years of older men?[6]

The move to Rugby turned Arnold into a public figure, 'Arnold of Rugby', or 'Dr Arnold'. His recently acquired doctorate became part of his persona; he is one of the two famous Englishmen who are customarily known as 'Doctor', the other being Samuel Johnson. Arnold's name and reputation remain familiar through two very different books which stay in print and continue to attract readers: Thomas Hughes's *Tom Brown's Schooldays*; and Lytton Strachey's *Eminent Victorians*. Before long it was evident that Edward Hawkins had spoken no more than the truth when he said that Arnold would change the face of public school education.

Tom Brown's Schooldays is more than a fictional record of its author's experiences; it is something of a historical novel with a compressed time-scheme. The earlier chapters look back to the early, unreformed, Rugby, with its rowdiness, drunkenness, fights, bullying—particularly as practised by the egregious Flashman—poaching, and intimidation of the local population. Arnold was familiar with all this from his years at Winchester, and he was determined to clean up the school. He used corporal punishment sparingly, and preferred to expel pupils who were unsatisfactory; they were not all notorious malefactors like Flashman, but were somehow not right for the school. In fact, Arnold introduced a non-punitive form of exclusion called 'superannuation' in order to get rid of pupils who were not personally at fault but could not fit in with the school as he wanted it; he would go to some trouble to help such pupils in their future lives. Another feature of the school that Arnold found disgusting was the practice of letting the boys sleep four or five to a bed; parents who wanted their sons to have the luxury of sleeping alone, or even with only one other boy, were required to pay extra. Arnold insisted that all boys would sleep only one to a bed, without extra charge.

His most potent innovation was his use of the sixth form, previously a collection of ill-behaved and underemployed youths. Arnold made it his business to become close to them, to win their trust and share their interests, and to employ them as prefects charged with supervising and directing the lower forms. The system proved very effective, though at one point some sixth-formers proved over-zealous in exercising discipline and Arnold narrowly survived a vote of no-confidence by the trustees. His overriding method was to encourage an spirit of inner-directedness or, as he would have put it, an active conscience, in all the boys. They would not behave badly, or neglect their work, because they knew that was wrong. They also knew that Dr Arnold would be pained, and have to apply sanctions. His aim for the school was that it should produce

Christians, gentlemen, and scholars, in that order. Though intellectual work took third place—Arnold always believed that virtue was more important—it was taken seriously. He moved away from the exclusively Classical curriculum he had followed at Winchester to introduce, as additional subjects, mathematics, modern languages, and history. Science, though, he could not see the significance of.

Thomas Hughes presents a schoolboy's eye-view of Arnold in the latter part of his novel. 'The Doctor' appears there as remote and firm but benign, a mildly god-like figure. Lytton Strachey, in full reaction against the gods of the Victorians, showed Arnold as a posturing hypocrite with no sense of the values that made for a civilized existence. Arnold's grand-daughter, Mary Ward (who had never known him) read Strachey's essay and was outraged, describing it as 'none the less foolish because it is the work of an extremely clever man . . . one can only regard it as one proof the more of the ease with which a certain kind of ability outwits itself.'[7]

Present-day readers are likely to respect Arnold's seriousness, but to feel uneasy at his demands for total control, inner as well as outer, suggesting an enlarged superego, a control freak, Big Brother. Arnold would not have understood such criticism; as far as he was concerned control, sur-veillance, governing by directing sympathies were all justified if the cause was right. He was a man of prodigious energy, who once said he would like to dictate to twenty secretaries at once. If the school took up much of his effort, there was still enough left over for him to engage in work for and among the poor of Rugby; here, no doubt, it was appropriate for him to appear in his role as clergyman. He established a dispensary for them, where they could obtain free medicine, and gave lectures at the local Mechanics' Institute. He even launched a newspaper, indebted to Cobbett but Christian in spirit, to further the cause of the poor. This project was over-ambitious and soon folded, but it led to Arnold con-tributing a regular column to a Sheffield magazine. He rapidly generated opinions and liked to propagate them, either by his journalistic writing or in pamphlets. He became increasingly a commentator on national affairs, with a clear sense of what he wanted for the country. This, in short, was an Anglican theocracy, where church and state would be indistinguish-able, and the law of God would be the law of the land, in what now looks an Islamic model. The Church of England would incorporate so-called Dissenters, and would play down divisive doctrines to do so. The only belief that Arnold insisted on was in the Divinity of Christ, so Unitarians, who denied it, had regretfully to be excluded from the Christian polity.

So, too, were Roman Catholics; and Jews, who had to accept the status of resident foreigners and not be allowed to vote. Such a plan for a whole nation remained chimerical, but Arnold was able to institute it in the smaller community of the school, and the still smaller one of his family.

Arnold was intensely hostile to the Tractarian movement that emerged in Oxford under the leadership of Newman and Arnold's old Corpus fellow-student John Keble. They emphasized that the Church of England was a sacred entity, which participated in the Apostolic Succession. They favoured Catholic forms of devotion, though rejecting the authority of Rome. All this was anathema to Arnold, looking for a Protestant national church, embracing the whole population, with a minimum of doctrinal distinctions. He particularly rejected the idea of a special and privileged priesthood. He attacked the Tractarians in a notorious article, 'The Oxford Malignants and Dr Hampden', published in the Whig *Edinburgh Review* in 1836. The phrase 'Oxford malignants' was an editorial insertion, harking back to a word used disparagingly of the royalists in the seventeenth century, but it reflected the vehement tone of Arnold's article. It was unsigned, and its principal target, Newman, was never mentioned, but informed readers knew what it was about. The article concluded that the Tractarians' attack on the liberal theologian Dr Hampden was personal and had the character 'not of error, but of moral wickedness'. It established Arnold as a hard-hitting Broad Church polemicist.

Arnold's children grew up with a father who was already a father-figure; though he could be stern, he could also be relaxed and playful, but his concern was unfaltering. Fifteen years after his father's death, Matthew commemorated him in 'Rugby Chapel':

> O strong soul, by what shore
> Tarriest thou? For that force
> Surely has not been left vain!
> Somewhere, surely, afar,
> In the sounding labour-house vast
> Of being, is practised that strength,
> Zealous, beneficent, firm!

Thomas Arnold was a force as much as a human being. His children remembered him as 'Zealous, beneficent, firm'; he was a father to live up to in a family where one was never off duty.

Another of his sons left a literary memorial of his father, albeit of an oblique kind. William Delafield Arnold (1828–59) spent much of his short adult life in India. After Rugby and Oxford he became an ensign in the army of the East India Company, and drew on those experiences in his novel *Oakfield; or, Fellowship in the East*; the first edition appeared under a pseudonym in 1853, and the second under his name a year later. Despite its many autobiographical elements and references, it is as much an expository moral story as an autobiographical novel in the usual sense. The hero, the eponymous Oakfield, tries to lead a Christian life among his crude, insensitive fellow-officers; he allows himself to be insulted without fighting a duel in response and is henceforth despised as a coward. He is described as having as a 'painful, anxious, darkling search after truth' (the word 'darkling' tends to appear at crucial moments in nineteenth-century texts). William Arnold was a fluent but uneven writer, very interested in ideas, so that he holds up the narrative with page after page of quasi-platonic dialogue, in which Oakfield holds forth on life, religion, and India (a country which, like his author, he deeply disliked). Kenneth Allott, in his excellent introduction to the 1973 reprint of *Oakfield*, said that it 'combines cumbrous plotting with genuine psychological and moral insight'. Arnold and Rugby are never mentioned in the book—Oakfield has been to Winchester—but G. M. Young remarked, 'On the whole, William Arnold's *Oakfield* seems to me to convey most completely the effect that Arnold made on those who came under his influence.'[8]

Arnoldian religion, as it pervades the book, is a matter of unrelenting striving to do right; it is said of a much admired character, the middle-aged Mr Middleton: 'He has felt a consciousness of right and wrong, duty and sin, every day through twenty years of service.' It is a religion lacking any sense of the numinous, the aesthetic, the ritual, the mystical, the paradoxical. Matthew and Tom Arnold broke away from it: Matthew in pursuit of a religion that was poetic rather than dogmatic; while Tom eventually turned to Catholicism. Allott has said that William Arnold was closer to his father's spirit than any of his brothers, and *Oakfield* is a record of his adherence. William came back to England after some years of service, then reluctantly returned to India to take up a good position in the educational service. But the climate destroyed the health of both William and his wife. She died in India, and he died at Gibraltar on his way back to England; his death was poignantly commemorated by Matthew in 'Stanzas from Carnac' and 'A Southern Night'.

Though Rugby was the centre of Arnold's activities, educational, ecclesiastical, and political, he never liked the place; he remained nostalgic for the Thames Valley, where he had spent his early married life. He found Warwickshire flat and featureless, and detested the prospect to the east of Rugby: 'It is no wonder we do not like looking that way, when one considers that there is nothing fine between us and the Ural mountains. Conceive what you look over, for you just miss Sweden, and look over Holland, the north of Germany and the centre of Russia.'[9] Arnold determined to find a second home in a more congenial setting. He was a tireless traveller, both in Britain and on the Continent, and in the summer of 1831 the Arnolds, four of their children, a governess, and a servant embarked on a grand tour which took them as far as Edinburgh. On the way back they stopped off in Westmorland and visited Wordsworth, whom Arnold had previously met, in his house at Rydal Mount. Arnold decided that in the Lakes he had found his Great Good Place, and told Wordsworth so. The poet was encouraging, and mentioned to Arnold that a convenient house nearby was available for holiday lettings. Matters were arranged, and the Arnold family were back in Westmorland for the Christmas holiday. For the next few years they spent their summer and winter vactions in rented houses near Rydal; Arnold and Wordsworth became good friends, despite the fact that one was a Whig and the other a Tory who complained about what he regarded as a subversive sermon that Arnold had preached in Rydal chapel. The next step was for Arnold to build a house in the district to serve as a permanent holiday home and a base for his eventual retirement. For Arnold, to decide was to act, and he resolved to build it at Fox How in the Rothay valley, near Ambleside, a couple of miles from Rydal. De Quincey had lived in an adjoining house, Fox Ghyll, for some years. The position had fine views of the mountains; Fairfield in one direction; in another, and closer to the house, Loughrigg Fell. Arnold liked the contrast between the small, secluded green valley and the snow that was often visible on the surrounding mountains. Norman Wymer suggests that the move to build the house was made with Wordsworth's active encouragement, but in fact he was grumblingly cautious, as he showed in a letter dated 28 August 1832:

Dr Arnold has determined to purchase the little estate that we looked at together. I am rather sorry for this, as I think it will involve him in more expense and trouble, should he build, than he is aware of. Mr Hamilton is of the same opinion. He has purchased Mr. Dillbrook's, for 1700, very dear I think, but he is likely to have his enjoyment of it, and promises to make a pleasant neighbour for us, only I fear he will draw around him some persons whom this quiet village would rather be without.[10]

Nevertheless, Wordsworth was supportive once the house was started, and oversaw the progress of the building when Arnold was back in Rugby. Fox How was built of Westmorland greenstone in a local style; it had six bedrooms and two staff bedrooms. The sitting-room measured 22 feet by 18 with a large window that gave an uninterrupted view of the mountains. There were also a dining room, a school-room, and a study. An interesting feature was that the principal living rooms were built facing north; they did not get the sun themselves but provided a fine prospect of the sun on the mountains. By 1834 the house was finished; Mrs Wordsworth commented approvingly that Fox How had 'not the least of a modern appearance'.[11] Fox How provided an ideal holiday home for the Arnolds, where family life could flourish away from the demanding presence of the adjoining school. The family was growing: three more children were born during the Rugby years: Susanna, Frances, and Walter. The Arnolds were in occupation of Fox How for ninety years; after Dr Arnold's death his widow made it her permanent residence, and after she died, in 1873, her unmarried daughter Frances—'Aunt Fan' to the family—lived there for another fifty years.

When the family began their twice-yearly peregrinations from Rugby to the Lakes, the journey took three days, with two overnight stops on the way. But within a few years the railways arrived and reduced the travelling time to a day. Long afterwards, Tom Arnold looked back nostalgically to the coaching days:

This way of travelling was sometimes a little tedious; but how familiar one became with country and town in the parts of England traversed! What joy it was to rattle through the streets of every town that we came to, wondering at all that met our eyes, and ourselves the objects of a not unfriendly curiosity to the passers in the street! Now we wait outside in a dull station, where nothing of the town is brought to our cognisance except its name. Not that I mean to say anything against the railways, to have originated which always seemed to me a real glory for England; but it is natural that those who remember the earlier state of things should sometimes think affectionately of the old turnpike roads, the bad macadam here, the excruciating *pavé* there—the long hills, the post-boys in their buff or blue jackets, and the much-loved horses—bay, brown, gray, and chestnut.[12]

Fox How was the centre for a wealth of outdoor activities, in which Dr Arnold joined eagerly, with his boyish high spirits and disconcerting, often exhausting, energy. Tom Arnold remembered:

The Fox How portion of our life was a time of unspeakable pleasure to us all. Loughrigg, the mountain at whose foot we dwelt, was bountiful to us of joy. In the winter there were the frozen tarns, which would bear for several days before Rydal Lake was safe, the deliciously pure and bracing air, the slides, the little streams, each forcing its way down its own obstructed gully through a succession of lovely ice grottoes, which wrapped round and hushed its noisy little waterfalls. But in the summer Loughrigg had still better things in store . . . As for the rowing on Lake Windermere, the sailing and rowing just for the amusement's sake, the picnics, the building up of fires on lonely shores where dead wood was abundant, the fishing for perch, pike and eels—all these things found the day too short to exploit them fully.[13]

Dr Arnold would have been uneasy about things being done 'just for the amusement's sake'; he believed that recreation should involve purposive activity. There must, though, have been many days at Fox How when the occupants were kept indoors by Lake District rain, and it was probably on such occasions that they produced a delightful compilation, the 'Fox How Magazine'. This was a small holograph brochure, one compiled on each holiday, to which all members of the family, except the very youngest, contributed verse or prose or drawings. The magazine shows what a formidably cultivated family the Arnolds were. Mrs Arnold wrote rather more elegant verse than her husband, and their daughter Jane provided drawings as well as literary items. There are translations from the Classical languages and German and Italian, as well as playful pieces by the younger children. One item by an unidentified child, dated December 1837, calmly indicates the hazards of the new method of travelling: 'A dreadful accident has recently happened owing to the engineer being intoxicated—they were just come to a station, when instead of stopping they went on & ran against some coaches that were standing there. Luckily only two lives were lost.'[14] Matthew's verses are significant as the juvenilia of an important poet; one can make no such claim for Tom's, as he had neither the talent nor the ambition. Nevertheless, they are vigorous and make a cheerful noise, as when he commemorates the receipt of the good news that the summer holiday of 1838 was to be extended by a week to mark the coronation of Queen Victoria; Tom was 14 when he wrote it:

> Is't true? Another week at Fox How dear.
> How joyfully the summons we receive,
> How joyfully we break the letter now,
> Which tells us of our much-loved week's Reprise.

Another week! How the news is spread,
From mouth to mouth it flies with lightning speed
And soon by every one the letter's read
And Walter even does the letter read.[15]

Walter, the youngest, would have been 3 years old.

The 'Fox How Magazine' makes it clear that Arnold had his children educated to a high level, in directions that went beyond the Classical curriculum. He also, which was truly advanced for the time, believed that girls should be as well educated as boys; his daughters did not go to school but seem to have been well taught by competent governesses, with Arnold taking a considerable hand in the process himself. His eldest child Jane—'K' in the family code—was an intellectual woman who was regarded as a considerable German scholar, and gave Harriet Martineau, a neighbour and family friend, help with the language. It is Jane whom Matthew writes to in later years as an intellectual equal, sharing and debating ideas with her.

Matthew and Tom were so close in age that they were treated for educational purposes as a single unit, though Matthew was always the dominant partner, Crab to Tom's Prawn. Matthew was obstreperous, sometimes agressive and given to violence, while Tom was gentle. At one point both boys developed a stammer; Matthew's disappeared in time but Tom's led to the appointment of a special tutor for him in 1833, though to no avail. It persisted and worried him all his life. Because of Matthew's reluctance to study he was sent away for a time to the school run by his father's brother-in-law and former colleague, John Buckland. After his return, the brothers were taught at home, either at Rugby or Fox How, by Herbert Hill, a graduate of New College and a cousin of Arnold's acquaintance the poet Robert Southey. Then, in 1836 Arnold decided that the boys should follow the normal practice and go to school. They were sent to Winchester for a year. It was a suprising move, given his discontent there in his own school days, and his conviction that Winchester as he knew it represented everything that was wrong with the public schools. On the other hand, he was loyal to it as a venerable institution, and he may have had reasons for thinking that conditions had improved since his day. He may even have believed that a little hardship might be good for the boys; it would only be for a year.

In fact, the year at Winchester passed uneventfully for Tom, though not altogether so for Matthew, who made himself very unpopular in the school by casually remarking to the headmaster that he thought the lessons were too easy; he won a verse-speaking competition, and injured his arm in an experiment with a firearm. Tom remembered the beauty of the services in Winchester Cathedral, and the pleasure of games on St Catherine's Hill. In 1836, visiting the Whatelys in Ireland, the brothers travelled by train for the first time, on the new line from Kingstown—now Dun Laoighire—to Dublin. The following year they repeated the experience in England, travelling by coach from Winchester to Birmingham, and then by train as far as Manchester, en route to Fox How. There was also a taste of metropolitan glamour, as Tom recalls:

At Easter 1837 we spent the short vacation in London, and I had the unspeakable pleasure of hearing Grisi, whose voice was then at the acme of its power and sweetness, in Don Pasquale, and Mario as Count Almaviva. I think it must have been on the same occasion that we saw the wonderful cast of King John at Covent Garden, in which Charles Kemble played the bastard Faulconbridge, Macready King John, and Helen Faucit the Lady Constance.[16]

At about that time the genius of Dickens exploded across the nation. Dr Arnold did not approve:

Childishness in boys, even of good abilities, seems to me a growing fault, and I do not know to what to ascribe it, except the great number of exciting books of amusement, like Pickwick and Nickleby, Bentley's Magazine, etc., etc. These completely satisfy all the intellectual appetite of a boy, which is rarely very voracious, and leave him totally palled, not only for his regular work, which I could well excuse in comparison, but for good literature of all sorts, even for history and for poetry.[17]

Nevertheless, Matthew and Tom were devoted to Dickens, and Wordsworth sympathized with their father over this lapse in taste: 'Dr Arnold told me that his lads seemed to care for nothing but Bozzy's next number.'[18]

In August 1837 Tom made his first trip abroad, though, strangely, he does not refer to it in his *Passages in a Wandering Life*. The Arnold parents, Jane, Matthew, and Tom, accompanied by a son of John Buckland's, made a rapid, ten-day tour of northern France, ending up in Paris and returning via Boulogne. When the autumn term of 1837 began Matthew and Tom joined their father's school as regular pupils. In time they rose to become prefects, or 'praepositors' as they were known at Rugby, and in that capacity joined their father in welcoming William IV's widow, the Dowager Queen Adelaide, on her visit to the school in 1839.

Soon after the brothers joined the school, one of their father's favourite pupils, Arthur Hugh Clough, left it for Oxford. His career at Rugby had been brilliant, marked by a succession of prizes, culminating in the triumph of the Balliol scholarship in 1836. He was an athlete as well as a scholar, and Tom Arnold remembered him playing the game named after the school: 'He wore neither jersey nor cap; in a white shirt, and with bare head, he would face the rush of the other side as they pressed the ball within the line of the goalposts; and not seldom, by desperate struggles, he was the first to "touch it down", thus baulking the enemy of his expected "try at goal".'[19] Clough made his mark in a number of ways. His appearance was striking, with a mass of black hair falling over a broad, white brow which contrasted with a small, delicate mouth. The academic successes took their toll; Clough was what would later be called 'highly-strung', and he was liable to periods of exhaustion. He was a loner, whose family were living in America, and he spent his vacations with members of the family in England, or with friends. The headmaster invited him to Fox How, and it was here that he got to know Matthew and Tom, who were a few years younger. Both brothers became his close friends. Clough went to Oxford in triumph, but left it, after he had graduated, in disgrace, at least in his own eyes. He failed to achieve the First that everyone had been expecting; he had been working too hard for too long, and had become bored and stale. Balliol had not been a helpful environment; as Clough's biographer, Katharine Chorley, put it, 'he was transferred without a break from one atmosphere of tension to another'.[20] Tom Arnold remembered his return to Rugby: 'I remember—it must have been, I think, after his comparative failure in the schools in 1841—his coming up to my father in the front court of the Schoolhouse, standing in front of him with face partly flushed and partly pale, and saying simply, "I have failed". My father looked gently and kindly at him, but what he said in reply I do not remember, or whether he said anything.'[21] Out of the quarrel with ourselves we make poetry, said Yeats; and Clough went on to become one of the outstanding poets of his age. But the cost was great. Walter Bagehot, reviewing Clough's posthumously published poems, offered shrewd observations not only on Clough but on the Arnoldian system which had formed him. They are worth quoting at length:

Dr Arnold was almost indisputably an admirable master for a common English boy,—the small apple-eating animal whom we know. He worked, he pounded, if the phrase may be used, into the boy a belief, or at any rate a floating, confused conception, that there are great subjects, that there are strange problems, that knowledge has an infinite value, that life is a serious and a solemn thing. The influence of Arnold's teaching upon the majority of his pupils was probably very vague but very good. To impress on the ordinary Englishman a general notion of the importance of what is intellectual and the reality of what is supernatural, is the greatest benefit which can be conferred upon him. The common English mind is too coarse, sluggish, and worldly to take such lessons too much to heart. It is improved by them in many ways, and is not harmed by them at all. But there are a few minds which are very likely to think too much of such things. A susceptible, serious intellectual boy may be injured by the incessant inculcation of the awfulness of life and the magnitude of great problems. It is not desirable to take this world too much *au sérieux*; most persons will not; and the one in a thousand who will should not. Mr Clough was one of those who will. He was one of Arnold's favourite pupils, because he gave so much heed to Arnold's teaching; and exactly because he gave so much heed to it was it bad for him. He required quite another sort of teaching: to be told to take things easily; not to try to be wise overmuch; to be 'something beside critical'; to go on living quietly and obviously and see what truth would come to him. Mr Clough had to his latest years what may be noticed of others of Arnold's disciples,—a fatigued way of looking at great subjects. It seemed as if he had been put into them before his time, had seen through them, heard all which could be said about them, had been bored by them, and had come to want something else.

A still worse consequence was, that the faith, the doctrinal teaching which Arnold impressed on the youths about him was one personal to Arnold himself, which arose out of the curiosities of his own character, which can only be explained by them. As soon as an inquisitive mind was thrown into a new intellectual atmosphere, and was obliged to naturalize itself in it, to consider the creed it had learned with reference to the facts which it encountered and met, much of that creed must fade away.[22]

Bagehot's account of the way Arnold's influence worked seems to me convincing, certainly in respect of Clough. Matters were not quite the same with Matthew and Tom; sons, no matter how devoted, may be to some extent innoculated against the extremes of paternal influence. Clough, Matthew, and Tom all broke away from Dr Arnold's doctrines. Clough and Tom did so with considerable unhappiness; Matthew, at little apparent personal cost. William Delafield Arnold, on the other hand, remained committed to them, and embodied them in *Oakfield*. In 1841, Matthew, aged 19, competed for one of two Open Balliol Scholarships, and was successful, though it seems to have been a near thing. Both he and his father thought he was lucky to have got it: "'I had not the least expectation of his being successful", wrote a father who had scarcely seen a Clough or a Stanley lurking in his lazy son. "The news actually filled me with astonishment."'[23] In that year Arnold had received a signal honour from the Whig government of Lord Melbourne, just before it fell from office. Melbourne had long wanted to do something for Arnold, who was one of the few prominent churchmen with Whig convictions. A bishopric had been discussed, but Arnold's intemperate polemical style made him unacceptable to the ecclesiastical establishment. Now he was offered the Regius Professorship of Modern History at Oxford. His edition of Thucydides and his writings on Roman history made it a respectable appointment. Having ascertained that the post required only limited residence in Oxford, and could be easily combined with the headmastership, Arnold happily accepted.

Much as he loved Fox How, he could never stay there for very long at a time; 'What a Velocipede he is', Wordsworth remarked in 1839, when Arnold had suddenly taken off for the Continent with Jane.[24] In 1841 he was back in France with Matthew and Tom, touring the west of the country; they took in Tours, Angoulême, and Bordeaux, ending up at Bayonne and the Pyrenees. But they had a wet time of it; Tom complained to Fan on 12 July, 'Every day since we landed at Calais it has been more or less cold & rainy, and though I expected it to mend as we got farther south, yet we have been to the very Frontier of Spain & still it has been as bad as ever.'[25] Dr Arnold kept a journal of this holiday, which is for the most part a severely factual account of places and things, combined with complaints about the weather. He has little to say about his sons, but he notes that Tom had taken a header into the Loire at a point where it was unexpectedly shallow and had cut his face. He gives, too, a charming description of Tom walking up and down on the balcony of their hotel in Tours, singing in the night.[26] Matthew was the poet, but Tom was inclined to the romantic gesture.

With Matthew installed at Balliol, Arnold began to think about his second son's university career. At first he considered Cambridge, but Clough reported in November 1841, 'Tom Arnold is not to go to Cambridge, but to come up here to University, which I am sorry for.'[27] Clough was presumably sorry because University College—the abbreviation 'Univ' seems not to have been in use at that time—was considered rather dull, certainly compared with Balliol. But it had the glamour of antiquity, vying with Merton for the title of the oldest college in Oxford, and gave itself an additional mythic advantage by claiming Alfred the Great as its founder. Dr Arnold may have been drawn to it because his beloved pupil and disciple, Arthur Stanley, had recently become a fellow, and could keep a benevolent eye on Tom.

In December Arnold travelled to Oxford to deliver his inaugural lecture as Professor of History to a large and enthusiastic audience in the Sheldonian Theatre. He returned in the New Year to give the remainder of his lectures. Tom Arnold recalled:

The whole family went up to Oxford in January 1842 when my father read his first course of lectures as Professor of Modern History. My brother, in all the glory of a scholar's gown and three months' experience as a 'University man' welcomed his rustic *geschwister* with an amused and superior graciousness. We visited him at his rooms in Balliol at the top of the second staircase in the corner of the second quod [quad]. When he had got us all safely in, he is said to have exclaimed, 'Thank God, you are in!' and when the visit was over, and he had seen the last of us out on the staircase, 'Thank God, you are out!'. But this tradition is doubtful.[28]

On 2 February 1842 Arnold went to dine at his old college, Oriel, where Newman was still a fellow. Although Arnold was initially apprehensive and ill at ease, the encounter of these old opponents was courteous and good tempered; they talked of non-controversial subjects such as North African myths. Newman reminded him of their previous encounter, when Arnold was examined for the degree of Bachelor of Divinity. Arnold had not identifed him on that occasion and in fact believed him to be another leading Tractarian, Edward Pusey. Nearly fifty years later, after Newman's death, Tom recalled his father's account of the meeting: 'I recollect as well as if it were yesterday how pleased and radiant dear Papa looked when he came back to the Beaumont St lodgings, and how he described Newman's cordiality (which was evidently more than he quite expected) . . .'.[29]

Arnold was to give no more lectures. In June, at the end of the summer term, he and his wife and Tom, and Arnold's former pupil William Lake, were at Rugby; the Arnolds looked forward to travelling to Fox How in a day or so, where Matthew and other members of the family were already assembled. Arnold invited some of his sixth-formers to supper before they departed from the school, and reflected 'How strange the chapel will look tomorrow!' Early the next morning he woke with sharp pains in his chest, which became steadily worse. A physician was sent for, who could do little for him, and made it clear how serious his condition was. Mary Arnold was praying by her husband's bedside:

At this point she was joined by her son, who entered the room with no serious apprehension, and, on his coming up to the bed, his father, with his usual gladness of expression towards him, asked, 'How is your deafness, my boy?' (he had been suffering from it the night before); and then, playfully alluding to an old accusation against him, 'You must not stay here; you know you do not like a sickroom'. He then sat down with his mother at the foot of the bed, and presently his father said in a low voice: 'My son, thank God for me;' and as his son did not at once catch his meaning, he went on saying, 'Thank God, Tom, for giving me this pain: I have suffered so little pain in my life that I feel it is very good for me: now God has given it to me, and I do so thank Him for it.'[30]

Arnold died of angina pectoris a little before 8 a.m. on 12 June, the day before his forty-seventh birthday. He had succumbed to the heart condition that had killed his father at the age of 53, and which ran on in the family. Matthew's son William died at the age of 18 after running a mile in a school sports event, and Matthew himself collapsed in the street at the age of 65 and died soon afterwards. Mary and Tom comforted each other, while Lake hastened north to break the terrible news to the waiting family at Fox How and bring them back to Rugby. A beloved father and husband, an admired clergyman and schoolmaster, was no more, but a legend was established, and endured. Stanley's vivid account was not based on direct observation, and must have been derived from Mary's and Tom's memories. It provides a good example of what A. O. J. Cockshut has called 'the death scene' in Victorian biography;[31] the biographer constructs a careful composition in which the dying Christian rounds off earthly life and prepares for eternity. Arnold's wish to thank God for giving him the experience of real pain expresses, *in extremis*, a characteristically Arnoldian religious attitude: a deep submissive devotion combined with a disconcerting assertion of the individual ego.

For Stanley, Arnold's death was the most shattering experience of his life. It could hardly have been less so for Tom, who endured at the age of 18 so heavy and unexpected a loss and so transforming a rite of passage. There may, too, have been a sense of release, accompanied by guilt at such a sense. But life went on. In August Tom visited the Whatelys in Dublin, accompanied by his sisters Mary and Susanna. Then it was time to prepare for Oxford.

CHAPTER 2

Oxford and London

In October 1842, when Tom Arnold arrived in Oxford as a scholar of University College, reminders of Rugby lay all around. Matthew was starting his second year at Balliol, and Clough was back in Oxford, having successfully competed for an Oriel fellowship. Tom's tutor was Arthur Stanley, a new fellow of the college; Stanley was a brilliant, delicate, sweet-natured young clergyman who had been one of Arnold's favourites and had become a close friend of the family. William Lake believed that Stanley 'never was a boy; he left school as he entered it, something between a girl and a man'.[1] When Tom entered the college Stanley was already at work on his life of the headmaster.

Oxford at that time was much as it was when Thomas Arnold Senior had been an undergraduate at Corpus Christi thirty years before; essentially a collection of colleges, churches, libraries, and other academic structures built between the thirteenth and eighteenth centuries, with a rural hinterland that came up to their walls. Cattle were regularly driven across Magdalen Bridge and along the High Street to Gloucester Green. The neo-Gothic remaking of Oxford was still in the future, as were the expansion and reform of the university. In the 1840s the colleges still looked as they did when Ackermann's artists had depicted them in the early years of the century, in their sleepy and sometimes crumbling beauty. Gown dominated Town, and the gown was clerical, as indicated in the little figures of clergymen scattered about in the Ackermann prints. Oxford was a closed Anglican community, where undergraduates had to subscribe on matriculation and again on taking their degrees to the Thirty-nine Articles. Fellows of colleges were expected to become clergymen and to remain celibate; once they married they moved out of college, usually to take up a living in a country parish. As a result the fellows of colleges tended to be young men, with a sprinkling of older bachelors. The unity of university and Church was imposingly evident at Christ Church, the grandest of the colleges, whose chapel was, and still is, the cathedral of Oxford.

If religion was everywhere apparent, education and scholarship, the traditional concerns of a university, were less universally in evidence. Much depended on the colleges. Some insisted on doing things their way, with closed scholarships for undergraduates, and closed fellowships for those who wished to remain on the foundation. Fellows were not obliged to teach, or indeed to do anything in particular, or even to remain in residence. But there was also a strong impulse to reform, and energetic heads of houses could make a difference if they wished. Oriel was an instance, with its competitive open fellowships. A few senior members of the university were uneasily aware that in other countries, particularly Germany, scholarship was taken much more seriously. But systematic reform did not come to Oxford until it was imposed by the government in the 1850s. When Tom Arnold came up the quality of college teaching was a hit-and-miss affair, and undergraduates who wished to do well in the Final Schools needed to pay private tutors as a form of insurance. At university, though, he was fortunate in being taught by the earnest and conscientious Arthur Stanley.

Not, indeed, that all young men were interested in shining academically. Oxford's peculiar burden was to serve both as a finishing-school for the sons of the upper class and as a place of learning. Young gentlemen were content to scrape through examinations and to fill their three years with riding, hunting, shooting, driving, and drinking. There was a category of 'gentleman commoner', scathingly presented in Thomas Hughes's *Tom Brown at Oxford*, who paid for and enjoyed a life of luxury and privilege in the college, and who were not expected to do any more than the minimum of work required to scrape a pass degree. Tom Arnold—as products of Rugby tended to be—was in the other camp, of those who were serious about reading. Study at Oxford in the 1840s was overwhelmingly Classical, continuing and extending the curriculum of the public schools, and the only honours schools were Classical and mathematical. The intellectually ambitious or academically athletic could read for both schools, a demanding business which not many attempted. Most students concentrated on Classics, in the paradoxical process whereby the texts of pagan antiquity were studied with tutors who were clergymen of the Church of England. At that time the BA in Classics was a three-year course; a few years later it was extended to what is still its present form, a four-year degree divided into two equal parts, 'Mods' and 'Greats'. Katharine Chorley showed in her life of Clough that the degree course had become narrower and less demanding than in the early years of the century. On the face of it, there was no reason why an undergraduate who had been well taught at school and was prepared to work steadily should not get a good degree. But matters did not always work out that way, as the case of Clough showed. When Matthew Arnold took his finals in 1844 he too ended up with a Second, but that was no surprise to anyone, least of all himself; he was able enough, but had given way to the distractions of Oxford and done little work. A last-minute burst of study was not enough to save him. Tom himself did what was needed and gained a First in the Schools. He was certainly as clever as Clough and Matthew, but he lacked their intellectual curiosity and waywardness, and whatever qualities of imagination it was that made them poets. He took easily to study, and was by temperament a scholar, as he showed later in his career when he came to edit medieval historical and literary manuscripts. His First Class was a matter of satisfaction to himself and his family, and proved invaluable in later life. He says as much in a rather dispirited comment in his autobiography, imbued with the priggishness that was one of the less attractive aspects of the Rugby inheritance: 'I held on to the Oxford life, though it had become distasteful to me, till I had taken my degree, knowing that an Oxford degree, and a good place in the class-list was an assurance against further embarrassment and want, which whoever had the power to provide himself with, was inexcusable if he did not do so.'[2]

Study and friendship are traditional aspects of a balanced student life, and Tom was not short of friends at Oxford. As well as Matthew and Clough, another Rugby man, Theodore Walrond, became an intimate. Walrond was a Scot, who had been Head Boy at school and entered Balliol at the same time as Tom went to university; he had been tutored for the Balliol scholarship by Clough at Grasmere in order 'to keep him from the office in Glasgow'. Walrond remains an attractive but rather shadowy figure, since few of the letters that he wrote or received have survived. He was an admired all-round athlete and an academic high-flyer who took a First in 1845; he returned to Rugby to teach for some years, and then held a Balliol fellowship for several more. He finally broke away from these familiar environments in 1856 to become a Civil Service examiner, then Secretary, and finally Commissioner to the Civil Service Commission. He was affectionately regarded by both Arnold brothers; he was a guest at Matthew's wedding, and Tom named one of his sons after him. He was equally close to Clough; indeed, one commentator has suggested that Clough was chastely in love with Walrond, and another that he was strongly attracted to Walrond's sister, Agnes.[3] Tom preserved idyllic memories of the outings of the four Rugbeians: 'After I came up to University in October, Clough, Theodore Walrond, my brother and I formed a little interior company, and saw a great deal of one another. We used often to go skiffing up the Cherwell, or else in the network of river channels that meander through the broad meadows facing Iffley and Sandford.'[4] An entry in Clough's diary refers to sailing on the Cherwell with Matthew and Tom on 15 May 1843.

Matthew, writing to Tom in May 1857, just after he had been elected Professor of Poetry at Oxford, fondly recalled the traces that those experiences had left in his poetry:

You alone of my brothers are associated with that life at Oxford, the *freest* and most delightful part, perhaps of my life—when with you and Clough and Walrond I shook off all the bonds and formalities of the place, and enjoyed the spring of life and that unforgettable Oxfordshire and Berkshire country. Did you ever read a poem of mine called 'the Scholar Gipsy'—it was meant to fix the remembrances of those delightful wanderings of ours in Cumnor hills before they were quite effaced—and as such Clough and Walrond accepted it—and it has had much success at Oxford, I am told, as was perhaps likely from its couleur locale.[5]

There were regular indoor meetings too:

After a time it was arranged that we four should always breakfast in Clough's rooms on Sunday morning. These were times of great enjoyment. Sir Robert Peel was in power; he was breaking loose more and more from the trammels of mere party connexion, and the shrewd Rentoul [Rintoul], who then edited the *Spectator*, welcomed in the Tory chief the only true statesman we had seen since the days of Canning. The *Spectator* of the day used to arrive at breakfast-time and the leading articles were eagerly read and discussed.[6]

Years later, Tom told Clough's widow that the weekly Sunday morning breakfast party at Oriel was one of the most interesting events of his life.[7]

There were more extended and formal opportunities to discuss the events of the day at the meetings of a select debating society called the Decade. It had a strong Rugby–Balliol orientation—a Balliol college servant always called it the 'Decayed'—but it was open to undergraduates and young dons from other colleges. Members were elected without their knowledge so as to eliminate canvassing, and it now appears a nursery of heavyweight talents. Among its members were Benjamin Jowett and Frederick Temple, who became, respectively, Master of

Balliol and Archbishop of Canterbury. Clough and Arthur Stanley and the Arnolds attended, as did their friend John Duke Coleridge, great-nephew of the poet, who in time was to become Baron Coleridge and Lord Chief Justice. Another close friend in the society was John Campbell Shairp, a Scot from Glasgow University who had come to Balliol on a Snell exhibition, part of a tradition of bright Scottish students at the college. At Glasgow he had acquired intellectual tastes which were well in advance of Oxford, such as reading Kant, whom few of the local philosophers knew anything about. Shairp was also a poet, winning the Newdigate prize, and in years to come was elected Professor of Poetry. He made an academic career back in Scotland and eventually became Principal of St Andrews University.

Debates at the Decade were liable to be to be tough and searching, as J. D. Coleridge sardonically recalled: 'we discussed all things human and divine—we thought we stripped things to the very bone—we believed we dragged recondite truths into the light of common day and subjected them to the scrutiny of what we were pleased to call our minds. We fought to the very stumps of our intellects.'[8] The debates provided an opportunity for Clough and Tom Arnold to display their political radicalism. The latter had put forward a motion in support of Lord Ashley's Ten Hours Bill, which aimed to limit the hours women and young people could work in factories, and was hotly discussed throughout 1844. Clough spoke in support: 'in supporting the resolution he combated the doctrines of *laissez faire* and the omnipotence and sufficiency of the action of Supply and Demand, then hardly disputed in England, with an insight marvellous in one who had so little experience of the industrial life . . .'.[9]

Tom had not had much experience of it either, but the resolution showed their hearts were in the right place. Clough was a regular debater at the Decade, but one wonders how much good such fierce clashes of intellect did him, given his anxious and depressive temperament, which had been undermined when he was at Balliol by the ruthless ratiocination of his mathematics tutor, W. G. Ward. Clough and Tom and Matthew remained a close trio, at Oxford and afterwards, in what must have been a complex relationship, given that brothers are likely to be both more and less than friends. There was enduring affection between Clough and Tom, which continued in the correspondence they conducted when the latter moved to the Antipodes. Clough enjoyed such epistolary friendships, like the one he conducted with J. P. Gell, a Rugby contemporary who had emigrated to Tasmania.

Where Tom was concerned, Matthew remained the dominant elder brother. In later years Tom took to calling him the 'Emperor', picking up a phrase of Emerson's to the effect that a poet is an emperor in his own right. Matthew was very fond of Tom, but he was inclined to patronize him. 'My misguided Relation' he called him, in a letter to Clough in 1844;[10] a few years later, when Tom was in New Zealand, Matthew remarked, 'my dear Tom has not sufficient besonnenheit for it to be any *rest* to think of him any more than it is a *rest* to think of mystics & such cattle—not that Tom is in any sense cattle or even a mystic but he has not "a still considerate mind".'[11] 'Besonnenheit' means prudence or self-possession; lapsing into German had become a fashion with the younger men at Balliol in the 1840s. It is not easy to focus on Tom as an individual, distinct from his brother and circle of friends, during his years at Oxford; none of his letters from that time appears to have survived. He was popular and known to be clever, moved in intellectual circles, and was famously handsome. He was dark, slender, tall, with a Celtic aspect to his appearance which may have derived from his Cornish maternal grand-mother. Matthew wrote to his mother from Paris in 1859: 'I could not but think of you in Brittany, with Cranics and Trevenecs all about me—and the peasantry with their expressive rather mournful faces—long noses and dark eyes—reminding me perpetually of dear Tom & Uncle Trevenen...'.[12] When finalists were being vivaed in the summer of 1845, an undergraduate encountering a friend in the High Street told him that if he stepped into the Examination Schools he would see the handsomest don in Oxford examining the handsomest undergraduate.[13] The don was Henry Liddell, subsequently Dean of Christ Church, co-author of the Greek–English Lexicon, and father of Lewis Carroll's Alice; the under-graduate was Tom Arnold. At Oxford he was troubled by the stutter or, as he called it, the 'hesitation', which afflicted him all his life; it may have affected his participation in debates, but it seems never to have been a really disabling handicap. He may have been cheered by Carlyle's convic-tion that 'a stammering man is never a worthless one'.[14]

Mary Ward recalled towards the end of her own life:

There is a sketch of my father made in 1847, which preserves the dreamy, sensitive look of early youth, when he was the centre of a band of remarkable friends ... It is the face—nobly and delicately cut—of one to whom the successes of the practical, competitive life could never be of the same importance as those events which take place in thought, and for certain minds are the only real events.[15]

One picks up here the slightly patronizing tone that occurs in Matthew's comments. Mary's description of her father's appearance as a young man is accurate enough, but the conclusions she draws are no more than half right. Tom Arnold did indeed have an impractical streak, but she exaggerated it; one would not imagine from her remarks that he had held a number of serious jobs in his life—as a précis-writer in the Colonial Office, as head of educational services in Tasmania, as a schoolmaster in Birmingham, and a university professor in Dublin—and performed satisfactorily in all of them. She contrasts her father's appearance with his brother's: 'Matthew Arnold was very different in outward aspect. The face, strong and rugged, the large mouth, the broad lined brow, and vigorous coal-black hair, bore no resemblance, except for that fugitive yet vigorous something which we call "family likeness", to either his father or mother—still less to the brother so near to him in age.' Mary Ward had been writing novels for many years when she set down these accounts, and she presents her father and uncle as significantly contrasting characters: the Holy Fool and the Mensch. She leaves implicit the further point that, though Tom had the sensitive, dreamy face of a Romantic poet, it was Matthew, with his rugged, rather coarse, features, who actually became one. (The contrast was even more marked in later life: Tom, with his thin, sensitive face and white whiskers, made a remarkably handsome old gentleman; Matthew's features became coarser and redder—his liking for drink accentuated the process—and he was once described as looking like a prosperous working man.)

There was a more significant difference between the brothers. Despite the variety of their talents and temperamental inclinations, they were equal in intelligence and range of knowledge. But Matthew's consciousness was divided. His letters to Clough make entertaining reading, with their irony and wit and jokes, their baroque exaggerations and camp endearments and flights of facetious fancy; these were the qualities evident in the young Matthew's dandyish public persona. Refined and modified, the wit and irony recur in his critical and polemical prose. But they are absent from his poetry; the sombre, sometimes tormented, lyricism of *The Strayed Reveller and Other Poems* was a revelation to those who thought they knew him well when the book appeared in 1849. There is a comparable division and duality in Clough, though less under control, evident in the tension between jokes and despair in his letters. The ironic capacity of both writers is evident in their greatest works in verse and prose, respectively, *Amours de Voyage* and *Culture and Anarchy*. Tom Arnold had a simpler temperament and in some respects a simpler mind, without the ironic dimension; what you saw was what you got. Matthew did not write to Tom in the way that he wrote to Clough.

All three were subject to religious crises and transformations during their years at Oxford. The university, virtually an institution of the Church of England, was deeply affected by the conflicts between Tractarians and Liberals and Evangelicals that had raged ever since the first of the *Tracts for the Times* had appeared in 1833. The Tractarians, under Newman and Keble and Pusey, wanted the Church to return to its Apostolic origins; the Liberals, of whom Dr Arnold was the loudest spokesman, rejected much of this as irrelevance or superstition. In such a climate, religion took on the aspects of both politics and popular entertainment. Newman was for many years vicar of the university church of St Mary, and his Sunday afternoon sermons had a wide following among undergraduates; college authorities opposed to his Tractarian influence unsuccessfully tried to counter it by arranging dinner-time to coincide with the sermons. Matthew, though ceasing to be an orthodox believer, was one of those who were captivated by Newman's preaching, as he recalled many years later: 'Who could resist the charm of that spiritual apparition, gliding in the dim afternoon light through the aisles of St Mary's, rising into the pulpit, and then, in the most entrancing of voices, breaking the silence with words and thoughts which were a religious music—subtle, sweet, mournful?'[16] Tom Arnold, who once or twice crossed the High Street from his college to listen to Newman in his final months at St Mary's, did resist that famous charm: 'the delicacy and refinement of his style were less cognizable by me than by my brother, and the multiplied quotations from Scripture introduced by "And again"—"And again"—the intention of which I only half divined, confused and bewildered me.'[17]

Accusations and counter-accusations of heresy were common. Tom Arnold heard a sermon by the Tractarian Dr Pusey which was judged to be heretical by a panel of six doctors of divinity and for which he was suspended from preaching for a time, though his views remained unaltered. Matthew was prevented from reading his poem 'Cromwell', winner of the Newdigate prize, at a Commemoration ceremony in the Sheldonian Theatre because Tractarian undergraduates were noisily demonstrating against the award of an honorary degree to the American ambassador, who had the misfortune to be a Unitarian. Tom witnessed the ultimate defeat of the Tractarian cause in February 1845, when W. G. Ward, a fellow and mathematics tutor of Balliol, was solemnly stripped of his degrees in the Sheldonian because of the ultra-Catholic sentiments expressed in his book *The Ideal of a Christian Church*: Tom wrote, 'I heard the sermon in Christ Church for which Pusey was "six-doctored", and tramped up and down in the mud of Broad Street on that day of pouring rain on which Ward was degraded.'[18] Other witnesses described the weather on that day as snowy; as Owen Chadwick puts it, 'as Ward came hurrying out of the theatre his clumsy frame slipped in the snow and fell headlong, scattering papers and pamphlets in all directions. Sixty or seventy undergraduates cheered and escorted him to Balliol. They hissed the vice-chancellor.'[19] By the end of the year Ward and Newman had followed the logic of their convictions and entered the Roman Catholic Church.

Clough and the Arnolds were interested in these public dramas but not deeply affected. Their concern was less with the various divisions within Christianity than with the possibility that it might have had its day. In Chapter 26 of *Tom Brown at Oxford*, the hero, who was at the university at the same time as the Arnolds, remarks facetiously on the opposed schools of the Tractarians and the Germanizers, and says the latter are more dangerous. When asked why, he replies, 'Why? Because one knows the worst of where the Tractarians are going. They may go to Rome and there's an end of it. But the Germanizers are going into the abysses, or no one knows where.' Hughes, writing in the 1860s, may have been indulging in historical hindsight; Newman had gone to Rome, and Mark Pattison, religiously speaking, into the abyss. Mary Ward says that Tom and Matthew and Clough 'discovered George Sand, Emerson and Carlyle, and orthodox Christianity no longer seemed to them the sure refuge that it had always been to the strong teacher who trained them as boys'.[20] They were succumbing to what Dr Arnold would have condemned as 'infidelity', though it stopped well short of atheism. It is not easy to know what Matthew Arnold really believed, but anguish over the retreat of traditional faith is powerfully expressed in 'Dover Beach'; he came to think that the poetry of religion should be preserved and its theological doctrines surrendered, whilst maintaining the Church of England as an essential pillar of the state; it was desirable to go to church, but it did not matter very much what you believed when you got there. Clough's movement away from the strong belief of his days at Rugby was a painful process, as we see in his letters and poems. He was reluctant to abandon Christianity but had to in the end, with the result that he left Oxford because he could no longer subscribe to the Thirty-nine Articles. The struggle is dramatized in his two poems called 'Easter Day'. The first of them rings with the sad refrain 'Christ is not risen'; the second wistfully asserts the opposite: 'in the true creed | He is yet risen indeed'. But the 'true creed' is something very different from what Dr Arnold would have recognized as Christian faith, though Matthew would have sympathized; it implies a radically demythologizing approach to religious belief.

The 'Clougho-Matthean circle', as Tom called it, found intellectual excitement and a degree of spiritual sustenance in the post-Christian writers mentioned by Mary Ward: Carlyle, Emerson, George Sand, to which can be added the Goethe of *Wilhelm Meister*. They offered a possibility of liberation; Scoto-German, American, and French, they wrote from outside the English and Anglican traditions which had dominated the young men's education. George Sand, in particular, was a cult figure; once, when Tom and some friends were in the Highlands they arrived well after dark in the village where they had arranged to meet another Oxford party. They were not even sure which was the inn, but when Tom found a likely looking house he climbed in a window to explore. He emerged with a copy of George Sand's *Consuelo*, which confirmed that they were in the right place: 'Assuredly a book from Oxford'. Matthew was a particular admirer; when he was travelling in France in 1846 he asked George Sand, otherwise Madame Dudevant, if he might call on her. She agreed; he was kindly received, given tea, and introduced to her lover, Chopin.

Tom Arnold's spiritual crisis, following his loss of faith, lasted intermittently for several years. As his daughter observes, he had a profoundly religious temperament, which made unbelief very painful to him. He was badly shaken by David Strauss's demonstration of the presence of myth in the New Testament, which was profoundly unsettling to those brought up in a Protestant conviction of the literal truth and sufficiency of Scripture. George Eliot, who was translating Strauss's life of Jesus during Tom's time at Oxford, was similarly affected. Tom gave a compelling account of his desolate state of mind, presented in the third person, in the 'Equator Letters', a series of letters, addressed to John Campbell Shairp but intended for circulation among his friends, that he wrote when he was sailing to New Zealand in 1847–8:

Meanwhile the perplexing questions to which I have before alluded returned upon him again, and now he could not shake them off so easily. Moreover he read about this time one or two works by materialists; in one of which especially a fatalistic view of nature and of man was sustained with wonderful ability and power of expression.—However it was, he fell into a state of dejection, such as he had never before known, and which, by the mercy of God, has never since returned. Outward nature seemed to harmonize with the gloom of his mind. The spring of that year (1845) was unusually cold; and the blasts of the North East wind shook the large Oriel window of his room, and made him shiver with cold as he crouched over the fire. A universal doubt shook every prop and pillar on which his moral Being had hitherto reposed. Something was continually whispering, 'What if all thy Religion, all thy aspiring hope, all thy trust in God, be a mere delusion? The more thou searchest into the mystery of thy Being, findest thou not that iron relentless laws govern thee, and every impulse and thought of thee, no less than the full stones beneath thy feet? What art thou more than a material arrangement, the elements of which might at any moment, by any accident, be dispersed, and thou, without any to care for or pity thee throughout the wide universe, sink into the universal night. Prate not any more of thy God and thy Providence; thou art here *alone*, placed at the mercy of impersonal and unbending laws, which, whether they preserve or crush thee, the Universe with supremest indifference will roll onward on its way'.—The misery of the incessant recurrence of such thoughts to a believing mind he only who has experienced them can understand. They took away the charm from the human face—the glory from the sky; the beauty from the flowers—all these seemed to be the garlands round the victim's neck; designed to cheat it for a time into a little ease and forgetfulness of the cold inexorable necessity that lay beneath. For months he was haunted by these doubts, which at last passed away of themselves, without his having been able to find any means of facing and overcoming them.[21]

It is a powerful account of a state of feeling that was becoming common among sensitive Victorian intellectuals, well before Darwin brought biblical religion to a condition of public crisis. Tom Arnold draws on the familiar forms of Romantic rhetoric, such as the 'pathetic fallacy', which regards Nature as echoing and enlarging human moods. His reading of Carlyle is evident in tone and cadence; and when he writes, 'thou art here *alone*', the phrasing and emphasis as well as the sentiment anticipate a poignant stanza from his brother's 'To Marguerite—Continued':

> Yes! in the sea of life enisled,
> With echoing straits between us thrown,
> Dotting the shoreless watery wild,
> We mortal millions live *alone*.
>
> ll. 1–4

In later years, Tom, though liable to recurring moods of dejection and discouragement, was more inclined to look on the bright side of life, sometimes to an unrealistic extent. There is a contrast with Clough's more fundamentally depressive temperament. As religion crumbled, Tom turned to politics and a confused idealistic radicalism that wanted to pull down the mighty from their seats, and was excited by rumours of revolt on the Continent.

There was solace, too, in the company of his family; he spent university vacations at Fox How, where Mrs Arnold had made her home after her husband's death. In 1843 Arthur Stanley stayed there, working on his life of Dr Arnold, which Clough reported as 'approved of highly' by the family. The book was published the following year and was an instant success, selling a thousand copies of the first edition in a week. It was a remarkable achievement to produce so monumental a work in under two years; Stanley was only 29 when it appeared, but the effort seems to have left him in a state of permanent mental exhaustion; nothing he wrote subsequently achieved a comparable reputation. It is a virtual mausoleum of a book, that reflects nothing of the intense grief that Stanley felt on Arnold's death. Frances Woodward acknowledges that 'it seems to have been deliberately desiccated of emotional content', but pertinently adds, 'to be Arnold's biographer gave sufficient release to his emotions: he did not allow himself to become his encomiast'.[22]

In the summer of 1844 Clough was a guest at Fox How. Despite his heavy frame he was a determined walker; having gone with Tom and some other friends as far as High Raise, he continued alone across Helvelyn. That October, shortly before he returned to Oxford, Tom and his mother visited Wordsworth, who had been striding the mountains for many years:

It was my good fortune to see and hear him once in one of his moods of inspiration. In the autumn of 1844, at the time when plans and prospectuses were flying about, proposing the continuation of the railway from Kendal to Windermere, my mother paid a morning call at Rydal Mount, and I accompanied her. We were shown into the dining-room, a small apartment very plainly furnished. Presently the poet appeared, having a sheet of paper in his hand; his face was flushed, and his waistcoat in disarray, as if he had been clutching at it under the stress of fervid thought. 'I have been writing a sonnet,' he said. After a few more words, standing up in front of the fire, he recited it to us; it was the sonnet, 'Is then no nook of English ground secure from rash assault?'. The force and intensity with which he uttered the lines breathed into his hearers a contagious fire; and to this hour I recollect the precise manner and tone of delivery more exactly than in the case of any verses I ever heard.[23]

A year or two later Tom and his brother attended a public meeting to protest against the extension of the railway; Wordsworth delivered a rambling and sentimental speech and was briskly hauled back to the point by the chairman, the Scottish man of letters John Wilson, who wrote as 'Christopher North'.

After his disappointing but not surprising Second, Matthew returned to Rugby to teach for some months, and then competed for an Oriel fellowship, and, like Clough, was successful. He was back in Oxford in the spring of 1845, coinciding with Tom's last term. On a hot day in June there was a meeting between Tom and Matthew and their younger brother, Edward, who was about to go up to Balliol. Edward was accompanied by the youngest of the Arnold siblings, the 10-year-old Walter. The boy had been taken off by Tom and Matthew was unable to find him, until he heard him running along the street behind him, freshly bathed under Edward's supervision and with his hair parted in the middle. Walter dined with his brothers in Matthew's rooms in Oriel; Matthew remarked in a lettter to his sister, 'I trust he was not made ill at dinner', and added, 'Tell Mamma his cloth jackets are a hideous cruelty in this weather, poor child.'[24] This was an early instance of Matthew's tendency to be bossily considerate about his younger brothers.

In August and September, after Tom's Finals, he and Clough took a vacation in Scotland, staying at Waldron's family home, Calder Park, outside Glasgow. Tom and Waldron walked to Loch Aird; they were then joined by Clough, who reported:

I came back and slept at Inversneyd; they remained and attended a Highland reel party in a shoemaker's hut at Loch Ard and after staying up dancing and drinking milk and whiskey till 2 past 2, rose 2 p.4, walked 11 miles to a hasty breakfast with or rather after me and then took steam down to the foot of Loch Lomond, and so by Dumbarton we came home, dirty and dusty and bankrupt.[25]

After a further expedition to Loch Long, Tom and Clough and Waldron stayed with J. C. Shairp and his family in Edinburgh, and met J. G. Lockhart, Sir Walter's Scott's biographer and son-in-law and ferocious editor of the *Quarterly*, sometimes known as 'the Scorpion'. Tom returned to Fox How via Carlisle.

Back at home, Tom took his time about finding employment. His First Class degree meant that he could have picked up a fellowship at University College; indeed the college elected him to a foundation scholarship with that in mind. In November Clough noted that Ward's

Tractarian colleague at Balliol, Frederick Oakley, had resigned from his fellowship to become a Catholic: 'This will cause another vacancy at Balliol; perhaps Tom Arnold will have the benefit of it . . .'.[26] But Tom did not want to return to Oxford; his loss of faith would have prevented him from subscribing to the Thirty-nine Articles in order to take up a fellowship. Tom had a much more remote goal firmly in mind. As he later wrote of himself:

When he had been about two years at Oxford, he began to look forward, and consider what he was to do after leaving the University, but he could not settle on anything until (in 1844) some words casually dropped led him to think of New Zealand and the life of a Colonist. It is not to be described how this idea took possession of his whole nature. For some time before this, he had felt himself very poor in thoughts and intuitions, and used sorely to regret the raptures of his first awakenings.—But now he was carried away by a flood of feelings and fancies, which attended him all day long, and assumed a thousand beautiful forms to his imagination. It is needless to detail all the plans that formed in his brain. Suffice it to say that his mind was soon made up to follow the impulse thus communicated, and to emigrate to New Zealand.[27]

But first he needed to take a good degree, as his father would have wished for him; and in this, despite a lack of personal inclination, he succeeded. In aspiring to go to New Zealand he was, in a different way, influenced by his father, for Dr Arnold had long been interested in the Antipodean colonies and more than once expressed a desire to end his days there. In 1840 he wrote to Sir Thomas Pasley, 'I have often thought of New Zealand, and if they would make you Governor and me Bishop, I would go out, I think, tomorrow,—not to return after so many years, but to live and die there, if there was any prospect of rearing any hopeful form of society.'[28] More concretely, Dr Arnold had purchased from the New Zealand Company, which administered some of the territory until it became officially a colony in 1840, two pieces of land, totalling 200 acres, in the vicinity of present-day Wellington. This property meant that Tom would have a firmer reason to go to New Zealand than the pursuit of a romantic reverie. But he delayed, either because of the vacillation to which he was prone before finally and firmly making up his mind, or as a tactical manœuvre to keep his family happy. Clough reported in January 1846, 'Tom Arnold has for the present given up New Zealand—why, I do not yet know.' He also noted that Tom had been treated for his stammer by mesmerism, following the example of the Arnolds' intellectual friend Harriet Martineau.

After travelling on the Continent with Edward Whately, son of the archbishop, Tom played the part of the dutiful son by settling in London to study law at Lincoln's Inn. He was not very familiar with the metropolis, having so far spent his life, after his early childhood in rural Middlesex, at Rugby, Fox How, and Oxford. In 1846 London had been a Victorian city for nine years, but it was not yet looking like one: the prevailing styles and materials of building, the Georgian brick and Regency stucco, reflected the taste of earlier reigns. The streets were noisy, dirty, full of hurrying or dawdling crowds. Dickens had already published half a dozen novels reflecting the misery and vitality of life in the capital. Henry Mayhew was embarking on the studies published in 1851 as *London Labour and the London Poor*. A young German businessman had been impressed by his first sight of the capital when he arrived in it in 1842:

I know nothing more imposing than the view which the Thames offers during the ascent from the sea to London Bridge. The masses of buildings, the wharves on both sides, especially from Woolwich upwards, the countless ships along both shores, crowding ever closer and closer together, until, at last, only a narrow passage remains in the middle of the river, a passage through which hundreds of steamers shoot by one another; all this is so vast, so impressive, that a man cannot collect himself, but is lost in the marvel of England's greatness before he sets foot upon English soil.

But Friedrich Engels found that the greatness had been dearly purchased:

the sacrifices which all this has cost become apparent later. After roaming the streets of the capital a day or two, making headway with difficulty through the human turmoil and the endless lines of vehicles, after visiting the slums of the metropolis, one realizes for the first time that these Londoners have been forced to sacrifice the best qualities of their human nature to bring to pass all the marvels of civilization which crowd their city.[29]

Carlyle had expressed similar sentiments about what he called 'The Condition of England Question', and they were shared by his admirer Tom Arnold. In London he was appalled by the lives of the poor, whom, like Engels, he made it his business to seek out—'almost with the feelings of a Sister of Mercy'—and 'was brought into daily contact with the extremity of human suffering and degradation, and forced to behold our common human nature "not struggling but sunk"'.[30] The radical idealism he had professed at Oxford had come to seem altogether inadequate. He told Clough:

Those are indeed happy who can still hope for England, who can find, in identifying themselves with our political or social institutions, a congenial atmosphere, and a suitable machinery for accomplishing at last all that they dream of. Of such sanguine spirits, alas! I am not one. To imagine oneself called upon to 'do good' in the age in which we live, is an illusion to which I was long subject myself, but of the utter fallaciousness of which I am now convinced.[31]

He tells Clough that the desire to escape, to fulfil his old ambition of emigrating to New Zealand, is as strong as ever, but he is prepared to defer it for a time to satisfy his family. He tried to settle down to his legal studies with Walter Coulson, a barrister and an expert on conveyancing, but he found them uncongenial: 'a hardening worldly profession', as he later described it. After some months an opportunity for change presented itself: 'being by this time much interested in Colonies, I accepted a clerkship in the précis-writing department of the Colonial Office at the beginning of 1847'.[32]

The change in his fortunes reflected the political upheavals of 1846, arising from the famine in Ireland. Sir Robert Peel, the Tory prime minister who had been admired by Tom and his Oxford friends, was resolved that the policy of agricultural protection enshrined in the Corn Laws had to go. That was an obviously humane move; at the same time he proposed an unrealistically tough policy with an Irish Coercion Bill, designed to deal with the unrest prompted by the famine. As a result of these manœuvres, Peel split his party and lost his parliamentary majority. In those days of loose party discipline governments could change without the necessity of a general election; the Whigs under Lord John Russell came back into office.

The change would have been good news for Mrs Arnold, always ambitious for her sons. It was an age when patronage was a customary way for young men to advance in their careers; Dr Arnold had been one of the few eminent Whig churchmen and his name carried weight with the Whig aristocrats now installed at ministerial desks, such as Lord Grey at the Colonial Office, and Lord Lansdowne, Lord President of the Council, with special responsibility for education. It would have been natural for Mrs Arnold to engage in some discreet networking. Tom moved to the Colonial Office early in 1847; in April of that year, Matthew, who had been rather marking time at Oriel, decided to seek his fortune in London; Clough remarked, 'I did not expect him to stay here long.'[33] He found an agreeable and not too exacting post as private secretary to Lord Lansdowne. Both Clough and Tom displayed a hint of Rugbeian priggishness in disapproving of Matthew's move, which deprived Clough of his company in Oxford and may have seemed unsuitably glamorous to Tom in his more humble appointment.

At that time the Colonial Office was situated at the bottom of Downing Street, in premises originally built as a private house in the seventeenth century, like the two that now survive in the official ministerial residences of Nos. 10 and 11. The building had long been recognized as overcrowded and unsuitable for government use. It was eventually replaced but the Colonial Office was still there in the 1860s, when Trollope's Phineas Finn MP was appointed under-secretary, with a large office looking out on St James's Park, though the clerks were presumably still in their cramped conditions. (In the real world Tom's brother-in-law William Forster briefly held this post in 1865; his career and Phineas's ran interestingly parallel; in a later novel, *The Prime Minister* (1876), Trollope's character becomes chief secretary for Ireland, a post that Forster took up in 1880.)

Tom worked conscientiously, but the pace was relaxed, as he described it to Jane:

My manner of life is uniform and simple. I breakfast at half past 8, practise a little, and read or write, till a quarter past 11, when I go down to the office, generally through the Parks. I have my luncheon or rather dinner at 2. Soon after 5 I leave the office, and have a very enjoyable walk through the Green Park, and in and about Hyde Park, for an hour or more, before going in to tea.[34]

Mrs Arnold would have doubtless been gratified by a report she received from Baron Bunsen, the Prussian ambassador, an anglophile intellectual and great admirer of her husband:

Now I must tell you what Lord Grey told me this morning, at the Queen's Levee, when I enquired after your excellent Son Tom. He said he had given him 3 or 4 difficult tasks, & he had done himself *great honour*. Among others he had given him an abstract to make of a great heap of papers, referring to that very complicated question, the property of the land to New Zealand, and he had made a capital report on the subject.

When we were speaking on this subject, the Marquess of Lansdowne joined our conversation by saying: 'That the eldest is with me as private secretary, and does very well'. I was very glad to hear this, to me new, piece of intelligence, for a confidential place like that of private Secretary to Lord L. is exactly a place where a young man of talents & acquirements can distinguish himself, & find that sort of steady intellectual employment, which I always thought so particularly desirable for your eldest Son.

I am sure it will be gratifying to you to hear what those two Ministers said about your Sons: both are honest admirers of your great husband.[35]

Bunsen's letter is revealing about the political culture of the day, and on the status of the Arnolds. Tom, for the time being, was content to deal with New Zealand matters only on paper; but not for much longer.

He described himself as being much on his own during his time in London, when he lived in lodgings in Mount Street (as did a fictional bachelor, Adolphus Crosbie in Trollope's *The Small House at Allington*). Despite his loss of faith he sampled services and sermons. Once or twice he heard F. D. Maurice, the Christian Socialist, preach in the chapel of Lincoln's Inn, but was unimpressed: 'he made upon me the impression as of a man who was immersed in a thick metaphysico-theological fog, and I felt quite unable to look to him as one capable of helping other people find their way into sunshine'. For a time he was attracted by the spiritual fervour of the Methodists, but was put off by a visit to a Wesleyan chapel: 'In the pulpit was a large elderly man, who ranted and raved in a manner painful to listen to; yet he was regarded as a shining light in the Wesleyan body.'[36] Tom was quite unsure what he wanted in religion, but he was getting an increasingly clear idea of what he did not want. A visit from Clough provided an opportunity for a significant discussion, as Tom recalled:

In the evening before bed-time the conversation had turned on the subject of prayer; and it had been argued that a man's life, indeed, ought to be a perpetual prayer breathed upward to Divinity, but that in view of the dangers of unreality and self-delusion with which *vocal* prayers were beset it was questionable how far their use was of advantage to the soul. Clough slept ill, and in the morning, before departing, gave his host a sheet of paper containing the noble lines above mentioned.[37]

He is referring to Clough's poem, 'Qui Laborat, Orat'; the stanza which Katharine Chorley calls 'the heart of the poem' runs:

> O not unowned, Thou shalt unnamed forgive,
>   In worldly walks the prayerless heart prepare;
> And if in work its life it seem to live,
>   Shalt make that work be prayer.
>
> ll. 17–20

('Laborare est orare' was the motto of the Benedictines, and 'Orando Laborando' that of Rugby School.)

During his time in London Tom fell unhappily in love with Arch-bishop Whately's daughter Henrietta. Details of the affair are very sketchy, and what is known of it has to be picked up from the muffled Weltschmerz of the letters Tom wrote after he had left England. Archbishop Whately was well disposed to Tom, but perhaps not to the extent of finding him an acceptable son-in-law. Henrietta, either under pressure from her father, or from her own inclinations, refused Tom's proposal of marriage. The matter was closed after Henrietta became engaged to a lawyer called Mr Wale, as Tom's sister Jane reported to him in 1848, tactfully adding, 'you know that I have long thought that she was not altogether the person who would make you happy as a wife'.[38] There was a curious sequel, when, many years later, Tom's son William married Henrietta Wale's daughter, also called Henrietta. Disappointment in love might have reinforced Tom's determination to leave England.

There is an indication of his state of feeling in his devotion to George Sand's novel *Jacques*. At first he did not share his brother's admiration for the French novelist, but when he read *Jacques* he was won over: 'my inter-est was completely excited both in the book and the writer'. *Jacques* is an oppressively sad story of marital breakdown, told in the epistolary form made popular by Richardson. It was not well received by the critics when it appeared in 1834, but it was a great popular and financial success. The eponymous Jacques, said to be based on George Sand's sometime lover Alfred de Musset, is a country gentleman and veteran of the Napoleonic wars; he is 35 when the story begins, and regards himself as already middle-aged. He embarks on a misguided marriage with a vain and empty-headed girl of 17 whom he loves deeply. In time she is unfaithful to him with a younger man; Jacques' devotion to her is such that he plays the *mari complaisant*, leaving her free to act as she will. Jacques is a Byronic figure: sombre, taciturn, noble, long-suffering. Outwardly he presents a stoic front to the world, but inwardly he is racked by turbulent and destructive feelings. At the end, finding he has nothing left to live for he removes himself from the world by disappearing into an Alpine crevasse; his suicide is arranged to look like an accident. Tom Arnold identified with Jacques, and in the 'Equator Letters' described his own state of mind in fervid language which is close to George Sand's:

There was something in the divine stoicism of Jacques which was perhaps con-genial to my nature, and the fate of his love impressed me with sad forebodings, which were but too soon destined to be realized. It was so then;—in the age in which we live, and in the society in which we move, there is a curse on love and marriage for those who will not bow the knee to the world's laws; those who have resolved to put away illusions, and to live for truth, be it at the risk of all that is held precious here below, rest, happiness, nay, of love itself, which is the very life of life.[39]

The archbishop's daughter would have been alarmed by *Jacques* if she had been allowed to read it, and Tom's admiration for the book would scarcely have helped his claims as a suitor. His regard for George Sand declined in later years, but he continued to be a great admirer of a more substantial monument of European Romantic literature, Goethe's *Wilhelm Meister*, which he read in Carlyle's translation. (Though like many of the Arnolds he was a competent reader of German.) He tended to identify with the wandering, vacillating nature of Goethe's character, and in 1853 he told Jane, 'I believe I am by disposition a rover, and the rules of the "Bond" in Wilhelm Meister would have suited me exactly.'[40]

Tom found a certain release for his feelings in his rapture over the 'Swedish Nightingale', the singer Jenny Lind, who came from Stockholm and took fashionable London by storm in 1847. The critics' hyperbole was unrestrained: 'a new perception of musical art has burst upon us; it is as though we now learned for the first time what singing really is, and have been, with all our fancied knowledge and taste, groping, till now, in darkness', wrote one; and another, 'We might as well send for a pot of paint in order to paint the lily, or cover a sovereign with a layer of Dutch metal, as endeavour to paint Jenny Lind's splendid achievements in their appropriate colours.'[41] Her acting in operatic parts was as expressive as her singing, and, though not beautiful, she had a very pleasing appearance. Her private life was, reassuringly, said to be impeccable.

In May 1847 Clough wrote to his sister, 'You will see by the paper that the adorable Swede Jenny Lind has enchanted all the world. I greatly rejoice at it; and think I *must* go and see her, though I don't like spending the money. One can't go under a sovereign, I believe, and if either Matt or Tom goes with me they will make it 30/- I dare say.'[42] Clough's caution about the cost is understandable; the tickets were stiffly priced. Tom had heard her sing in Bellini's *La Sonambula*, and had been overwhelmed, like many other Londoners:

Jenny Lind is such a singer as appears once in a century, and who, once heard and seen, can never be forgotten. The mere sight of her is enough to drive from one's mind for ever all ideals but that of the pure guileless Northern maid, in whom stormy passion is replaced by infinite supersensual Love, and intellectual power by the direct contemplation of and communication with the Divine.[43]

Tom's swirling romantic fervour was easily aroused. He told Clough that he had got two tickets for the pit at her next performance 'at the very moderate price of half a guinea'. But he had made a mistake about the date and the tickets were returned. It is not clear whether Clough heard Jenny Lind sing in London, but he did so in Manchester two years later, in Mendelssohn's *Elijah*. He told Tom in a letter, 'Not seldom I thought of her distant devotee, who would have died upon the smiles with which she beamed approbation when anything pleased her in the performance.'[44] Other members of Tom's circle shared his enthusiasm and joined in the hyperbole. In March 1848 Theodore Walrond wrote, 'In a few weeks I trust to hear Jenny Lind again. It is strange that Stanley & I, so unlike, agree in looking to Jenny Lind & your Father as the two beings who have most powerfully testified to us the presence of a Deity in the World.'[45] It was left to Matthew to insert, not uncharacteristically, a cooler and coarser note, remarking to Clough, 'by the way what an enormous obverse that young woman and excellent singer has'.[46] Tom would have detested this comment; his enthusiasm continued, and Jenny Lind's portrait hung in his various lodgings in New Zealand.

In August 1847 Tom went to Scotland for his annual vacation. Clough was already there, staying near Loch Ness with a 'reading party'. This agreeable institution had been invented by Benjamin Jowett; a group of undergraduates went with a tutor to an area of rugged and impressive scenery—the Highlands and Lakes were favourite areas—to study and to engage in strenuous walking. Clough enjoyed these occasions and often went on them; he gave memorable literary expression to one of them in his long poem in hexameters, *The Bothie of Tober Na Voulich*; when it was first published in 1848 it was called *The Bothie of Toper Na Fuosich*, but Clough found he had unwittingly reproduced a Gaelic obscenity and changed the title in later editions. In the Highlands Tom met up with Clough, Walrond, and Shairp. It was the last time they were to be all together. Shairp and Tom Arnold went off on a walking expedition from the western end of Loch Rannoch and along the western shore of Loch Ericht, which Shairp described as 'one of the wildest, most unfrequented lochs in the Highlands'. They attempted to track Prince Charlie's haunts on Ben Alder, before making their way to Dalwhinnie to join up with Clough and their other friends. Clough liked their account of this walk so much that he later repeated it himself, and reproduced parts of it in the *Bothie*. Tom Arnold was generally thought of as providing the basis for 'Philip Hewson' in the poem, though Tom himself played it down. But Philip's radicalism seems to be drawn from Tom's:

> Hewson a radical poet, hating lords and scorning ladies,
> Silent mostly, but often reviling in fire and fury
> Feudal tenures, mercantile lords, competition and bishops,
> Liveries, armorial bearings, amongst other matters the Game-laws . . .
>
> I. 25–8

At the end of the poem, Philip has graduated from university, married a girl he met in the Highlands, and set off to farm in New Zealand. When the poem was published marriage was not yet part of Tom's experience, but the departure for New Zealand was.

By the time he left Scotland he had definitely made up his mind to go. On his way back to London he stayed at Fox How, but later wrote that he had not found a good opportunity to talk to his mother about his intentions; perhaps not, or perhaps he was simply scared. Back in the Colonial Office he wrote to her on 21 August, making his plans clear:

I do not think you will be surprised to hear that I cannot give up my intention. It would really be unjust to myself, if I were to speak of what leaving you all will cost me, and I am sure that though you may think me wrong, you will believe that no cold-heartedness towards home has assisted me in forming my resolution. Where or how we shall meet on this side of the grave, will be arranged for us by a wiser will than our own; nay, if we only walk by faith, may we not believe that that was a true word which said, 'all these things shall be added unto you'? To me, however strange and paradoxical it may sound, this going to New Zealand is become a work of faith, and I cannot but go through with it.[47]

A week later Tom wrote to his mother thanking her for her reply: 'Your letter was a great pleasure to me. I care little for the disapprobation of all the world beside, if those nearest and dearest understand me and sympathise with me.'[48] Mary Ward commented, 'His mother, indeed, with her gentle wisdom, put no obstacles in his way.' But friends of the family tried to dissuade him, notably Baron Bunsen, who gave him well-meaning but ineffectual advice: 'Give yourself time. Try a change of scene. Go for a month or two to France or Germany.'[49]

When Tom had made his mind up, nothing would shift it. The move to New Zealand had the quality, he felt, of a spiritual quest, even though it was anchored to the family's 200 acres of land. His aspiration might well have been reinforced by a passage in *Jacques*; at the end of the novel the passionate and enigmatic Sylvia (who may or may not have been Jacques' sister) begs him not to commit suicide but to move to a new country and a new life: 'Ne peux-tu abandonner pour jamais cette maudite Europe où tous tes maux ont pris racine, et chercher quelque terre vierge des tes larmes, où tu pourras recommencer une vie nouvelle?'

In September Tom told Jane, 'There is such an indescribable blessedness in looking forward to a manner of life which the heart and conscience approve, and which at the same time satisfies the instincts of the Heroic and Beautiful.'[50] After the inequalities and misery and injustice of life in England, he looked forward to a purer, more egalitarian society. He recalled near the end of his life, 'Some kind of Pantisocracy, with beautiful details and imaginary local establishments such as Coleridge never troubled himself to formulate, seemed to my groping mind the thing that was wanted. I suppose, too, that I was a rover by nature.'[51] It may have been a spiritual journey, but Tom plunged into the practicalities. He took 200 pounds as his share of his father's estate, and set about ordering tools and agricultural implements: 'There are a light plough and a pair of harrows among the things ordered, and yet the whole bill is under £18. In ordering, I went upon the calculation of what would be sufficient for two or three men, working together.'[52] His friends gave him useful leaving presents: a gun, a saddle, an iron bedstead, a Dutch oven; but Clough's gift was severely intellectual: a volume of Spinoza. As James Bertram has pointed out, Clough recalled these gifts in the *Bothie*, in the mock-heroic list of objects that Philip Hewson takes to New Zealand. And he took many books with him, which Tom described to Clough as 'a mass of heresy and schism': 'Rousseau! Spinoza!! Hegel!!! Emerson!. Stanley observed that Spinoza and Hegel had probably never crossed the Line before.'[53]

Carlyle's name is not invoked, and Tom Arnold seems to have cooled about him: 'He is much to be pitied; having a philosophy that teaches him to be discontented with the life of other men, without showing him how to attain to a higher.'[54] Emerson was a new object of admiration for the Clougho-Matthean circle; he arrived in England in November 1847, though Tom did not meet him, and enthusiastically accepted Clough's invitation to visit him in Oxford. The two men became friends, and when he returned to America in July 1848 Clough lamented, 'What shall we do without you? Think where we are. Carlyle has led us all out into the desert and has left us there.'[55]

Tom was affectionately seen off by his brothers and friends. His last days in England were engagingly described in a letter to Mrs Arnold from Edward, who was then in his last year as a Balliol undergraduate, and had been given permission by the Master, Dr Jenkyns, to go to London to see his brother off. On the evening of Saturday, 20 November 1847, Tom, Matt, Edward, Clough, and Walrond went to see a farce, *Box and Cox*, at the Lyceum Theatre; Tom, he reported, 'was in very good spirits & laughed at part of the play a great deal'. The following day the party made their way to London Docks, where Tom's ship, the *John Wickliffe*, was moored at Shadwell Basin. 'Matt joked a great deal about the smallness & closeness of the hold, but Tom did not in the least mind. Clough indeed says, that it is a good-sized one for an emigrant ship, & that Tom is very lucky. I did not like to laugh at what was so serious a matter to Tom, but my firm conviction was that *I* could not live out a voyage of 5 months there . . .'.[56] Clough knew something about these matters, as his family were living in America and he had crossed the Atlantic.

On Monday evening, Clough, Tom, Edward, and their brother Willy dined at Long's Hotel; the following morning Tom and Edward break-fasted together and Clough returned to Oxford. The *John Wickliffe* had moved down river to Gravesend, where Tom was to join it and where Edward would be seeing him off; Matthew had hoped to do so too, but Lord Lansdowne required his services later that day. Matt and Edward met up with Tom at London Bridge, and they travelled on by train from Fenchurch Street to Blackwall, where a steamer was taking them on to Gravesend, though Matt would have to return to his office. Edward gives a good account of the departure, which recalls Engels and looks forward to passages about the Thames in Conrad and Eliot; and suggests, too, the moonlit Victorian townscapes of Atkinson Grimshaw:

When we got out on the Quay at Blackwall, Tom's spirits quite rose. After leaving the smoke & dirt of London here was the River with vessels of all shapes & sizes & a blood-red sun going down over London—the very image as Tom remarked of Turner's picture of the Old Temeraire. Tom was rather affected at leaving Matt. From the steam-boat he watched him until he disappeared in the Station & then I saw the tears in his eyes, as he leant over the Gunwale to look at the water. About 5 minutes after 3 we started & though it was very cold, yet it was a brilliant sunset, & the river with all its shipping is always beautiful, besides the banks above Erith and Greenhithe are very pretty. We paced the Deck talking till we arrived at Gravesend at ¼ to 5. I asked him if he had the least inclination to change his mind were it possible. He said, not the least, that when he had made up his mind fully, he looked upon the thing as inevitable, besides that his wish to go was as strong as ever. The last I saw of him was his being pulled in a boat with his luggage out to the *John Wicliffe*, sitting in the stern, & then in the dusk I could see a light hung over the ship when the boat was alongside, & he went on board his home for the next 5 months. In 10 minutes I had to start back again: it was a lovely night: an almost full moon shining on the water & the ghostly ships which flow silent past us.[57]

It was a good while before the *John Wickliffe* was out on the open seas. As Tom recalled some years later, 'After the usual tug of war with the elements in the English Channel, after pitching four days at the Downs, taking refuge from a furious gale behind the Isle of Wight, with the cabin all afloat, lying a week at the Mother Bank and narrowly missing ship-wreck on the Scillys, we got clear of the narrow seas, and felt the long roll of the Atlantic.'[58]

CHAPTER 3

New Zealand

Most of the passengers on the *John Wickliffe* were Scots, members of a dissident Free Church faction. Under the leadership of a Peninsular veteran, Capatain William Cargill, they were headed for the new Presbyterian settlement at Otago, on the South Island of New Zealand. Tom Arnold did not have a lot in common with them, but maintained friendly relations. He shared a cabin with a young Londoner named Cutten, who was going to Otago to take up work as an auctioneer. When Arnold was laid low with sea-sickness as the ship plunged through heavy seas in the Bay of Biscay, Cutten recommended a glass of Bass. 'The composing and invigorating effect of this was wonderful', Arnold recalled, in the accents of one offering a testimonial; 'I lost all feeling of sea-sickness, and have seldom been troubled by it ever since.'[1]

During the first part of the voyage Arnold worked at the 'Equator Letters' quoted in the previous chapter, the confessional account of his state of mind and feelings at the time he left England. They express an anguish about religion which is the more acute because it defines the separation he felt from his father's ideas. Dr Arnold would have sympathized with Tom's rejection of creeds and 'churchmanship', but would have insisted on the Divinity of Christ and the literal truth of Scripture. He would certainly have identified with his son's concern for the poor, but would have held back from the vehemence of his political radicalism. Tom Arnold reveals himself as a Romantic, though his Romanticism is not that of his father's Lakeland friends, Southey and Wordsworth, but has a stronger, Continental flavour. Continuing sadness over the loss of Henrietta Whately provides a further strand of feeling; Goethe's Wilhelm offered a model for the young voyager; and so, perhaps, did his Werther. Tom's devotion to George Sand took an extreme form: 'thanks be to God, and to George Sand, the interpreter of His truth . . .'.[2] The 'Equator Letters' are a remarkable fragment of Romantic autobiography, but there is something unconvincing about their expressions of feeling; Tom Arnold seems to be forcing the note a little. He was at pains to exclude the cheerfulness and the optimism—sometimes ill-founded—that marks his other correspondence at that time.

As the *John Wickliffe* sailed south he was struck by the beautiful appearance of Palma in the Canaries: 'Clearly, when colonies were first served out to the nations, Spain had the pick of them! New Zealand might be as beautiful, but it was on the other side of the globe; here were islands forming an earthly Paradise, not a thousand miles from Cadiz.'[3] Tom Arnold's radicalism was not developed enough to let him see that colonies are not served out but taken. After the ship had crossed the Line, he criticized one of the splendours of the Southern Hemisphere, noting on 9 February 1848, 'The Southern cross is not a very fine constellation, one of the stars which form the cross being so small.'[4] As a relief from reading and writing, he found a useful manual occupation:

There is a boat on board for the the use of the Otago settlement, and young Cargill, who has been a sailor, has had to make the sails for her, as she will be wanted immediately upon our arrival to carry food from the ship to the shore. He has taken me as his apprentice in his work; as we call it in joke, and I have learnt to sew the cloths together, to table the edges (a sort of hemming), to make grummets, eylet-holes and what not. I sewed together the cloths of the jib almost entirely myself, and the Captain said it was very neatly done.[5]

The captain, an Irishman named Bartholomew Daly, took the ship well to the south, believing that this shortened the route. One night he came dangerously close to land; daylight revealed the looming cliffs of the desolate island of Kerguelen, in the south of the Indian Ocean. Tom was impressed by the sombre appearance of the island with its towering mountain, and described it in detail. He expressed the hope that he could sail back there when he was settled in New Zealand, but it was one of his many aspirations that were not fulfilled. As James Bertram has remarked, he was not used to sailing anything more demanding than a small boat on Windermere. Soon afterwards, although the day was fine, the air grew chill; there were icebergs nearby.

Tom became bored with the long voyage, and felt that he had had enough of the travelling companions with whom he had been on friendly terms. He was still brooding over Henrietta, and reverted to the mood of the 'Equator Letters': 'I find no peace or happiness except when alone.'[6] Then, on 19 March, the ship came in sight of Stewart Island, at the far south of New Zealand. A few days later it sailed into Otago harbour, where the Presbyterian settlers and their stores disembarked. The *John*

Wickliffe was in no hurry to continue its voyage north and Arnold spent much of the time on shore, though Otago had few attractions. The real New Zealand was more than a utopia or the shimmeringly beautiful site of an ideal community; at Otago it resolved itself into solid ground, dull surroundings, and poor weather. Nevertheless, it was a strange country, made singular by its geographical isolation; there were no indigenous mammals, and had only known human inhabitants for about a thousand years, when the Maoris mysteriously arrived from elsewhere in the Pacific. If it resembled Britain, it was Britain painted with a broader brush, with higher mountains, faster rivers, stronger winds, a warmer climate. And it was very empty.

After a brief visit from the Dutch explorer Abel Tasman in the seventeenth century, New Zealand was subsequently circumnavigated and investigated by James Cook. From early in the nineteenth century the country was occupied by settlers, traders, and adventurers, many of whom came across the 1,300 miles of ocean from Australia. In the words of one historian, 'the tale of early European enterprise in New Zealand is substantially the tale of an Australian frontier'.[7] Indeed, as plans for an Australian federation were developed, it was taken for granted in the larger country that New Zealand would be part of it as an outlying province. But there were important cultural differences. Although all sorts of dubious characters ended up in New Zealand, it had never been a convict settlement; everyone who came was notionally a 'free settler'. The indigenous populations were also very different; the Australian aborigines were brutalized and vastly diminished in number by the European invaders. The New Zealand Maoris had an elaborate tribal system, and were very warlike; they bought firearms from European traders and were prepared to use them. The British government licensed the New Zealand Company to settle and sell tracts of land, but the system was regarded as failing. New Zealand was an anarchic territory without an adequate civil administration; there was friction between groups of European settlers, and between Europeans and Maoris. British attitudes varied. There were those who wanted a straightforward colonial occupation, with the Maoris treated as a subject people. Missionary groups wanted the Maoris to be converted but otherwise left alone with their culture and traditions; their ideal was a free Christian Maori nation. Others believed that any British presence should be restricted to trade, with no attempt at political control. The British government was reluctant to intervene; the imperialist fervours of the high Victorian era were still in the future, and the officials in the overcrowded Colonial Office in Downing Street felt they had quite enough problems already. Nevertheless, in 1840 the government reluctantly declared New Zealand to be a British colony, and attempted to set up an administration. A humanitarian concern to protect the Maoris from uncontrolled exploitation by the settlers was a factor in the decision.

Tom Arnold lived in New Zealand for a total of twenty-one months, many weeks of which were spent waiting for ships to take him from one place to another in the colony, for communications were still largely seaborne. He fulfilled nothing of the high dreams and hopes with which he had embarked; while he was there he made plans, sometimes attempting to put them into effect by physical labour, sometimes only putting them on paper. They were all frustrated. Yet failure can be character-forming; Arnold's New Zealand experiences gave him a better understanding of himself and of humanity at large.

While he was marking time at Otago, waiting for his ship to sail north, Tom decided to do some exploring in the surrounding mountains. He was ludicrously underprepared, and he seems to have regarded the expedition as not much more than the kind of strenuous walk that he was used to in the Lake District. The enterprise was a predictable failure; it was not until three years later that Tom described it in a letter to his mother, which has a certain deliberate symbolic resonance, underlining the failure of a Romantic pastoral ideal, and recalling the collapse of his other enterprises in New Zealand. But, as he says, the misadventure cured him of the pursuit of extreme self-sufficiency:

I think the greatest mistake I have ever made was that of fancying that an honest man was sufficient society to himself, and that the growth and vigour of the intellect was compatible with loneliness. I remember well the first practical check that this feeling received. It was at Otago; I had made up my mind to go on foot a journey of three or four days into the unknown interior. I could get no one to accompany me, and I did not care for anyone. On the evening of the first day I reached a narrow mountain valley, partly clothed with wood, partly with high fern and flax and rushes. I camped by the side of the clear stream, and made my fire out of the drift wood that lay on its banks and had probably never before been disturbed by the hand of man. I boiled my tea, baked a cake of flour in the ashes, and after the meal spread my plaid on the soft long grass by the water side, and tried to go to sleep. I had nearly succeeded when I felt the plash of rain drops on my face. It came on harder and harder, till I was quite wet through and cold. I got up and stamped about in a little circle, to keep up the circulation. The rain at last ceased, and I lay down again but could not sleep for the cold. The morning came and the sun rose gloriously, but I was chilled through and faint from hunger. I saw too that my provisions would not hold out for more than another day, and I resolved to return. I could not light a fire; everything was too wet; and I could not eat flour; so I started without any breakfast. As I struggled back over the mountains, almost sick with hunger, I could not help remarking within myself a longing to get back to the settlement and the haunts of men equal to that which I had felt a day or two before to penetrate into the silence and solitude of the bush. No, I said to myself as I leaned on a great boulder at a spot whence the eye commanded a far stretching plain, on which not the faintest curling smoke told of the presence of man, Thou wast not made to be alone! A sort of horror fell upon me, the might of Nature seemed to rise up irresistible,—all pervading, and to press down upon my single life. From the hour that I reached the settlement, I became, I think, a wiser man . . .[8]

Arnold finally got to Wellington at the end of May 1848. He lodged with a friendly clergyman, the Reverend Robert Cole, who introduced him to the Bishop of New Zealand. The bishop took Arnold to an official reception to mark the Queen's Birthday, which provided a convenient way of extending his acquaintance. He had breakfast with one of the most interesting men in the colony, Alfred Domett, a Cambridge graduate and a barrister of the Middle Temple, who had emigrated a few years earlier. Domett was a close friend of Robert Browning, whom he had known since his boyhood; Browning lamented his departure in 'Waring': 'What's become of Waring | Since he gave us all the slip?' When Arnold met him he was a rising man in the colonial administration, and one of those who wanted to take a hard line with the Maoris. After representative government was established Domett became an MP, and was briefly, and by all accounts not very successfully, prime minister in the 1860s. He returned to England in 1871 and turned poet, producing a saga based on his Antipodean experiences.

Arnold made other acquaintances in Wellington. Frederic Weld was a sheep-farmer from an old English Catholic family; one of his relations was Cardinal Weld, a titular bishop in Rome. Weld later turned from farming to public administration; he, too, became prime minister of New Zealand, and was subsequently governor of Tasmania, of Western Australia, and of the Straits Settlements in Malaya. He was knighted at the end of his life. Arnold got to know some of the army officers who marked the British presence; one of them, Thomas Collinson, a young captain in the Royal Engineers, was to become a lifelong friend. Soon after his arrival in Wellington, Arnold went off to inspect the family property, which consisted of two parcels of land of 100 acres each, situated in the Makara valley, about 8 miles to the west of Wellington. He sent an account of them to Jane on 29 May, with a sketch map; he is not very enthusiastic, but tries to make the best of the prospect. In his autobiography he describes the drawbacks of this inaccessible piece of land:

For about half the distance there was a good road; for the rest of the way only a bridle path which had been recently cut through the bush across the steep ridge which bounded the Makara valley on the east. The sections were near one another, but on opposite sides of the valley; about half of each was pretty level; the rest lay on the slopes of the bounding ridges. If I remember right, not an acre of land on the Makara had as yet been cleared; a dark bush, consisting mainly of red pine, everywhere obstructed the sight.[9]

Dr Arnold had not done very well with his unseen purchase. Perhaps acknowledging this, the New Zealand Company's principal agent in Wellington told Arnold that there were still some unallotted sites in better situations, and that if he wished he could exchange one of the Makara sites for one of these. A lawyer confirmed that there was no objection to such an exchange; it would need to be confirmed by the Arnold trustees in England, and Arnold wrote to them, in the confident assumption that they would agree to what was a desirable move.

A much more accessible parcel of level land was available, on one of the best roads out of Wellington, which meant it would be easier to reach and to work. Having decided on it, Arnold took time off on an expedition and an errand. He made his way on foot to the Maori settlement of Otaki on the west coast, where Mr Cole had a horse that he wanted brought back to Wellington. The trip gave Arnold his first sight of the Maoris and their style of building; he returned on horseback.

Although a better piece of land had been found, Arnold was already showing characteristic signs of vacillation about the whole project. Perhaps, after all, he was more fitted to be a teacher than a farmer. Writing to his mother on 25 June, he tells her about his trip to Otaki, then goes on 'to something of nearer and more personal interest':

You must know that of late I have often been revolving in my mind, how I might turn to use, if possible, whatever of natural faculty or acquired knowledge I may have, and make these minister to the good of those amongst whom I am now to live. For I am well aware that I have no particular genius for farming, and that I am better fitted to teach little boys English History than to invent improved methods of cultivation or breeding fat cattle. So I had been forming various schemes of getting together the neighbours' children when I go to live in the bush, and teaching them, in short of making myself a sort of village pedagogue.[10]

It is the sort of proposal that Dr Arnold would have thoroughly approved of, though it is not clear whether Tom saw pedagogy as something he would combine with farming or to substitute for it. But that was not all that was in his mind, for he had been shown a grander possibility. Domett told him that the New Zealand Company was planning to build a college at Nelson, the town across the Cook Strait on South Island that the Company had founded. Funds were available, he said; 'He then asked me whether I would consent to be the Principal or Provost, or whatever the name might be, of such a college supposing the appointment could be got for me.' Arnold said he would, provided he 'were left entirely unfettered in the matter of opinions'.[11] Domett assured him he would be, and spoke as if Arnold were a certainty for the appointment, though it would take a year to be established, as the Company in England would have to approve it. It was an unsettling prospect for a 25-year-old who had not yet started on the farming that he had gone to New Zealand to undertake. It went to his head, and a few days later he sent the news to Clough, in a vein of unrestrained castle-building: 'Supposing then that I were elected Principal, do you think there would be any chance of your accepting a Professorship? Here there are a heap of contingencies, I allow; but what I want to know is, whether there is the slightest chance of your accepting the thing if it was offered; because if I thought there was, I would move heaven and earth to obtain the power of offering it to you.'[12]

Meanwhile, there was ground to be cleared of bush and trees. Arnold found lodgings in the home of a small farmer, originally from Kent, called Barrow, who lived about 3 miles from the site. He paid Barrow and his two sons, later augmented by a Tahitian and a Maori, to start the clearances, though he regretted that so many exotic trees had to be cut down. He kept his hand in as a pedagogue by giving lessons to the Barrows' younger children. Only 5 acres out of the total 100 acres were cleared; Barrow also built a two-roomed hut, for which Arnold supplied the timber. He entertained vague thoughts of a pastoral existence; he thought he might raise potatoes and a little wheat, grow garden vegetables and keep a few animals. Indeed, in July 1848 he told his 15-year-old sister Fan that he was now the owner of a cow. He also told her how he had met the governor of the colony, Sir George Grey: 'Today, as I was down at work in the bush, dressed in a blue serge shirt, such as labouring men wear and employed in patching up a temporary ladder, three horsemen came galloping up the road. When they had reached me, they pulled up, and one of them, Thomas the Auditor General, whom I knew, said, "Arnold, the Governor is come to see you."'[13] Grey had been appointed as a trouble-shooter, whose task was to bring some order into the chaotic affairs of the colony. He approached his task in the spirit of a benign despot, without much trust in representative institutions, which made him a controversial figure. He was already aware of the young recent arrival who was a son of Dr Arnold with a First-class degree from Oxford. As Arnold describes the encounter, after some general conversation Grey asked him if he would agree to serve as the head of a new college on Anglo-Catholic principles that the bishop was establishing. Arnold was already expecting to head the New Zealand Company's proposed college at Nelson; as he remarked to Fan, 'I am in the ludicrous position of having two colleges thrown at my head at the same time.' He declined the governor's invitation, regarding himself as potentially committed elsewhere and in any case objecting to such a sectarian project. In *Passages from a Wandering Life* (1900), Arnold gives a different account of Grey's proposal, describing it as the offer of a post as his private-secretary. He says that he turned it down because he did not wish to throw up his work on the land, and, in a sentiment worthy of Philip Hewson in Clough's *Bothie*, 'the radical idea influenced me that men of independent character ought not to have any-thing to do with the Colonial Government so long as it was carried on by means of nominee, not representative assemblies'.[14] In his autobiog-raphy Arnold seems to have confused two separate offers; writing to Clough on 9 September he refers to the governor's offer of the secretary-ship as one which he had just received and was, at that point, inclined to accept on a temporary basis until the proposed college materialized. He indulges in further pipe-dreams, developed with mocking exaggeration, about Clough joining him:

Here, where we could work with a free activity, we might lay the foundations deep and wide, of an institution, which like Iona in the middle ages, might one day spread the light of Religion and Letters over these barbarous colonies and throughout the great archipelago of the Pacific, where hitherto only the white man's avarice or lust or his imbecile Theology have penetrated.[15]

He had recently received a long letter from Clough written some months before, describing the revolutions then convulsing Europe in that portentous year, which aroused Arnold's fervent republican nostalgia. He wondered if by then England itself might be in the throes of revolution. According to *Passages in a Wandering Life*, at the end of September 1848 Arnold received a reply from the trustees to his request to exchange the parcels of land. I am sceptical about this dating, as Arnold only made the proposal for the exchange in June, and it is very unlikely that a reply could have reached him so soon. Arnold's autobiography, written more than forty years after these events, provides sharp recall of particular details, but is not always reliable about their sequence, and presents simplified narratives. It is likely that Tom misdated the trustees' reply; in a letter to Jane written in August of the following year he refers to it as if it were a recent event. The trustees were Tom's maternal uncle Trevenen, and Dr Arnold's close friend the lawyer John Taylor Coleridge (father of Tom's Oxford acquaintance, John Duke Coleridge). As Arnold describes it, the reponse was shattering, a flat refusal to authorize any exchange of plots of land. Perhaps he had not given enough information in his letter, or not been persuasive enough. From so many thousand miles away, any departure from clearly defined legal arrangements may have looked doubtful and not to be tolerated. There is also the consideration that though Tom was regarded with great affection in the family he was not thought of as a man of sound judgement. And perhaps he had not been in this instance; it would have been more cautious to have waited for the trustees' permission before taking up the exchange, though he had been assured locally that there could be no objection to it. Whatever the motives and underlying issues, the short-term result was disastrous for Arnold. He had spent most of his capital in paying for the clearing of a site which was not legally his, and which reverted to the New Zealand Company for the benefit of another occupier. The hut, which he had jokingly dubbed the southern Fox How, had to be surrendered; he had been negotiating with potential smallholders who wanted to rent portions of the land, and those arrangements had to be cancelled. The result was to put Arnold off farming; someone of more determined temperament would have returned to the original plots in the Makara valley, even though they were difficult to get at and consisted of inferior land. But even if he had been willing to, he could not have afforded it. Taking a longer view, the trustees' refusal may have been a blessing in disguise, notwithstanding the heavy financial loss. Given Arnold's temperament and his basic lack of interest in farming, he is unlikely to have made a success of it. Leaving aside pastoral dreams, small-scale mixed farming was difficult to make a living at; in Keith

Sinclair's words, the smallholder 'often led a semi-barbarous existence for many years living in rough huts and eating mutton and damper [unleavened bread baked in a fire]'.[16] The only profitable agricultural pursuit in New Zealand in that era was sheep-farming; this was demonstrated ten years later by another young English immigrant with intellectual interests but a good deal more capital, Samuel Butler. He spent five years as a sheep-farmer in the colony and did very well out of it.

According to the account in Arnold's autobiography, after the trustees' refusal Domett urged him to cross over to Nelson and open a school there—for which there was an urgent need—that could later be merged in the proposed college. Arnold had meanwhile turned down Grey's secretaryship, one of his reasons being that he did not wish to move north to Auckland, where the governor was then based. Notwithstanding the blow of the refusal, it is, I think, likely that Arnold had already decided to abandon farming for teaching before it arrived.

He decided to go to Nelson and investigate the prospects. Transport across Cook Strait was irregular, but Frederic Weld was travelling to his sheep-station at Flaxbourne in North Island, and gave Arnold a ride in his small cutter, the *Petrel*. Once there he spent three weeks as Weld's guest, talking about books and ideas and enjoying his austere but warm hospitality. He went shooting with Weld in order to replenish the larder with teal and quail. As Arnold put it, 'the larder needed replenishing: the fare consisted of mutton chops and damper for breakfast; ditto for dinner, and ditto for supper. There was no milk or butter, but plenty of tea and claret, and abundance of sauces and pickles. The teal, therefore, which were superior in flavour, I think, to the English teal, were always acceptable.'[17] In the small hours of 16 October he was shaken awake by an earthquake; it was very alarming, but daylight revealed that it had done no damage though it left large cracks in the ground, and after-shocks continued for some time. The locals were familiar with these disturbances; the boundary between the Indo-Australian and the Pacific tectonic plates passes diagonally across South Island.

When it was time for Arnold to move on to Nelson, Weld took him some of the way by boat around the coast, and for the rest he needed to make a difficult trek overland. However, Arnold was good at finding people to give him a helping hand, and he met a Mr Sweet, a settler from Nelson who was returning there and offered to accompany him and even lend him a horse. But Sweet had business to transact on the way, and they did not reach Nelson until 8 November. He was warmly received by the people he met there, particularly the New Zealand Company's local representative, Francis Dillon Bell. Arnold was impressed with the beauty of the area:

The country round Nelson is of singular loveliness. Like Athens, the town slopes towards the sea and the midday sun . . . Standing on the Fort Hill in the middle of the town, and looking westward, one saw a range of mountains stretching for twenty miles or more from south to north, apparently about 2000 feet high, and forming the western boundary of the bay. Through gaps in this range could be seen the higher peaks beyond, usually capped with snow.[18]

For all its remoteness, someone in rural Yorkshire had heard of Nelson. In Chapter VII of Anne Brontë's *Agnes Grey*, published in 1847, the eponymous heroine reflects on her isolated situation: 'But this gives no proper idea of my feelings at all; and no one that has not lived such a retired, stationary life as mine can possibly imagine what they were: hardly even if he has known what it is to awake some morning and find himself in Port Nelson, in New Zealand, with a world of waters between himself and all that knew him.'

At the end of December Arnold returned to Wellington to sort out his affairs; he had agreed with a number of Nelson parents to start the school if a minimum number of boys could be enrolled. Early in February 1849 he was given a farewell party by his friends, including Bell, Collison, Domett, and Weld. He proved his radical *bona fides* by singing the Marseillaise: 'They drank my health in a very pretty manner, as one who was about shortly to leave Wellington, and I returned thanks with great conciseness.'[19] By March Arnold was back in Nelson and had launched his school in temporary accommodation. The determined cheerfulness that marked his letters to his mother and sisters, with their careful descriptions of natural beauty and interesting people encountered, was wearing thin. He had his treasured picture of Jenny Lind on the wall, but he wanted something more; everything would go swimmingly, he told his mother, if only he had a wife. But there were few women in New Zealand, and there was no equivalent to the convoys of eligible girls who visited India searching for husbands among the young officers and civilian officials. The school had enrolled nineteen local pupils and one boarder from Wellington, which was the minimum number Arnold had wanted.

On 1 April 1849 he belatedly thanks Clough for a long letter written the previous year and received in January, in which his friend gave a colourful account of the days he had spent in revolutionary Paris in May 1848.

Arnold unenthusiastically brings him up to date about his own affairs: 'I have just begun to keep a small school here; it is rather a bore, as the boys are young and unruly; but I find that it suits me better than digging, and it is just as honest a way of earning a living. But it leaves me some time to read for myself; and I find myself more and more drawn to study as to my natural vocation.'[20] But study was thwarted by the difficulty of obtaining books; Arnold described it as a 'serious evil', and said it might be a factor forcing him to return to Europe before much longer. Returning becomes a motif in his correspondence during 1849; Tom tells his mother that if he finds a wife he will stay in the colony, but if not he will eventually be back.

In July Arnold received a response from Clough, written the previous November, to his letter of June 1848, in which he had set out the glad news of the projected college at Nelson, the virtual promise he had received from Domett that he would be the head of it, and his hopes that Clough might join him. Clough, in his reply, says he might be interested; as he flirtatiously put it, 'The thing is not QUITE impossible, my dear Tom.' His own life was changing; unable to accept the Thirty-nine Articles any longer he was resigning his Oriel fellowship and leaving Oxford. He would need to go somewhere. An interest in the Antipodes was part of the Rugby inheritance; Dr Arnold had more than once expressed a wish to end his days in Australia, or in New Zealand, where he had made his unwise purchase of land. One of his first pupils, J. P. Gell, had gone to Van Diemen's Land and Clough, a close friend, kept up a regular correspondence with him.[21] As Clough's letter proceeds he starts setting out difficulties and reservations; it becomes apparent that though he is fascinated by the idea of New Zealand he has no real intention of going there. He had not, however, abandoned thoughts of Australasia. After leaving Oxford, Clough became principal of University Hall, which was part of the recently established London University. He was not altogether happy there—feeling happy was never Clough's *métier*—and in 1851 he resigned. He submitted an application for the Chair of Classics at the University College in Sydney which had opened the previous year. It was unsuccessful; Clough had been stymied by Provost Hawkins of Oriel, who declined to write a reference for him on the grounds that 'no one ought to be appointed to such a situation who is at all in a state of doubt or difficulty as to his own religious beliefs'.[22]

By the time Tom Arnold received Clough's letter, the prospect of the college had vanished like the mirage it had probably always been. As he glumly explained in a reply dated 7 July:

Domett thought, when he first spoke to me about the College, that it would really come into operation in a year's time, and I thinking his authority unimpeachable, wrote to you as I did; but twelve months have passed, and there is, as far as I can see, no immediate prospect of the Company's handing over the funds. I had no idea of the difficulties accompanying the forcing of a public body to act, especially when the action implies putting their hands in their pockets from the distance of 16,000 miles.[23]

The whole project had been misconceived and wrapped in wishful thinking. The urgent need in the colony was not for higher but for basic primary and secondary education. Many of the early settlers were illiterate, and only a minority of children went to any sort of school.[24] Arnold was not very impressed with the boys he taught, as he told his mother: 'The day scholars are a very heterogeneous set; as might be expected, not one of them is decidedly clever, though several are anxious to learn and take pains. The most advanced of them is Richmond, son of Major Richmond, the Superintendent of this place, and he is very far from bright.'[25] A further difficulty emerged when Arnold found that though the parents wanted their sons educated, they were slow at paying the fees: 'one has the greatest difficulty in getting any money due to one, and those to whom you owe are always dunning you'.[26]

By August 1849 he seems to have decided that the school at Nelson would have to be written off as one more failed enterprise, even though it had just moved into a new building. (But it was far from complete, and he grumbled that he could not get the carpenters to finish off their work.) He told Jane, 'I want a fixed income, regularly paid, however small it be; for the bore and trouble of collecting and asking for money, is, to a man of my disposition, most irksome.'[27] A way out, or a way forward, unexpectedly presented itself. He met a young officer on a brief visit to Nelson, Lieutenant Andrew Clarke, who was aide-de-camp to Sir William Denison, lieutenant-governor of Van Diemen's Land. He told Arnold that Denison's secretary was Arthur Stanley's younger brother Charles, whom Arnold had known well in earlier years. On his return Clarke told Stanley of Arnold's whereabouts. Arnold had been thinking of applying to a large school that was being launched in Hobart and needed teachers, but the Rugby network was effectively in action. He received a friendly letter from Stanley, dated 25 June 1849, asking if he would be interested in the post of Inspector of Schools for Van Diemen's Land, to replace an official who had recently died. It provided a salary of 400 pounds plus travelling expenses. Stanley enclosed a letter from the governor offering

Arnold the post; he urged him to go to Hobart Town, as it was then called, even if he could not accept the offer, and stay at Government House as his guest. This was deliverance, on exceptionally good terms. There was, though, a delay either in sending the letter or in Arnold receiving it; he still did not know about Denison's offer when on 1 August he mentioned to Jane the possibility of applying for a teaching post in Hobart.

But by 20 August the offer had arrived and he had no hesitation in accepting it. On that day he wrote to his mother in a spirit of shrill but understandable triumph, invoking Psalm 37:

How good is God; how he watches over the children of the righteous. 'I have been young and am now old, yet never saw I the righteous forsaken, nor his seed begging their bread'. Shakespeare says 'What's in a name?'; but our father's name has been to us, not only a source of proud and gentle memories, but actually and literally better and more profitable than houses and land.[28]

Certainly the Arnold name would have played a large part in this offer; it was an age when such patronage was taken for granted, and when there was also a belief—mystical rather than scientific—in the inheritance of exceptional qualities. Tom Arnold, always given to looking for outside support, was very ready to invoke his father's name (and did so to excess, Matthew complained years later). The Arnold name triumphed even though there were local candidates for the post. Tom told his mother that he expected to be in Hobart by the end of September, but the arrangements took a lot longer to set up than he expected.

While he was waiting for transport to Wellington, he engaged in an unusual and profitable task by acting as arbitrator in a land dispute that the local branch of the New Zealand Company was involved in; evidently the Arnold name was seen as a guarantee of fair and disinterested judgement. His friends in Nelson gave him a farewell dinner at the principal inn of the settlement, and on 20 October he finally embarked for Wellington on a coaster which took a fortnight to get there. When he left he was still owed money by the parents of some of the children he had taught. By December Matthew, in London, had heard from the Colonial Office something of Tom's possible move; he told Clough that he did not know if Tom would accept it but thought he probably would: 'I think I shall emigrate: why the devil don't you.'[29] The last part of Tom's slow journey to a new life was summarized in a letter to his youngest brother, Walter:

In October 1849 I left Nelson in a small coasting craft, and crossed the straits to Wellington. From Wellington I took the 'William Henry' a schooner of some 120 tons, to Sydney; it was about a fortnight's voyage. I arrived in Sydney about the middle of December, stayed broiling there for more than a fortnight, and then took my passage by the 'Shamrock', a steamer of 250 tons, for Launceston. We stopped at Broulee and Two-fold Bay, where there is a most desirable settlement, all sand and gum-trees, called Eden, from which Dickens might have got the idea in Martin Chuzzlewit.

Doubling Cape Howe, we came to the heads of Port Phillip, sailed over the little inland sea, forty miles over, which divides the heads from Williamstown the port of Melbourne, and steamed up the Yarra to Melbourne itself . . . At that time the gold slept undisturbed beneath the turf, and people were flocking in crowds to California . . . Sailing from Melbourne, we crossed Bass's Straits, and steamed up the winding Tamar to Launceston, where we arrived on Sunday the 14th January 1850. The next day I crossed the island by coach to Hobart Town.[30]

CHAPTER 4

Van Diemen's Land

Things looked up for Tom Arnold after he crossed the Tasman Sea. Van Diemen's Land, as Tasmania was known until 1856, was a more developed colonial society than New Zealand; it was to provide him with a wife, a family, and work that he found, for the most part, constructive and satisfying. As his ship approached the coast on 13 January 1850 he was cheered by the sight of mountains, 'those dear old friends, the sight of which is always a comfort to me', as he told Jane.[1] He disembarked at Launceston in the north of the island, and next day he left early for the capital, Hobart, 120 miles to the south along a good road built by convict labour. Such evidence of the colony's origins and recent past lay all around. Van Diemen's Land, like its parent colony, Botany Bay, later New South Wales, had been established and built up partly as a depository for convicts from the homeland. The practice of transportation was on the point of being abolished, after much delay and many arguments both in England and Australia, but it was still in force in Van Diemen's Land.

Arnold was pleased with the appearance of the country, as he observed it on his journey south. 'There is far more flat land in proportion to mountains than in New Zealand; but on the other hand it is not nearly so well watered.'[2] Hobart had been founded at the beginning of the nineteenth century. John West, in his history of Tasmania published in 1852, describes the town as it was when Arnold arrived:

It is finely situated on a rising ground, and covers a surface of nearly two square miles. On the western side it is bounded by a range of wooded hills, with Mount Wellington, a snow-capped mountain, 4,000 feet high, in the background. On the southern side of the harbour there are many beautiful residences, and, on a commanding eminence, fine military barracks. Close to the harbour, on the western side, stands the government-house, an extensive range of wooden buildings, erected at different times. Mulgrave Battery is on the southern side of the harbour. The streets are regular and well made; and many of the buildings—some built of freestone—are commodious and handsome. The wharves are extensive and well constructed, and are lined with numerous large stone warehouses and stores. St David's church is a large well-built brick edifice in the Gothic style, stuccoed and well fitted up.[3]

West concludes his account with the information that at that time the population of Hobart was 23,107, and there were 4,050 houses, 2,392 of which were built of stone or brick; five bi-weekly newspapers and a government gazette were published.

In Hobart Arnold stayed with his cousin John Buckland, who had gone out there as a headmaster in 1846. He had been looking forward to seeing Charles Stanley again but he had died suddenly; Arnold had a sad meeting with his widow. He was introduced to the governor, Sir William Denison, who was a military engineer and looked the part: 'He is rather short, but strongly built, and with the solid compact brow and intelligent but unimaginative eye, which you see so often in men of science. He has a straightforward decisive manner of delivering himself, which I like. He spoke generally of the duties of my office, and said that he would talk over the subject with me at greater length on future occasions.'[4]

Another significant encounter soon followed. Arnold wrote about it many years later in a memoir of his wife written after her death and intended for his children:

I think I had been about a month at Hobart Town before I met your mother. It was at a dance at the house of a Mr Poynter, a lawyer. She was a great favourite with Mrs Poynter. Looking round the room on entering, I saw a lady in black, wearing a single white camellia in her black hair, with a singularly refined and animated face, seated on a sofa talking to Charles Clarke. After a while he took me up and introduced me to 'Miss Sorell'. The usual arrangements for dances were made, and we had much to talk about together that evening. I remember how strong the feeling was upon me I *must* have met her before; a sense of moral like-ness, an overpowering attraction and affinity, drew me to her. For me it was certainly 'love at first sight'.[5]

A rapid romance followed. Tom had previously written to his mother about his need for a wife, and she had responded in her characteristically gentle and gracious fashion: 'It is my earnest wish that I may love your wife, whoever she may be, and I could do so, I am sure, unseen, if she were good and made you happy.'[6] But Mrs Arnold might have had difficulties in whole-heartedly approving of Julia Sorell. Her father was in a highly respectable position, as registrar of the supreme court at Hobart, and the Sorells were a well-known family in the colony—there was a township named after them—but their reputation was tinged with notoriety. They could trace their descent back to the seventeenth century, and they claimed Huguenot and Spanish connections. They were a military family and Julia's grandfather was Colonel William Sorell, governor of Van Diemen's Land from 1816 to 1823. He scandalously disregarded accepted morality; while serving at the Cape of Good Hope he had seduced the wife of a Lieutenant Kent, to whom he had to pay a large sum for 'criminal conversation' with her. After Sorell moved to Van Diemen's Land as governor, Mrs Kent lived with him as his wife and bore him several children. Meanwhile his wife and legitimate children—the eldest of whom became Julia's father—languished in England, inadequately supported by their father. Sorell was a capable and popular governor, but eventually the colonial secretary in London took account of complaints about his moral turpitude and dismissed him. The early historian of Tasmania writes of Sorell in warm and admiring terms and describes a public meeting that was held in an unsuccessful protest against his recall, though he does not refer to the reason for it.[7]

Julia's maternal grandfather, Captain Anthony Kent, was another colourful character. After serving in New South Wales he became one of the leading settlers in Van Diemen's Land, with wide commercial interests, some of dubious honesty. He had republican views and a quarrelsome disposition; Julia's mother, Elizabeth Julia Kent, was one of his eighteen children. Kent seems to have had a hand in Sorell's dismissal by passing on complaints about him. Nevertheless, the families were united when Elizabeth Julia married William Sorell Junior, who had returned from England to Van Diemen's Land about the time his father left it. His wife had inherited her father's rakishness. When she took Julia and her two younger daughters to Brussels for their education, she decamped with an army officer and was never seen again. The girls had to return to Van Diemen's Land by themselves. Such was Julia's complex inheritance. She was 24 when she met Tom, rather old for an unmarried girl. She had been twice engaged and ugly rumours circulated in Hobart about more scandalous involvements; Tom Arnold, in his manuscript memoir, refers to the excellence of Julia's character but acknowledges that she had some 'female detractors'.

Tom described her as beautiful, and her daughter recalls:

Of her personal beauty in youth we children heard much, as we grew up, from her old Tasmanian friends and kinsfolk who would occasionally drift across us; and I see as though I had been there, a scene often described to me—my mother playing Hermione in the 'Winter's Tale', at Government House when Sir William Denison was Governor—a vision, lovely and motionless, on her pedestal, till at the words, 'Music! awake her! Strike!' she kindled into life.[8]

Mary Ward's own daughter, Janet Penrose Trevelyan, refers in her biography of her mother to some of Julia's other characteristics, such as her 'undisciplined and tempestuous nature' and her tendencies 'to extravagance in money matters and to passionate outbursts of temper'.[9]

Tom Arnold had wanted a wife for the traditional needs of help, companionship, and the relief of concupiscence; but now he was in love, and he became a pressing suitor. Julia, too, needed a husband, to avoid the fate of being left on the shelf, and to give her the respectable status of a married woman. Tom would have been a good person to marry even if she were not in love with him; but evidently she was. Even so, she brought certain rational elements to their courtship. If Dr Arnold's name was helpful in finding Tom employment, it also helped in his romance. Julia's father was familiar with Stanley's life of Dr Arnold and greatly admired him and his work; and so did his daughter, passing on the admiration to the younger Thomas. Julia professed to prefer the 'clerico-professional' strands of English society to the military, official, and settler elements that were commonly met with in the colony: not surprisingly, given the amount of scandal that military men had brought to the family. Years later, Julia told Tom, 'Few families have been blessed with such a home training as yours, and certainly very few in our rank of life have been cursed with such as mine.'[10]

Tom proposed on 20 March 1850 and was at once accepted. His work was already taking him on tours of inspection to outlying parts of the colony, and he sent a succession of love letters while he was away. They are infused with high Romantic sentiments, and are what the Victorians would have regarded as 'warm' in tone; he writes of his impatient desire to give Julia 365 kisses. He would certainly have written to his mother with the news of his engagement, though no letter has survived. Whatever she thought about Julia—and Tom would have given a carefully selected account of his beloved's character and antecedents—Mrs Arnold was in no position to affect his decision. Nor is it likely that she could have done even if she had been there; Tom was utterly devoted to his mother, but when his mind was made up he did what he wanted to do. Probably, by the time Mary Arnold received the letter with the news, the marriage was a *fait accompli*. It took place on 13 June 1850, Dr Arnold's birthday, in St David's church, Hobart. The elderly officiating clergyman,

Dr William Bedford, had christened Julia in her infancy. On 18 June a newly wed Tom wrote to his mother with an account of the ceremony. In order to indulge what he called the 'weak minds' of his younger sisters he described first his own attire: 'I had on a blue frock coat, white waistcoat with lappels, light grey doeskin trowsers, and a tie of brown and white silk, tied in large bows.' Early Victorian dandyism had not yet been extinguished by dark broadcloth. He continued:

Julia looked pale, and was more moved than I had expected she would be. She was dressed as follows: I tell you from her own mouth. She wore a white hook muslin dress over muslin, high to the throat, with two deep flounces;—a white lace mantle, white chip bonnet with a small feather and lace veil; and white satin shoes. Both the dress and mantle were richly trimmed with lace. She also wore a massive Indian gold chain round her neck . . . whether from these data you will be able to form any sort of notion of the actual appearance of my beloved bride, I know not; but I know that in my eyes a thing so beautiful has rarely been seen.[11]

Julia's younger sisters, Augusta and Ada, also in muslin, were bridesmaids. After the ceremony there was a wedding breakfast at Mr Sorell's house; the cake, Tom approvingly remarked, was of 'ponderous proportions'. Some of it was despatched across the world to Fox How. The honeymoon was deferred, and the couple went straight to the house that was to be their home for the next three years. It was a stone cottage with an ironwork verandah, in the suburb of New Town, about 2 miles from the centre of Hobart. On 24 July Julia sent an affectionate note to her mother-in-law, enclosed in a longer letter of Tom's. She wrote, rather plaintively, 'We shall both be so glad dear Mrs Arnold when we hear from you in answer to Tom's letter telling you of our marriage.'[12]

By the following year Tom and his wife had received Mary Arnold's blessing. In March 1851 he wrote to Jane, who had herself married William Forster the previous August, 'Your note and Mother's gave great joy to my darling Julia, but I shall leave her to reply to them herself.' He continued with a detailed account of their daily lives:

Between 6 and 7 I get up, and when I am dressed, take a walk around the yard, to see how the pigs and poultry are getting on, and generally go round the garden also, which, as it is not more than a rood in extent, does not take me long. Then I come in, and sit down to read or write in the diningroom, into which our bedroom opens and whither I have now removed all the books from the study, which is at present in the transition or chrysalis-stage of a *workroom* but is intended to develop itself into a full grown nursery, should the Fates and Lucina be propitious. I jest, but yet you may well believe that I am anxious; who would not be? At

8 Julia gets up and we breakfast a little before 9. In little more than half an hour, I set off for town, 10 being the office hour. It is rather more than a mile and a half from our house to the office. At the office I answer letters, see persons who call on business, examine the accounts of the department; and so on. If my time is not fully occupied in this way, I go out and visit one of the town schools. About half past 1, I go to Luncheon at Mr Sorell's and talk over the gossip of the day with Gussie and Ada. I am very fond of them both; though I do not always approve of things that they do. Julia sometimes comes in to town at this time in the gig, driven by 'Joey' as we call him . . . After luncheon I return to the office or visit schools—generally the former—until 4. Then I walk out home, and when there we either go out for a short walk, or I dig potatoes in the garden while Julia looks on. At half past 5 we dine. In the evening Julia sometimes plays on the piano . . . or else works while I read aloud to her, or else I read to myself. At 9 Julia goes to bed, and I follow about 11 . . .[13]

Julia was pregnant and on 11 June Tom wrote to tell his mother that Mary Augusta had been born that morning.

A few weeks earlier Matthew, in a letter to Jane, had reflected on Tom's marriage: 'There is a great change in Tom certainly: something a little pedantic still in his style perhaps, which comes from reading books of sentiment so much and in such pure faith—but on the whole he seems greatly cleared. What his relations with his wife are does not exactly come out in his letters I think: I dare say there is no very deep reaching sympathy between them.'[14] Matthew is disagreeably supercilious, though he is perceptive about Tom's sentimental tendencies. He had not yet had direct experience of marriage himself but a month later he married Fanny Lucy Wightman.

Their brother William, himself recently married, wrote to Tom from India when the news reached him: 'I wonder whether it has changed you much?—not made a Tory of you, I'll undertake to say! But it is wonderfully sobering. After all, Master Tom, it is not the very exact *finale* which we should have expected to your Republicanism of the last three or four years, to find you a respectable married man, holding a permanent appointment.'[15]

In 1853 Tom started writing a novel, looking back on his experiences in New Zealand and Van Diemen's Land. It had no title beyond 'Fragments of a Novel' and the remnants of it in Arnold's papers at Balliol are very fragmentary indeed and partly illegible. It has a colonial setting, and a protagonist who mourns the failure of the European revolutions of 1848: 'After the Fall of Venice, I made the best of my way back to England, much sobered in mind, not to say soured.' One thinks of

Clough and his Roman experiences. The idealized picture of the heroine, Lucy Winthrop, is evidently drawn from Julia:

The sweet girl, draped in pure white with a camellia in her hair, looked even more cheerful and sunny than was her custom. She danced beautifully; indeed she did well everything she attempted . . . Her receptive many-sided nature seized upon every variety of thought, feeling or pursuit which life had to offer her, and tried it to the end. It might be expected that she would be led sometimes into error and exaggeration, and we shall see that it was so.[16]

Tom, like his father, was philoprogenitive. His first son, William Thomas, was born in 1852. Julia was soon pregnant again, but mortality sadly intruded, as it did in so many families until modern times. On 19 May 1854 a second son was born, but the infant was subject to convulsions, and despite such medical attention as was available died within twenty-four hours. Before he died he was christened Arthur Penrose; a tribute to Stanley, and perhaps also to Clough. A replacement soon followed; in 1855 Julia gave birth to a healthy son, Theodore. Recording these events in the memoir that he wrote after Julia's death, Tom showed himself in a curious state of confusion and amnesia about who had lived and who had died. He refers to the 'first Theodore' who was born in 1854 and only lived for a week; he means Arthur, who lived for only one day, and who was his first son of that name. There was only one Theodore and he lived until middle age.

Despite a happy family life and absorbing work, Tom's thoughts often dwelt on the prospect of sooner or later returning to England. Julia seems to have shared in this aspiration; she had briefly seen something of life in Europe and perhaps wanted more of it. Her family's scandalous history might also have made Van Diemen's Land a homeland that she would have no particular qualms about leaving. Meanwhile, letters from England were a lifeline. And not only letters; Tom was eager to read the literary productions of the Clougho-Matthean circle. Writing to Jane from New Zealand in August 1849 he expressed impatience to see Matthew's debut as a poet, *The Strayed Reveller and Other Poems*, and was cross with its author for not sending him a copy. By September, it had arrived, together with *Ambarvalia*, the collection of poems which Clough published jointly with Thomas Burbidge, and *The Bothie of Tober-na-Vuolich*. He read them all eagerly. He does not say very much about Matthew's book, though he remarks that it was pleasant to recognize 'old friends' in it, and adds that he will be writing to Matthew about it.

Unfortunately, we do not know what he said, as his brother did not keep his letters. He recognizes the origins of 'Resignation' in a long walk over the Lake District fells that the older Arnold children, Jane, Matthew, and the 9-year-old Tom had taken with their father and a family friend, Captain Hamilton. Matthew's poem is elevated and Wordsworthian in its meditations on time and mutability, but Tom would have enjoyed its evocation of a well-loved landscape. In a note on the poem first published in 1869 Matthew wrote, 'Those who have been long familiar with the English Lake-Country will find no difficulty in recalling, from the description in the text, the roadside inn at Whythburn on the descent from Dunmail Raise towards Keswick; its sedentary landlord of thirty years ago, and the passage over the Wythburn Fells to Watendlath.'

Tom is enthusiastic about Clough's *Bothie*. It would have evoked memories of Highland reading parties, and though he always played down the supposed identification of himself with Philip Hewson, there were many things in the poem that would have stirred his feelings. There is a note of reservation in his praise, reflecting Rugbeian propriety, but he goes on to invoke Milton, whose *Areopagitica* he had been reading:

The 'Bothie' greatly surpasses my expectations. With a vein of coarseness cropping out here and there, it is yet on the whole a noble poem, well held together, clear, full of purpose, and full of promise. With joy I see the old fellow bestirring himself, 'awakening like a strong man out of sleep, and shaking his invincible locks', and if he remains true and works, I think there is nothing too high and great to be expected from him. I do not think Matt was right in saying that Clough 'had no vocation for literature'.[17]

Later critical opinion of Clough has agreed with Tom rather than Matthew, whose lack of appreciation of his poetry was a cross Clough had to bear. Writing to Clough from Wellington a little later, Tom goes on praising the poem, and even withdraws his criticism of its coarseness. It has, he says, been read and discussed: 'Domett, after reading it, said emphatically, in his deep gruff voice, "That will live".'[18]

Another family literary production that Tom looked forward to reading was his brother William's *Oakfield*; in January 1854 he told his mother, 'I am very anxious to see dear Willy's novel. I have read a review of it in the "Morning Herald".'[19] *Oakfield* arrived; Tom read it and passed it around to many readers, who, he says, were exceedingly interested by it, but there is nothing surviving in his correspondence to say what he himself thought of it. This may indicate a lack of enthusiasm, or just a missing letter. Writing to Willy in April 1854 he reports, 'I have lent Oakfield to several persons. John Buckland, as you fancy, did not much relish it; thought the conversations "unnatural" and too long. Dr Bedford, about the most intelligent person here, was very much pleased with the book; he was struck with the moral resemblance of the author to Papa. This no one could fail to be who knew Papa's writings well.'[20] Both remarks are to the point. Tom would have noted that at one point in the novel Oakfield thinks of New Zealand as the 'good place' and the opposite of India, in a hint of a paradisal–infernal polarity; William may have been affected by Tom's letters.

Tom enjoyed domestic life and delighted in his little daughter. When she was 2 he told his mother, 'She evidently understands the meaning of a great many words which she cannot speak. She is passionate but not peevish; sensitive to the least harshness in word or gesture, but usually full of merriment and gladsomeness. She is like a sparkling fountain or a gay flower in the house, filling it with light and freshness.'[21] The word 'passionate' is significant: Mary had inherited her mother's hot temper. By the time she was 4 rather more of her nature had emerged. In November 1854 Tom told his mother, 'Mary is distracting my attention very much, for she is very naughty this morning. A child more obstinately self-willed I certainly never came across. It is very painful to have to punish her (which I usually do by locking her up) for the resistance of her will and the profusion of her tears and cries are wonderful; still it must be done, I suppose.'[22] Mary's will was formidable and made her a difficult child to control.

The young couple became friends of the Reverend Thomas Reibey and his wife; it was Reibey who christened Mary, though not until she was 3 months old. The free-thinking Tom made it clear that he thought such ceremonies had no particular significance, scandalizing Julia, who was not particularly religious but who wanted the traditional observances. The Reibeys lived at Entally in the north of the island, and more than once Tom and Julia stayed with them when he was on a tour of inspection. They were there in November 1852 with Mary and William, when they went on a holiday outing with Governor Denison and Andrew Clarke, his private-secretary, who were on official business in the district. Denison was an authoritarian personality, but he had a young family himself and was prepared to unbend. Much of Van Diemen's Land was still unexplored, and on another occasion when the Arnolds were staying at Entally, Reibey and Tom set off on an expedition. They climbed the mountain called Dry's Bluff and spent the night encamped at the top. In the morning it was raining so heavily that they abandoned the expedition and returned to Entally and their wives: 'with what a quizzing and ironical welcome we were received by those from whom we had parted with a flourish of trumpets the day before'.[23]

Life in Hobart was not entirely idyllic, because it was beset by inflation. The discovery of gold in mainland Australia had an unsettling effect on the economy of Van Diemen's Land. There was an exodus of adventurers seeking a fortune in the goldfields, labour became scarce and prices rose. Eventually the Arnolds could not afford the rent of their stone cottage on the New Town Road, but they were helped out by Denison, who permitted them to live in the former Normal School, now converted into a dwelling house, at a reduced rent. This was a fairly spacious property, where Tom set himself up in his spare time as a smallholder, as he had dreamed of doing in New Zealand. He made use of his experience there as he erected fences, made a driveway and paths, drained some of the land for cultivation, and planted an orchard on the rest. He bought a cow, which supplied the family with milk and butter. He grew vegetables on a large scale and was able to sell the surplus. Perhaps reminded by these activities, he thought regularly of New Zealand, which he decided he preferred to Van Diemen's Land. With his customary measure of castle-building, he thought of going back there as a farmer; of running a projected college in Wellington; and even of returning to Nelson, where the long-deferred college now seemed to be becoming a reality. In his underlying thoughts, though, the idea of returning to England was never far away.

Meanwhile, he kept up the day job. His appointment had a dual aspect; he was both head officer of the Education Department and Inspector of Schools. The former meant he had to spend time at his desk in the government building in Murray Street, dealing with official business; the latter took him round the colony, either on horseback or driving his gig. As an administrator he had to deal with the governor; Denison was interested in education and had his own ideas about it, but he was rigid and dogmatic in applying them. In November 1850 Tom wrote to his sister Mary:

The Governor, although I have a sincere respct, and, in some points, admiration for him, is a man of very arbitrary temper, and thinks lightly of any opinion that does not tally with his own. The same temper leads him very often to assume a short and dictatorial tone towards his Government officers, which it is difficult to put up with . . . Now your dear brother, being naturally placid and civil towards others, has no fancy for being cavalierly treated himself. He has not been accustomed to it, and every better feeling within him revolts against it. The Governor has already somewhat taxed my patience and if he goes on in the same way, it will be impossible to put up with it.[24]

For all his gentle temperament, Arnold was not willing to be bullied, and perhaps the governor respected him for it. Despite the friction, in the longer run it was Arnold's ideas about education that prevailed rather than Denison's. There was a basic difference between them on how the school system would work. Denison was an articulate reactionary, who believed—on the French model—that the state should closely govern the content and process of education; whilst also believing, like a modern free-marketeer, that the state should not pay for it, and that schools should be supported by local taxes. Arnold believed the opposite, wanting schools to have control over their own affairs whilst being supported by central funds. He argued that no-one would be willing to pay a local tax if local people had no say in the running of their school.

Arnold's tours of inspection made it evident to him that the schools scattered over Van Diemen's Land were in a very bad way, with crumbling buildings and demoralized and underpaid teachers. Part of the problem was the 'penny a day' system, which had been imposed by the Colonial Office. It meant that teachers were paid by a kind of capitation fee based on the number of pupils enrolled; a penny-halfpenny for each of the first sixteen; one penny each for numbers between sixteen and forty; and a halfpenny for numbers over forty. It was a system open to abuse; infants well below school age were enrolled to boost the numbers (and hence the teachers' pay), and in thinly populated areas—that is to say, most of the colony—it was not working at all. No-one really believed in the system, but Arnold reported on it in terms that the governor regarded as unacceptably vehement in a newly appointed young official. Nevertheless, as Arnold later wrote, 'The Governor, the best among the clergy, and my unworthy self, were all agreed that the penny-a-day system was full of evils, and in 1853 we changed it; an ordinance being passed establishing a Board of Education, and granting fixed salaries to the teachers.'[25] There was a real problem in finding sufficient qualified teachers. The governor had established a Normal School, or teacher training college, with the idea that local youths could become qualified as teachers. A Mr Leach had come out from England to act as superintendent, and the school opened in 1850. But, in P. A. Howell's words, 'The

Normal School was a complete fiasco.'[26] There were insufficient students and, of those, some were judged to be incompetent for teaching, some were removed for misconduct, and others removed themselves because teachers' pay was so inadequate. The school collapsed and the unfortunate Leach had to pay his own fare back to England. Then the school building became a residence for the Arnolds.

Arnold attempted to take a systematic overview of the problems and prospects of education in the colony. He drew up a set of 'Rules and Regulations for the Government of the Public Day Schools in Van Diemen's Land', which codified current practices and defined the government's role in the system. They dealt with day-to-day problems in running schools: attendance, religious instruction, conditions of service of teachers, local management, the inspector's examination, and so forth. The regulations were approved by the heads of the principal religious denominations and by the governor, and were duly gazetted. One gets the impression that on a number of issues Denison was outmanœuvred by Arnold; but he would have had other things to think about in his official position, and his term of office was coming to an end. He was still inclined to turn down extra expenditure until circumstances forced him to change his mind. Arnold proved himself an efficient administrator, drawing on the skills supposedly bestowed by a First in Greats, reinforced by his father's precepts and example.

His solitary role as inspector was taken over by a Board of Inspection, consisting of himself and representatives of the principal religious denominations: Anglican, Presbyterian, and Catholic. This ecumenical foursome travelled from school to school in a wagonette and pair driven by the Anglican Archdeacon Davies; according to Arnold, Fr Hall, the Catholic, had a mortified countenance and spoke little. They did a conscientious job and their unanimous report was instrumental in abolishing the penny-a-day system and setting up a representative Board of Education for the colony. There was still a problem in finding qualified teachers, and Arnold drew up a plan for importing suitable applicants from Britain, to the number of twenty a year. He proposed that he be sent home in order to select and test the candidates. It was a good try; if it had succeeded he and his family would have had a trip back to England at public expense. But that bright idea did not work; eventually a modified version of such a scheme was brought in, but without any headhunter from the colony vetting the applicants. Another plan of Arnold's did take off: it established a scheme for pupil-teachers, who could, after taking annual examinations, themselves qualify as teachers at the age of 18. It remained in force in Tasmania until the end of the nineteenth century. Over the years Arnold's workload increased and so did his salary, though, as he pointed out, because of the prevailing inflation his pay was worth less than the corresponding amount in England. Nevertheless, 500 pounds per year was a respectable sum for a man of 30 at that time.

One feature of life in Van Diemen's Land that Arnold hated was the transportation of convicts, then in its final phase. Writing to his mother in October 1850 he remarked, 'The hateful red flag is flying at the signal staff, showing that another ship with male convicts is coming in. A thousand more of the *worst* among men are expected before the end of the year, to colonize Tasmania.'[27] The colony was notorious for receiving some of the hardest cases to be deported, and as Arnold goes on to complain, once they arrived the convicts were released as 'ticket of leave men' and left to make their own way in the world. In many cases they found it easiest to resume their life of crime, to the fear and discomfort of the free settlers. The movement to abolish transportation had been gaining momentum for several years, and Van Diemen's Land was the last colony still to engage in it. Denison was strongly in favour of keeping it; partly, no doubt, from bloody-mindedness, and partly from the one plausible case for it, that it was a reliable way of maintaining a supply of colonists. The governor's stand was another reason for Arnold to feel at odds with him, as did many of the population.

Transportation was finally abolished in 1853. Although Arnold was severe about the convicts, he was prepared to admire certain honourable exceptions, such as the old Chartist John Frost, who had been transported for high treason because of his part in a Welsh riot in 1839. He trained as a teacher and in 1852 was appointed master in an Anglican school. Arnold wrote, 'the old man did his work conscientiously, and wrapped himself in a kind of dignified reserve, behind which there lay the impenetrable obstinacy of a Welsh reformer. It is needless to say that I treated him with entire respect.'[28] A less respectable but more colourful figure among the convicts was Thomas Wainewright. He had been well known in London as a dandy and an aesthete, an artist and an art-critic. He was also believed to have poisoned several members of his family, but though these crimes were strongly suspected he was never convicted of them. In addition, he was a forger, and it was for this offence that he was transported. Oscar Wilde discussed his career in his essay 'Pen, Pencil and Poison'. In Hobart Wainewright was able to live in freedom, though he was not permitted to return to England; he opened a studio and resumed his career as an artist; according to Wilde, he had not altogether given up poisoning people. Wainewright's portrait of Julia Sorell is included in this volume.

If transportation was one grim aspect of the history of Van Diemen's Land, Arnold has nothing to say in his correspondence about another, grimmer one: the extermination of the native population, in an unqualified act of genocide. There were only a few thousand aborigines living on the island when the colonists arrived, and they were subjected to economic and sexual exploitation and arbitrary killing. Their attempts at violent resistance increased the pressure on them. They were inevitably defeated by British power and arms, and the remnants were 'translocated' to Flinders Island, off the north coast of Tasmania, where they died rapidly from diseases or the traumatic removal from their own soil and habitat. At length, more humanitarian sentiments emerged and the few remaining aborigines were brought back to the mainland, but it was too late to save them. In his autobiography Arnold refers to the cruel treatment of the natives, but blames it on the convicts; in fact, the free settlers were just as responsible. He recalls seeing three aboriginal children in a school for orphans in Hobart, who could read and write fairly well; they were part of the last tiny group of survivors: 'When it was too late to save them, the conscience of the governing class both at home and in the colony was awakened, and everything that humanity could suggest was done to ameliorate the condition and retard the doom of the survivors.'[29] The children he met would not have lived very long, as the last surviving Tasmanian aborigine, an old woman, died in 1876. The society of the convicts and the fate of the aborigines are vividly rendered in Matthew Kneale's historical novel, *English Passengers*, published in 2000. (Recently, though, it has been suggested that the genocide was not total, and that more of the aborigines survived than was generally believed.)

Writing to his mother in 1852, Tom Arnold refers to Denison's support of transportation more in sorrow than in anger:

I have a real hearty liking for the man at bottom; and had he but tried to relieve the country of Transportation, or even stood neutral upon it, not one of his public officers would have fought his battles more warmly than I would. But in sad seriousness I believe that in this matter he has ranged himself on the wrong side; that in striving to perpetuate this curse, he is fighting against God and God's eternal laws . . .[30]

Despite their deep disagreements about transportation and about educational policy, and despite the governor's abrasive manner, Arnold's liking and admiration for him continued to grow. In 1855 Denison moved up in the world and he was appointed governor of New South Wales; Arnold attended the farewell reception, and next day watched the Densions' departure by steamer, accompanied by a band and an artillery salute. His last sight of Denison is presented in idealizing language: 'A last farewell bow, and then we saw no more of the stout old Governor, who has been better hated and more warmly loved since he has been in the colony than almost any English Governor that ever ruled.'[31] Arnold's attitude to Denison—he was still writing admiringly of him at the end of his life—is psychologically interesting. It seems to have contained elements of the liberal's reluctant respect for the intelligent reactionary, and the intellectual's starry-eyed attitude to the brusque man of action. A few years later, when Arnold was working with Newman, whom he admired for very different reasons, he engaged in a strange hyperbolic fantasy about the complementary qualities of Denison and Newman, exemplifying action and contemplation: 'A combination of Sir William Denison and Newman would make the greatest man of the 19th century—as great a man perhaps as the world has ever produced.'[32] At this point an historical personality has been turned into a mythic figure.

Despite his tendency to glance longingly eastward towards New Zealand, and his hopes of some day returning to England, Arnold's growing family and his reputation for ability in his job might well have combined to keep him in Australia; not necessarily in Van Diemen's Land, for there would certainly have been opportunities in the rapidly expanding educational systems of the mainland colonies. Such a position would have given the opportunity of home leave from time to time. But his return to England came sooner than he expected, and for a reason that no-one who knew him would have suspected.

In matters of religion Tom Arnold remained nominally an Anglican. In practice, he was a theist who had shed any belief in a supernatural Christ but revered him as a teacher and exemplar. This was the default position of many Victorian intellectuals, who continued to be very interested in religion despite their lack of orthodoxy; Matthew Arnold, in his later career, is an obvious example, and so is Tom's daughter Mary Ward. At a lower level, a concern with religious matters was akin to an interest in politics, and not always distinguished from it. It is evident in Tom Arnold's correspondence. He went so far as to write a pamphlet (which has not survived) called 'The Freedom of the Church'; he sent it to Clough in the hope that it would be published in England and was disappointed when no more was heard of it. The first sign of a new attitude to religion appeared in a letter he sent to his mother in October 1854. He describes a visit he made, on a recent tour of duty, to Charles Wilmot, the likeable son of a former governor, who had recently become a Roman Catholic and was therefore, as Tom put it, 'an object of great suspicion' to a local clergyman, though he believed that Wilmot's conversion had done him a great deal of good. He continued:

I too, dear Mother, have had a religious change lately, but it is back to the old true ways from which I wonder and bitterly repent that I ever should have strayed. I will say more when I next write; now I have not time, for I am going again out of town. But a great wall of partition which stood between me and all you dear ones who have never strayed from Christ's fold is now quite broken down; of that you may feel sure. Pray for me and think of me now as looking up to the same Saviour as you yourselves, though less worthy.[33]

It seemed that, after venerating Carlyle and Emerson, George Sand and Goethe, Tom had returned to Jesus Christ and the practice of Evangelical Anglicanism. In a further letter he writes of his satisfaction at once more feeling at one with his father: 'And oh! since the scales fell from my eyes, how has that beloved father been reinstated in all the reverence, the unstinted admiration, which which I used to regard him, but which, seduced by vain theories, I had learnt partially to withhold.'[34] Mary Arnold was an undemonstrative woman, but she would have rejoiced when she read of her son's return to the path of faith. So, too, would the comparatively undevout Julia, to whom Tom wrote from the northern township of Perth with the news of his conversion. She knew that it was better to have a properly Christian husband than an infidel who was indifferent to the baptism of their children.

But their satisfaction would have been short lived, for his return to Anglicanism was only a transitional position. By the following spring Tom had decided that he must become a Roman Catholic. In the abstract, this was not necessarily a remarkable decision. In Meriol Trevor's words, 'In reading nineteenth century memoirs it is surprising how often we find, in the same family, a variety of religious belief or the lack of it; nearly every educated family had its dissenter, its freethinker, its Roman Catholic, as well as its members, more or less committed, of the established Church of England.'[35] But given Arnold's antecedents and his previous opinions it was a pretty unexpected move. In his letters home traditional anti-papistry was reinforced by radical anti-clericalism. In 1849 he remarked on the Pope's misfortunes in the Roman revolution that Clough had witnessed and was to commemorate in *Amours de Voyage*: 'The great scarlet iniquity is not prospering in the world, praise be to Heaven.'[36] He is scathing about Oxford acquaintances who had converted to Catholicism. He refers to Frederick Faber, a fellow of University College when Arnold was an undergraduate there, as 'slightly cracked', after reading in a review extracts from Faber's lives of foreign saints. He remarks of William Gifford Palgrave (brother of F. T. Palgrave, of *Golden Treasury* fame), 'So young Palgrave has been goose enough to turn Roman Catholic . . . I have little doubt that he will change to something else before long.'[37] He would have more to do with Gifford Palgrave in time.

Conversion is a mysterious process and there is little contemporary evidence about the processes that led Arnold to this unlikely step. He looks back on it in the idealizing and simplifying narrative of *Passages from a Wandering Life*. He refers to the moment of his original return to Christian belief in October 1854, when a passage in the First Epistle of Peter made a sudden impression on him: 'the words of Peter sounded to me rather as a command than as a theme for discussion, and made a direct appeal to the practical reason and the will. But who was this Peter? What was his general teaching? Who were his helpers and successors?'[38] Arnold does not say what the passage was that so impressed him, but it may have been 5: 35, 'For ye were as sheep going astray; but are now returned unto the Shepherd and Bishop of your souls.' This passage can be given an obvious Catholic interpretation, as did the command that Arnold says he took from Peter. It was not just to make a commitment to Christ, as it would be in a Protestant context, but to consider the nature of authority, the question which had led Newman and the other Tractarian converts to Rome.

He refers to other factors in his conversion. Spending the night in a country inn he came across Butler's *Lives of the Saints*, a work he had not previously heard of. Opening a volume he was fascinated by the life of St Brigid, a fourteenth-century Swedish aristocrat who married and had eight children; she was also a visionary and prophet who lived an ascetic life after she was widowed. Something in her story deeply touched Arnold, and he found a particular significance in the fact that her festival was celebrated on the day in October in which he had been so impressed by the Epistle of Peter. Arnold also read some of the *Tracts for the Times* about the lives of early saints and martyrs, which gave him a sense of the unity and continuity of the Church. His conversion was given an intellectual direction by his reading of Newman's *Discourses on the Scope and Nature of University Education,* which had been published in 1852. It is noticeable that Arnold's move was not like that of Newman, Ward, and the other Tractarian converts, who had become so close to Roman Catholicism in their stance and thinking that in the end they could not resist it. Arnold's conversion was more dramatic, a Pauline reversal of his previous positions. He had grown up with his father's dislike of the Tractarian enterprise, and only a year or so before he had complained of the spread of Tractarian influence in the colony; now he was deeply influenced by the Tracts. He had mocked Frederick Faber for venerating foreign saints; now he was inspired by one. And having had no regard for Newman as he had known him at Oxford, Arnold now wrote to him for advice.

On 6 July 1855, Newman, engaged in his copious correspondence, was writing to a recent convert, Lord Dunraven. In his letter he remarked, 'The same post, which brought your letter this morning, brought one from the other end of the earth, showing the working of God's grace in a way so wonderful, that it is distressing to have it all to oneself, and not be at liberty to mention it.'[39] The letter was from Tom Arnold, who apologizes for writing out of the blue, and refers to certain common Oxford acquaintances from the past, such as Faber and Ward. He gives a brief history of his personal and religious life, describing his move at Oxford from liberal Protestantism to doubt and uncertainty, and then his plunge into what he called 'the abyss of unbelief'. But the previous year, following a spiritual crisis, he had recovered his Christian faith. Now, he tells Newman, 'You who have said that a man who has once comprehended and admitted the theological definition of God, cannot logically rest until he had admitted the whole system of Catholicism' will not be surprised to know that he has followed a comparable course, and wishes to become a Catholic. That is his intention, but he is worried about timing, and the effects his conversion will have on his family. 'My dear wife, who is without any positive religious convictions (in a great measure, alas! through my fault) has imbibed the strongest prejudices against Catholicism, and I see no prospect, humanly speaking, of her altering her mind. My mother and sisters—all in England—are sincerely Protestant, and I cannot doubt that my conversion will be a serious blow to them.' He asks for Newman's advice on these human dilemmas; he would also like to know if he would be justified in keeping on with his employment after becoming a Catholic, assuming that he would be able to. In a final, very characteristic, touch, he asks Newman if he would be able to find work as a teacher if he returned to England.[40] Arnold's letter is undated and it exists only in a copy made by his daughter Julia, but it would have been written in the spring of 1855; it shows how rapid the process of his conversion had been. The previous October he had shown the general prejudices of the culture by recommending Julia not to take on a Roman Catholic servant.[41] Now he was about to become a victim of them.

Arnold's misgivings about Julia's anti-Catholicism proved to be entirely justified. However indifferent she was to religious questions in general, this was one position to which she was strongly committed. She responded in horror to the news of Tom's intended conversion. Mary Ward, using her practised novelistic imagination, refers to the supposed Huguenot antecedents of Julia's family; she sees her mother's resistance to Catholicism as going deeper than the English Evangelical tradition, taking on the sternness of French Protestantism: 'Had some direct Calvinist ancestor of hers, with a soul on fire, fought the tyranny of Bossuet and Madame de Maintenon, before—eternally hating and resenting "Papistry"—he abandoned his country and kinsfolk, in the search for religious liberty?'[42] Julia resolved to do all she could to keep Tom out of the embrace of Rome. She made him promise not to take any definite step until he had talked to his mother, Dr Arnold's representative on earth. This was a way of buying time, since it was likely to be months, even years, before he could go back to England and consult his mother. Mrs Reibey, equally concerned but less fanatical, urged him to consult a clergyman she named and to read a number of books supporting the Anglican position. She knew he had written to Newman and made him promise not to take any step for six months, which was the interval likely to elapse before a reply could be expected. She then returned to Entally, taking the young Mary with her for a long stay; it was the first of the girl's many experiences of being farmed out to family, friends, and schoolteachers. Tom read the books Mrs Reibey had recommended, but was not persuaded by them.

On 23 June Tom wrote to Julia saying that he is unhappy with the promise she had extracted from him, but that if she will not release him he will endeavour to keep it. Her reply was dramatic and anguished. She refers to the joy she had felt when he returned to Christian belief and practice:

How different were my first feelings on hearing that you had become a believer in Christianity, I thought (how utterly mistaken I was) that through you I, and our children would be led to God. But now for myself, I almost feel the utter impossibility of such ever being the case; a Romanist I cannot be, my whole soul revolts from a religion so utterly to my mind inconsistent with the true worship of Christ, and for our children I cannot but feel the prospects to be equally dreary.

She threatened to leave him if he became a Catholic: 'I love you dearest Tom most deeply and in separating from you I shall strike my own death blow, but as things are now it must be so.'[43] Julia was an intelligent woman, articulate and rational when her passions were not aroused, but when they were, she was consumed by rage and bitterness.

On 1 October Arnold received a reply from Newman, much more rapidly than he expected. It has not survived, but he described it as 'kind and most comforting'; it evidently recommended him to go ahead and become a Catholic, whatever the incidental difficulties. When Mrs Reibey knew that Arnold had heard from Newman ahead of the expected time, she sensibly released him from his promise to her; she no doubt felt that nothing would be achieved by it, as his mind was made up. Thanking Newman for his letter, Arnold says he has decided to become a Catholic, though he also refers to consulting his mother, attempting to stick to the letter of his promise to Julia. He also says that he will consult the local Catholic bishop, Robert Willson. He tells Newman apologetically that he may receive an abusive letter from Julia: 'forgive, I entreat you, its unjust and half-frantic language, and pray for the unhappy writer'.[44]

Towards the end of 1855 Arnold consulted Bishop Willson, who had just returned to the colony after a long absence; he described the bishop as 'a man whom it was impossible to know and not to love',[45] and he was clearly an admirable character. He was born at Lincoln in 1794, ordained in 1824, and after serving as a parish priest at Nottingham for many years was ordained as bishop of Van Diemen's Land in 1842. He campaigned on behalf of the inmates of the penal settlement on Norfolk Island, who were subject to a brutal regime in atrocious conditions. He had returned to London at his own expense in 1846 to give evidence to a Committee of the House of Lords, about the settlement, which was finally closed in 1855. He was also a pioneer in urging the humane treatment of the insane, which put him well ahead of his time.[46] Arnold refers to 'the holy zeal with which he burned for the conversion of wanderers', choosing the word deliberately. Willson's advice to Arnold was that his promise to Julia should not have been made and should not be kept, as it meant that he was unable to act in accordance with his conscience. Meanwhile Julia was doing all she could to make life difficult for him by spreading the news of his change of belief.

On 18 January 1856 Arnold was received into the Catholic Church by Bishop Willson. Julia did not leave him as she had threatened, but she made some kind of physical demonstration during the ceremony. Her grandson Julian Huxley says that she arrived with a basket of stones and smashed the windows of the Catholic Pro-Cathedral with this 'protesting ammunition'.[47] This is probably exaggerated; Huxley's account of Arnold's years in Van Diemen's Land is very inaccurate, and represents a garbled version of family lore. Newman may be closer to the mark when he says that Julia 'threw a brick through the Church window';[48] he had perhaps been told as much by Arnold. In February Tom wrote to his mother telling her that he had become a Catholic and giving his explanations; it was not an easy letter to write, and he delayed starting on it. For the second time since he had arrived in the colony he presented Mrs Arnold with a *fait accompli*, the first occasion being his marriage. He refers to Julia at the end of the letter: 'I earnestly pray, and so I trust will you, that God will have mercy upon her, and calm at last the unhappy perturbation of her mind.'[49]

Having taken the step of joining the Catholic Church and informing his family, Arnold now had to consider his official position. For several years he had done his job effectively without any religious beliefs beyond a vague theism and humanitarianism, and no-one had been concerned. But his Catholicism proved unacceptable to many people because of the prejudice deeply engrained in British culture. Julia's spreading the news in an alarmist way exacerbated the situation. On the very day he was received into the Catholic Church and before it was generally known about, a leading article in one of the local newspapers said it was 'generally understood' that he was becoming a Catholic and called upon him to resign his appointment. Other newspapers took up the outcry, and Arnold heard that a clergyman who had come out from England to be sub-warden of the college in Hobart had gone to the governor and asked for his job. The governor, Sir Henry Young, rebuffed this man and offered Arnold his support. But during the spring of 1856 his position was becoming increasingly difficult, with the press campaigning against him and the Anglican and Dissenting clergy united in their opposition to a Romanist being in charge of education in the colony; there was a widespread fear that he would use his position to propagate Catholic ideas and practices. Arnold did have some support in the press and he might have held on, despite the opposition. But he was not convinced that he ought to; with the zeal of a new convert, convinced that the only truth is Catholic truth, he was becoming uneasy about being in a post that required a neutral attitude to particular religious professions. Bishop Willson did not want to lose him, but confessed that he would rather see him in some other branch of public service. For a time Arnold entertained the hope that he might transfer to another administrative post, such as one of the new under-secretaryships that were to accompany the advent of representative government in the colony. But nothing came of that and he began increasingly to feel that he ought to resign and go back to England. The secretary of the colonial administration was of that opinion; he told Arnold that while he personally thought a change of religion should be no bar to his continuing his work, he could not ignore the wide hostility to him, not only in the press but in the legislative council. A gentlemanly deal was proposed, that Arnold should go home on leave for eighteen months, on half-pay, and then not return. He accepted the arrangement, which would get him and his family back to England, sooner than they expected and not in the fashion they might have hoped for. He told Newman in May that he expected to leave in six or seven months, but in fact they left in two.

CHAPTER 5

Dublin

I

The Arnold parents, with Mary, William, and Theodore, sailed from Hobart on 12 July 1856; they were accompanied by four other children, cousins of Julia's, who had been in India and were going to school in England, plus their nurses. Mary was 5 years old and remembered the journey to the end of her life:

> I can just recall . . . the deck of a ship which to my childish feet seemed vast—but the *William Brown* was a sailing ship of only 400 tons!—in which we made the voyage home in 1856. Three months and a half we took about it, going round the Horn in bitter weather, much run over by rats at night, and expected to take our baths by day in two huge barrels full of sea water on the deck, into which we children were plunged shivering by our nurse, two or three times a week.[1]

The voyage was uneventful though uncomfortable, particularly so because of the rats; one fell off a beam on to Tom's bed, and another chewed his leather braces. The ship was out of sight of land throughout the voyage. On 18 August, when they had been sailing for over a month eastward across the vast empty South Pacific, Tom began a journal-letter to his mother. He describes how they had passed Cape Horn but had been blown 300 miles south by a strong northerly wind. Then the wind veered round and the ship was able to sail into the Atlantic and head north.

The tone of Tom's letter is calm and cheerful, concealing whatever anxiety he must inevitably have felt at being in charge of a party of seven children, as well as Julia, who was four months pregnant when they left Hobart and was weak and seasick for much of the voyage. She was alarmed when the baby Theodore, who was teething, was troubled by a distressing inflammation on his thighs. But one of the nurses knew what had to be done: 'By means of cold applications, and keeping him on a low diet, all came right in a day or so.' Tom is clearly keeping his and Julia's spirits up, and they were fortunate that nothing worse afflicted the party during the long and isolated journey. As the birth of the next child approached, there might have been troubled memories of the infant who had lived for only twenty-four hours in 1854.

On 13 September the *William Brown* crossed the equator and entered the Northern Hemisphere. The weather was fine and the party made the most of it; it was winter when they left Tasmania and would be autumn when they got to England. Tom's spirits rose as it came closer:

Certainly it is very hot; and some of us feel it more than others; and there is a great deal of lying about on deck under the awning, and limejuice and water is much in request, and we have all with one consent abjured stockings, and a tropical warmth and intensity has infused itself into the children's tempers (always exceping Theodore); but yet on the whole it is most enjoyable weather. As you lie on the deck, shoals of flying fish, disturbed by the ship as she ploughs along, dart on silvery wings into the air, and descend with little splashes on the top of the next wave. The sunsets are generally gorgeous, and after them we have now the long moonlight nights. The moon is intensely bright, and wears now the dear old English face: how *homish* it seems. The Southern Cross, the glory of the Australian heavens, is sunk and lost beneath the haze which surrounds the horizon. Arcturus and Vega, the bright star in Lyra, are already high in the sky, and soon we shall see Cassiopeia's chair and Charles's wain, and the Pleiades.[2]

The last stage of the voyage went rapidly, helped by favourable winds. The ship entered the Channel; on 13 October they came in sight of Bolt Head in Devon. Tom tells his mother that a pilot boat will take his letter ashore, and asks her to write to him c/o the *William Brown* in London Docks. Mary remembered 'being lifted—weak and miserable with toothache—in my father's arms to catch the first sight of English shores as we neared the mouth of the Thames'.[3] The day after the ship docked Tom was supervising the unloading of his possessions when the custom house agent told him, 'Mr Arnold, your sister wishes to see you.' The efficient Victorian postal service and the Arnold family network had seen that Jane got there in time. There was a joyful reunion between Tom and Jane, who was accompanied by her husband, William Forster, the Quaker businessman and future Liberal politician, whom Tom had never met. Forster took charge of the situation; the family had spent their first night on land in a disagreeable inn at the docks—Mary recalled, 'the dreary room where we children first slept the first night, its dingy ugliness and its barred windows, still come back to me as a vision of horror'—and he installed them in a much pleasanter place, the 'Four Swans' in Bishopsgate.

From there Tom wrote to his mother on 19 October, telling her that he and his family hope to come to Fox How in the next few days, but that there are various bits of business to transact in London, not least getting urgent medical attention for Julia. He thanks Mrs Arnold for a money draft she had sent to him in Hobart, and raises the sensitive matter of his change of religion. He very much regrets that according to the regulations then in force, which did not permit Catholics to pray with members of other religions, he will not be able to join in family prayers at Fox How. He has no doubt that his Protestant family and friends are far better people than he is, and remarks that his membership of the Catholic Church is more an argument against it than in its favour (rather in the spirit of Groucho Marx saying that he wouldn't want to be in a club that would have him as a member). But whatever incidental difficulties and sadness, he is certain of the rightness of his course.

In a postscript written the next day Tom reports that he has been to the Colonial Office to see if his half-pay was yet available, but found it was not; it arrived a few weeks later. He adds, glumly, 'Not that it matters much to me, for I shall have to remit the greater part of the money to Van Diemen's Land as I get it, in order to meet obligations which I was obliged to contract there before leaving.'[4] Financial difficulty was to provide a steady ground-bass for Tom Arnold's activities for the whole of his life. Having reached England, his dominant concern was to find employment which would enable him to support himself and his family. He envisaged such work as being of an educational kind in a Catholic context. With this in mind he arranged to see Cardinal Wiseman, the Archbishop of Westminster. He does not seem to have got very far with Wiseman, though the cardinal told him that he would shortly be going to Ushaw, the Catholic college near Durham, and that Arnold might call on him there. Presumably the cardinal proposed this because the Arnolds would by then be in the north of England; but the journey from Ambleside to Ushaw was not an easy one, and Tom does not seem to have attempted it.

The family reached Fox How on 22 October. The grey stone house in the valley of the Rothay, which was to be her home for several years, made a good impression on the young Mary:

Inside, Fox How was comfortably spacious, and I remember what a palace it appeared to my childish eyes, fresh from the tiny cabin of a 400-ton sailing ship, and the rough life of a colony. My grandmother, its mistress, was then sixty-one. Her beautiful hair was scarcely touched with grey, her complexion was still delicately clear, and her soft brown eyes had the eager sympathetic look of her Cornish race.[5]

Writing to Newman, Tom says, 'I am staying for the present with my mother, who, as well as the rest of the family, has behaved most kindly and affectionately with regard to my change of religion.'[6] The happiness of the reunion and her love for Tom would in some measure have modified the dismay of Dr Arnold's widow that their son had become a Romanist and could no longer pray with them; in the words of his grand-daughter, Janet Trevelyan, 'Tom was, I think, the special darling of the family, and his lapse to Catholicism a terrible trial to them.'[7] Tom's wife got on well with his mother, despite the temperamental differences between Julia's hot temper and Mary Arnold's serenity; their shared Protestantism united them in the face of Tom's distressing lapse. Matthew called at Fox How to see his brother, taking time off from a tour of school inspections in Yorkshire. Tom told Clough, 'putting out of sight the whiskers (which considering their bushiness is difficult to do) I consider the old boy very little changed'.[8] Matthew, though, was discon-certingly cryptic about his brother; in a letter to Jane in December he re-marked, 'About Tom I say nothing. I thought of him on his birth-day the other day.'[9] One member of the family who had changed considerably was Tom's sister Frances, otherwise 'Fan', who had been only 14 when he left; he was fascinated by the fleeting traces of the child in the young woman.

In his letter to Newman, Tom Arnold presented his situation:

I am very anxious to get as soon as I can some employment, and, if it were pos-sible, in the service of the Church. I know well that the difficulties are great, the number of converts being so large, and many of them having such far higher claims and qualifications. But my expectations are not lofty; to do some useful plain work and to live in obedience, is what I most desire, so only that by my work I can support my family.[10]

He asks if there were any possibility of finding tutorial work for students intending to enter the Catholic University in Dublin, where Newman was rector. He acknowledges, 'I am in a state of great ignorance as to the present position of the University.' Newman's reply was prompt and emotional:

How strange it seems! What a world this is! I knew your father a little and I really think I never had any unkind feeling towards him. I saw him at Oriel on the Purification before (I think) his death (January 1842). I was glad to meet him. If I said ever a harsh thing against him I am very sorry for it. In seeing you, I should have a sort of pledge that he at the moment of his death made it all up to me.

Excuse this. I came here last night, and it is marvellous to have your letter this morning.[11]

Newman was given to seeing the direct intervention of Providence in the course of his own and other people's lives, and this looked like a shining example. More concretely, he offered Arnold a temporary post as Professor of English Literature at the Catholic University. This was gratifyingly more than he expected; in his reply of 28 October he expressed satisfaction at what he described as this tempting offer, though he wondered if his 'degree of impediment of speaking' would prevent him accepting it; he offered to come to Dublin to discuss matters with Newman if it would help. Newman was very pleased. On 30 October he remarked in a letter to his Oratorian friend, Fr Edward Caswall, 'Only fancy Arnold's son being our Professor of English Literature! there is a great chance of it.'[12] Arnold arrived in Dublin on 4 November, leaving his family at Fox How; it was less than three weeks since he had landed in England. In the immediate future, there were mutual needs to be satisfied: Arnold's for employment, and Newman's to replace a colleague who had resigned because of ill health. Arnold accepted the post on a temporary trial basis, and agreed to stay in Dublin for the rest of the term and start teaching at once.

Late in life he recalled the impression made on him by Newman, whom he had not seen since his Oxford days:

The air of deep abstraction with which he used to glide along the streets of Oxford was now in a great measure exchanged for the look of preoccupation and anxiety about temporal matters, which the features of a man to whom business was neither habitual nor congenial would naturally assume under the new circumstances; but otherwise he seemed to me quite as vigorous and little older than when I had first seen him at Oxford.[13]

As Tom acknowledged, he knew nothing about the Catholic University; and, like Newman when he had first arrived in the country five years before, he knew very little about Ireland, apart from what he had seen on his visits to Archbishop Whately. The Catholic University represented a splendid ideal that was destined to become a sad though interesting failure, not just in Newman's career, but in several adjacent histories: of nineteenth-century Ireland; of Catholicism in the British Isles; of the development of higher education.[14] The process of decline was already evident when Arnold arrived in Dublin. For centuries there had been only one university in Ireland: Trinity College, founded by Protestant colonists in the late sixteenth century on the site of a former monastery in Dublin. There was no provision for the higher education of the Catholic majority (nor indeed for their lower education); in the 1840s the government decided that education in Ireland should be extended and set up three new Queen's Colleges, at Cork, Galway, and Belfast. They were thought of as non-denominational, though both Catholic and Protestant religious instruction could be provided. In practice, they were more likely to cater for the educational needs of the Protestant Ascendancy than for the majority of the population, who were already handicapped by the lack of Catholic secondary education. The Queen's Colleges aroused a certain fleeting interest; in 1845 Clough considered putting in for a professorship in one of them, and Tom Arnold wrote a letter of enquiry to Archbishop Whately on his behalf. But that project, like most of Clough's, ran into the sand. In Ireland itself the establishment of the Queen's Colleges meant that the bishops had to decide on their attitude to them. They may have deplored the lack of higher education for Catholics as one more legacy of discrimination and neglect by the imperial power, but they were not deeply interested in the question; educated at seminaries or at the Irish College in Rome, they did not know very much about universities. And in the 1840s when their flocks were starving in the terrible famine they had far more urgent questions to contend with.

Nevertheless, the question arose, could suitably qualified young Catholics attend these colleges? The majority of the bishops disliked their mixed relgious ethos and were opposed; but a minority were prepared to tolerate them, on a 'half-a-loaf' principle. Eventually Rome decided in favour of the majority view and Catholics were told they should not attend the Queen's Colleges, though doing so was not made a matter of excommunication. The argument had brought the matter of Catholic higher education into consciousness; the solution proposed in some quarters in Ireland and enthusiastically accepted by Pope Pius IX was for a specifically Catholic university. There was a convenient model in Belgium. When the Belgian kingdom was set up in 1830 it was provided with secular universities run by the state; but the Catholics wanted one that would be pervaded by a Catholic ethos and practice. After negotiations such an institution was set up at Louvain in 1834; it proved to be an academic success and a distinguished centre of learning. In Rome the Protestant English-speaking world was *terra incognita*. But it was expanding over the globe, from the British Isles to North America and Australasia, and including more and more Catholics in the process. Their educational needs had to be met; schools came first, but there should be a university as well. What better place for it could there be than the one anglophone country that, by God's providence, remained solidly Catholic? Ireland was the ideal setting for a new Catholic university with an international constituency, a Louvain for the English-speaking world.

This was more than the Irish bishops had bargained for; what the Pope wanted they would, of course, endeavour to establish, but as a motive loyalty fell short of burning enthusiasm. In 1851 Newman, as the most distinguished of recent converts and a former Oxford don, was invited to Dublin to give lectures on higher education and to advise the bishops on the proposal; the lectures formed the nucleus of *The Idea of a University* (1873). After discussions with the bishops, Newman was invited to serve as Rector of the new university. He was initially reluctant, but before long he was seized with enthusiasm for the project and agreed to take on the task. In the years following his admission to the Catholic priesthood in 1846 Newman had lived a secluded life in the Birmingham Oratory, which he had founded. The Dublin scheme would provide an outlet for his ideals and energies, and the hope of accomplishing a great work for Catholic education. From the beginning his aim was for an international foundation, a second Louvain; the bishops' sights were set firmly on their own country; they wanted a university for young Catholic Irishmen, to counter the Protestantism of Trinity and what they saw as the indifferentism of the Queen's Colleges. From the beginning there was a rift between what Newman (and the Pope) envisaged and what the bishops hoped to see; it grew steadily wider during his years in Dublin.

The Pope permitted Newman to take temporary leave of the Oratory to serve as rector, but he retained many responsibilities there, and his years in Dublin were marked by frequent wearisome trips back and forth across the Irish Sea. In the preliminary discussions that went on after 1851 he was dismayed at the differences that emerged between the bishops and himself about the shape of the new institution. Some of them were genuinely enthusiastic; others barely disguised their hostility to the whole idea. The leading figure was Dr Paul Cullen, Archbishop of Dublin and later cardinal, who had originally issued the invitation to become rector (largely, it seems, on his own initiative), and Cullen had his opponents among the bishops. He was a man of autocratic temperament and strongly ultramontane convictions, who had spent most of his life in Rome, where he had been head of the Irish College. Although the bishops as a whole were supposed to have the ultimate responsibility for the Catholic University, with the rector acting as a chief executive, Cullen took more and more authority into his own hands, seeing himself as the Pope's representative. Newman found him increasingly difficult to deal with. The problem was not so much that Cullen was an autocrat—if they have the right ideas such figures can be very effective—but that he provided the deadly combination of an autocrat and a prevaricator. Newman wanted to take his time in putting the university on a firm foundation, but Cullen, it seemed, wanted to take for ever. Probably he had come to regret the whole idea; certainly he seems to have wanted something much more like a seminary than the concept that Newman embodied in *The Idea of a University*. Cullen refused to answer letters that urgently needed a response, or to authorize necessary decisions. Newman, who had his own autocratic tendencies and a clear idea of what, as rector, he wished to achieve, was driven close to despair at times. Indeed, his first biographer, Wilfrid Ward, who had known him, wrote that he took an increasingly gloomy view of the university's prospects, even before it had opened its doors:

he never seriously changed the view which he formed in February 1854, that, as a practical work, the University was doomed to failure. He indeed hoped against hope. He was slow to abandon without a fair trial the idea that Ireland with its great Catholic population might supply a University which should be to the Catholics of the Kingdom what Louvain was to the Belgian Catholics—the home of a liberal education enabling them to be a real power in the country in proportion to their numerical strength. But towards the realization of this hope no event seemed to point.[15]

The model of Louvain was beguiling but inappropriate. The Belgian Catholics had a better system of secondary schooling, and the degrees of the Catholic University were recognized by the Belgian state. Louvain could attract Catholics from francophone countries, and from further afield at a time when French was the second language of educated Europeans. The English-speaking world was larger and less homogeneous, being riven by historical and cultural divisions; and of these, none was greater than that between Ireland and England. One particular problem was that anti-Catholic prejudice in England made the British government reluctant to give the Catholic University a charter and validate its decrees. This was a problem that was still rankling more than twenty years later when Matthew Arnold addressed it in his essay 'Irish Catholics and British Liberalism'.

There was a double attitude in Dublin to Newman and the other post-Tractarian converts he was recruiting to the university; they might be revered as distinguished Catholics but still disliked as Englishmen. There seems to have been an element of this in Cullen's dealings with Newman, who referred to him as someone who trusted nobody; Cullen had a certain hostility to the English, but he was also opposed to the nationalists of the Young Ireland movement, some of whom Newman had also appointed; Cullen regarded them as dangerous revolutionaries. Despite everything, Newman attempted to deal charitably with Cullen, and seems even to have liked him personally.

Hope against hope is still hope, and it was in this spirit that Newman went on appointing staff and trying to attract students. Newman had a much broader concept of university education than the one he had grown up with in Oxford, or indeed than the one suggested by a superficial reading of *The Idea of a University*. Science and medicine were prominent, and from the beginning the medical faculty was regarded as successful, mainly because it had taken over a previous institution as a going concern. His programme for the Humanities reflected his own love of literature: primarily the Classics, but with a strong emphasis, too, on English Literature. In this Newman was a pioneer; most university courses in English Literature did not appear until much later in the century.

In making academic appointments Newman had to keep several balls in the air. The prevalent suspicion of his English identity and Oxonian ways made him anxious to appoint Irishmen where possible, and he did this with some success in the science and medical faculties, where one of his strongest supporters was the Professor of Chemistry, W. K. Sullivan, a former Young Irelander (and therefore disapproved of by Archbishop Cullen). In appointing to the Humanities Newman had to rely more heavily on English converts, for the most part former clergymen with degrees from Oxford or Cambridge, who, if they were married, could not follow Newman into the priesthood. Such appointments were inevitably seen as signs of pro-English bias, but in the last analysis Newman felt he had to appoint the best possible teachers, regardless of local opinion. The idea of a great international university was still just alive. In making his appointments Newman often proceeded intuitively, rating the quality of the man above specialist knowledge. He was prepared to ride his hunches, as he did in the case of John Hungerford Pollen, who in his Anglican days had been a fellow of Merton and then a vicar in Leeds. Among other things he was a gifted amateur painter who had designed the ceiling of Merton

College Chapel. On this slender foundation, Pollen, despite his own mis-givings, was appointed Professor of Fine Arts in the Catholic University. He turned to architecture and designed the University Church that Newman commissioned on St Stephen's Green. Newman's encourage-ment led Pollen to a successful and varied later career as painter, architect, and critic. He joined the Pre-Raphaelites in their abortive attempt at frescoes in the Oxford Union, and was subsequently Slade Professor and assistant keeper at the South Kensington Museum.

There was provision from the beginning for a professor—or lecturer, the terms were originally used interchangeably—of English Literature. When the first staff-list was issued in 1854 the post was held by Edward Healy Thompson, a friend of Newman's and another former clergyman. But Thompson soon dropped out and in the following year it was listed as vacant. There was also a professorship of Poetry, held by Denis Florence McCarthy, a lawyer who had turned poet and devoted himself to literature. In 1855 Newman tried to attract another Irish poet to the post in English Literature: Aubrey de Vere, a Catholic convert from a Protestant family, who had been giving lectures on an *ad hoc* basis. De Vere declined, mainly, it seems, because it involved tutorial work as well as lectures. In a striking instance of Newman's flexible attitude to aca-demic appointments De Vere then emerged as professor of Political and Social Science; in the autumn term of 1855 he gave a series of lectures on Literature considered in its relations with Political and Social Philosophy. In other respects his appointment seems to have been, as the *Dictionary of National Biography* puts it, 'nominal' and he gave it up before long. Meanwhile, the professorship of English Literature had been merged with that of Poetry, and McCarthy had taken it over. Then, in 1856, he stepped down, supposedly because of ill-health; Newman sent him good wishes for his recovery, but it may have been a diplomatic illness, a means of getting out of a job which he found onerous. At all events, McCarthy lived until 1882.

This was the vacant post that Arnold arrived to fill temporarily in November 1856. It goes without saying that he had no formal training in the subject, since no-one had at that time. Until well into the twentieth century university teachers of English Literature had taken their first degrees in Classics or Philosophy or History. Arnold's appointment may have had a touch of the traditional Oxford assumption that anyone with a First in Greats can pick up other subjects in a few weeks. More specifically, Newman felt that in addition to his attainments in Classics, the son of Dr Arnold and brother of Matthew Arnold came from a milieu that made his appointment respectable. There was a particular satisfaction for Newman in this final act of a psychodrama that had begun in the Tractarian wars of the 1830s, the symbolic revenge of the chief Oxford Malignant upon his principal foe. But in more everyday terms it was good public relations for the university to have a famous name associated with it, who would raise the prestige of the establishment and attract more students.

Indeed, the lack of students was a cause of continual difficulty. When the university was founded in a glow of idealistic fervour, it was meant to appeal to a three-fold constituency: Catholic students from beyond the British Isles; those from mainland Britain; and those from Ireland. The first group did appear and were courted. In an early letter from Dublin Arnold refers to a wealthy young French Canadian who was treated as a 'decoy duck' to attract others, and later he sardonically refers to Belgian princes and Polish counts among the undergraduates. But in the nature of things there could not be a large number of these exotic imports. Catholics in England were not inclined to support the Irish university and in any case there were not many of them with the right qualifications. In the past the Catholic gentry had educated their sons abroad, and now they were beginning to knock on the doors of Oxford and Cambridge. And the Irish Catholics, with whom the bishops were most concerned, were too poor and too badly educated at secondary level to provide a large intake of students.

This was the history that Tom Arnold had to discover when he arrived in Dublin, and it took him some time. He was warmly received by some of his future colleagues, all convert ex-clergymen. Thomas Scratton, the secretary of the university, was a Christ Church man whom Arnold had known slightly at Oxford. They had many friends in common and Scratton made him feel at home, though Arnold's opinion of his competence declined during his years in Dublin. Robert Ornsby, a former fellow of Trinity, Oxford, was Professor of Classical Literature; James Stewart, Professor of Classical Languages, had been at Trinity, Cambridge. Cullen had proposed that their appointments should be only temporary; Newman replied that distinguished men had to be better treated than that, and got his way (though the actual distinction of Ornsby and Stewart was open to doubt).

When he had been in Dublin a few days Tom responded to a note from Julia in a way that shows that, whatever their religious differences, the relaxed intimacy of married life was maintained (and, perhaps, that Tom, like Dr Johnson, was not greatly bothered by clean linen): 'I think I must get myself a hat if it can possibly be managed before I return. As to my flannel drawers, I have got a pair with me, my dear; what made you think I had not? If the weather gets cold I shall wear them for the last fortnight I am here. But it does not seem to be so cold here as it is at Fox How.'[16]

Later in the term he sent Julia his impressions of Newman:

I do not think he is likely to retain the Rectorship, at least the active duties of it, for very long. He is evidently very anxious to get quit of it, and to take to more congenial pursuits; and I really think, you will perhaps wonder at my saying so, that there are many who could manage the University affairs equally well, and perhaps some two or three who could manage them better. There is an immense deal of business connected with the office which many could manage as well or better than Newman, his mind is too refined, too polished, for such work; it is like cutting blocks with a razor.

I got through my lecture this morning with very little difficulty, and I think that by the blessing of God I shall find this the case more and more . . .[17]

Tom was right, up to a point. Newman's weariness with the frustrations of his position had made him resolve not to serve longer than the three years on which he had originally agreed in 1854; he was in any case under pressure from the Oratorians to return permanently to Birmingham. It is likely that his resolve to get out was becoming apparent. Tom may have underestimated Newman's considerable administrative ability, though it is true that he had difficulty in delegating. But there was not always anyone to delegate to; as Tom may not yet have understood, shortage of funds for staff meant that Newman himself took on lesser tasks that someone else could easily have done. The expressive image that for Newman's mind to be involved in such duties was like cutting blocks with a razor is apt; it reflects the recurring experience of eminent academics whose scholarly achievement plunges them into administrative labour. Tom's final remark that he had got through his lecture without too much difficulty is a reminder of the worry about his stutter that was a minor accompaniment to the major anxieties about money that dogged him throughout his career. Financially Dublin was a disappointment; when he arrived he worked out that he was being paid at a rate equivalent to 300 pounds a year; but when his post was finally established the stipend was only 200 pounds.

Tom was back in Fox How for the Christmas vacation, in time for Julia's imminent confinement; because of it he declined a proposal from

Newman that he should go to London with introductions to some potentially helpful people. At Fox How he responded to a letter from his
brother William in India, who had unwittingly made some dismissive
comments about Tom's new religion. Tom defends Catholicism resolutely as 'the religion of by far the greater part of the civilized world', and
adds, with emphatic underlining, it was *'the religion of your own country and
your own forefathers for nine hundred years'*.[18] He is anticipating later Catholic
writers, such as Hopkins, Belloc, Chesterton, and Waugh, in offering a
different reading of English history from the Whig-Protestant version
whose points of reference were the Reformation and the Glorious
Revolution.

Tom wrote to tell Newman that he definitely wanted to return to the
Catholic University, if the college authorities agreed and the perennial
matter of his stammer was not too great a problem. Newman certainly
wished to keep Arnold and to see him in a permanent position, but
Archbishop Cullen would take a lot of convincing. The new baby, a boy,
was born on 15 December; mother and child were well. The decision of
Tom and Julia about its name is likely to seem disconcerting nowadays.
To risk a truism, the lives and attitudes of these people a century and a half
ago were, in many essential respects, very like our own. But certain forms
of life have changed fundamentally, at least in Western culture, and make
earlier ways of behaving look strange. Nowhere is this more true than in
attitudes to children. The baby who had lived for only one day in 1854
had, during his few hours of life, been baptized as Arthur. Now the
Arnolds decided to call the new baby 'Arthur', seeming to deprive the
earlier infant of his unique identity and to write him out of the record. It
is as if they were very attached to the name, as a tribute to Stanley and to
Clough, and found the arrival of a new male child a good opportunity to
use it again.

One has a similar feeling about another action of the Arnolds. When
the family travelled to Dublin in January 1857 they did so with the new
baby but without the 5-year-old Mary, who was left behind at Fox How to
be brought up by her grandmother and Aunt Fan. In modern terms it
looks an extraordinarily unfeeling thing to do, but it was a way of dealing
with the fact of poverty when there were already three small children to
bring up. It was not uncommon: one thinks of Fanny Price in *Mansfield
Park*, plucked out of poverty in Portsmouth to be brought up in comfortable surroundings by her uncle by marriage, Sir Thomas Bertram.
Mary saw very little of her parents for several years. There can be no

doubt that she missed them greatly; she never forgot them, and in later life was devoted to them both. In her autobiography Mary Ward casts a golden glow over her years at Fox How, which she refers to as her 'second home' whereas in fact it was her only home. It would not be surprising if she was unhappy some of the time, and she was certainly given to fits of violent temper, which her Aunt Fan knew how to handle. Beyond that we know very little of her actual feelings. When she was a year or so older she was sent to a school in Ambleside run by Clough's sister Anne; she boarded there during the week and came home to Fox How at weekends. Her biographer, John Sutherland, who takes a harsh view of the way her parents treated her, says the fact that she lived as a boarder when the school was only about a mile away from Fox How shows that her grand-mother and aunt were keen to get rid of her. This need not follow. A mile on city streets would have been straightforward for a child in those days, though even there she would have needed to be accompanied; but a mile on Lake District terrain to the school, which was beyond Ambleside, on the slopes of Wansfell, would have been hard going, especially in winter. Staying as a boarder during the week may have been a sensible option, and gave Mary the excitement of living in two different worlds.

Dublin, when the Arnolds arrived, was a city that had been in steady decline since its heyday in the eighteenth century, when it had been the second city of the British Isles and one of the brilliant capitals of Europe. The elegant buildings remained, decaying and turned into tenements. The university had established itself in one of them, an imposing eighteenth-century mansion on the south side of St Stephen's Green, which has been preserved in literature in *A Portrait of the Artist as a Young Man* by James Joyce, who was an undergraduate at the end of the century. One of the poorest quarters in Dublin, the Liberties, was not far away, and the poor sometimes made unwelcome intrusions onto the Green. Dublin had been settled in the sixteenth century as an Anglican colony; by the time the Arnolds arrived the Protestant population was dwindling, but they still numbered about a third of the total, and were dominant in the pro-fessional classes. When Newman was organizing the Medical School he found that of 111 medical practitioners in Dublin who were in 'situations of trust and authority', 99 were Protestant. Not all the Protestants were gentlemanly; some were crude and aggressive, as Arnold noted; he saw placards in the street containing crude anti-Catholic gibes, and notices of Protestant missions to convert Catholics. The most prominent Protestant in Dublin, Archbishop Whately, would not have been guilty of such excesses. He lived on the north side of St Stephen's Green in one of the few eighteenth-century mansions still in private occupation, and was regularly to be seen on the Green smoking a cigar and exercising his dogs. The Catholic University was on the south side; Newman and Whately had once been very close in Oxford, when Whately was principal of Alban Hall and had invited the young Evangelical clergyman to act as vice-principal. But during Newman's years in Dublin they appear, remarkably, never to have met.

Whately was an old family friend of the Arnolds, whom Tom had visited in Dublin in the past. His presence was a potential cause of difficulty for Tom, as he discussed with Newman. He was evidently hoping for a miracle, in the form of the Pauline conversion of Julia, and Newman wondered if renewed acquaintance with Whately would impede that process. But Whately seems to have settled the matter by severing his acquaintance with Tom; on 15 December Tom told Newman:

I have just seen a letter from Whately to my mother, written not a fortnight ago, in which after saying that he has no objection at all to make against those who have been 'brought up in the system', he declares that he cannot excuse or think well of those who, like myself, have been educated in full Protestant light, and have then fallen away. Under these circumstances, I think that anything like intimacy between my wife and them is most improbable.[19]

This may not have been the final word on the matter. J. E. Axon quotes a letter from Tom's sister Fan, written in June 1857, in which she says, 'It is always interesting hearing about the Whatleys', and he concludes that there was, after all, a renewal of friendship with the archbishop and his family.[20] That seems unlikely; there are letters at Balliol from Whately to Arnold written in 1858 concerning some point of religious controversy, whose chilly formal tone contrasts with Whately's previous geniality towards him. Any news Tom passed on to his sister about the Whatleys was probably second-hand.

The Arnolds did, however, have an entry into official society by meeting the lord-lieutenant, Lord Carlisle, following an introduction from Harriet Martineau. He invited them to a St Patrick's ball:

the exertions of the good-natured Lord Carlisle, as with red and glowing face— the George round his neck and the Garter binding his knee—he laboured through the crowded country-dance, 'hands across, down the middle,' &c., &c., were exceedingly praiseworthy, and also slightly comic. As he passed us he said, with a laugh, 'Hot work, Mrs Arnold! was it as bad as this in Tasmania?'.[21]

After starting off in temporary accommodation, the family moved to Sandymount, and then to various other addresses in the Dublin suburbs; Mary Ward refers to

Years of straightened [*sic*] means and constant struggles, passed in dismal furnished houses in Rathmines or Kingstown [now Dun Laoghaire], with only the joys of the wide Kingstown sands, their gulls and their cockles, or the excitement of the storms in winter dashing against their little house on the sea-wall, or the delight of the yearly box, in which the kind Tasmanian relations sent presents for father, mother and children, to brighten a record marked by few of the pleasures now lavished on the modern child.[22]

There is no evidence that Mary Ward ever visited the family in Dublin— indeed, she greatly minded not knowing her younger siblings who were born there—and this impressionistic account suggests the novelist writing up her brother William's recollections.

II

It was while the Arnolds were living in Rathmines, at that time an area favoured by the Protestant professional classes, that they got to know the Benison family, an encounter that was to have a life-long significance. The Benisons were an Anglo-Irish family, landowners on a modest scale, from County Cavan in the north of the country, in the old nine-county Ulster (now part of the Irish Republic). James Benison was Protestant but he had married a Catholic; they had a son and several daughters. The eldest daughter, Josephine, and a younger sister had caused their father intense though not lasting annoyance by converting to Catholicism. In a sense they should have been Catholics anyway; according to the custom of the time, in mixed marriages the daughters were brought up in the mother's religion, the sons in the father's. (To invoke Phineas Finn again: he, like his father, is a Catholic, and his sisters are Protestants.) But James Benison had reneged on his promise and all the children had been brought up as Protestants.

In April 1858 Mr and Mrs Benison and their daughters Emily and Thomasina were in Dublin on a melancholy errand. Josephine remained behind in charge of the family home, Slieve Russell. Emily was very sick and they had brought her to be examined by a famous physician, Sir Henry Marsh, who confirmed her mother's fears that she was suffering from consumption; they stayed in Dublin so that he could give her what treatment he could, which was predictably little. They had had to leave their lodgings and were looking for new ones in Rathmines. The Arnolds at that time were living in 10 Leinster Square, in a rented house large enough to take in paying guests (Tom had bought new furniture for it) as a means of easing their financial burdens.

Emily, in the last letter she wrote, sent to Josephine on 23 April 1858, described how the families converged:

Yesterday morning Mama and Papa set off for Rathmines pretty early as we were obliged to leave Talbot St. that day. Well they had great hunting for lodgings and poor Mama nearly walked off her legs, well after a long time Mama chanced a house in Leinster Square which had no bill on it, and found that lodgings were to be had there, they pleased Mama very much and the lady of the house such a nice person, but far from worldly wise, Mama was not five minutes talking to her when she told her they were from the Colonies, that her husband had an appointment in Australia but becoming a Catholic he was obliged to give it up and he was now Professor at Dr. Newman's. This was enough for Papa, you may suppose, away he went and poor Mama, well they searched on, finding nothing to suit until they came at last to one that might have done but the terms were eight £ a month, Papa's pocket was touched and he said he saw nothing for it but to go back, and they engaged these lodgings for five £ a month—I have just seen Mrs Arnold, she is a very nice person, was never out of Australia till the last twelve months [nearly two years in fact; presumably Julia had diplomatically suppressed the early, disastrous trip to Belgium], her Grandfather was Governor of Van Diemen's land and her father has held an appointment for the last thirty five years.[23]

A day or so later Thomasina reported, 'Mrs Arnold is Church of England, but it is likely her husband will bring her round yet, at least one would fancy so, she has just sent Emily a volume of "Household Words" saying she can have another when she finishes that.' Thomasina's fancies were inaccurate. She was impressed with the Arnolds' connection with *Tom Brown's Schooldays*, then a wildly popular book: 'Mrs Arnold has just lent me Tom Brown's Schooldays! the Dr. Arnold mentioned was her father-in-law, the book is dedicated to his wife.' In a subsequent letter to her brother she gave her impression of Tom Arnold:

There was an obstreperous lock here that Mr Arnold came down to fix but failed in the attempt and afterwards sat with us for a good while, he is very quiet and gentlemanly but has a hesitation in speaking partly from nervousness I think, it is a great disadvantage. I could not suppress a smile listening to him and my father discussing Dr Newman's College,—it was something rare, that institution is only holding its own I fancy, its great disadvantage is the want of a Charter to enable it to give degrees recognised by law, of course it was Mr Arnold told us this. 'Tom Brown' is written by a school-fellow of his a Mr Hughes now a barrister in London, was it not strange our hearing so easily what many would almost give their eyes to know.

Writing to Josephine on 4 May, her mother Kate referred to Julia's kindness to the invalid, and her anti-Catholic prejudices:

I could not tell you all the attention Mrs Arnold pays, a pancake sent up so nice to Emmy for luncheon yesterday and today, cook has now told me Mrs A. ordered her to have a nice little rice pudding at E's dinner hour. There is a gentleman to dine with Mr A. today, a Mr Scott, a convert, a very high up person cook says and the last time he came here, Mrs Arnold would not sit in the room with him, but she has come round since then, she likes a good Catholic but she does not relish converts.

Emily, though not yet bed-ridden was visibly weakening. She wanted to see Josephine, and so did Kate, telling her daughter that she could safely leave her housekeeping duties—she was looking after her brother—for a few days. She came in the middle of May to find her sister now declining rapidly; Emily died at the beginning of June. She was buried back in County Cavan, but, according to the practice of those days, only her father and brother were at the funeral. The women remained a little longer at Rathmines; Kate was not fit to travel for a time. It was at this period that a particular friendship developed between Julia and Josephine, who was only five years younger. At intervals Josephine sent presents of country produce to the Arnolds—some fine grouse were much appreciated. Julia wrote affectionate and grateful letters to Josephine, beginning, with unusual informality, 'My dearest Josephine'. Julia, with her young and steadily increasing family, could not travel easily, but in August 1861, Tom, accompanied by his 9-year-old son Willie, stayed with the Benisons at Slieve Russell. The visit was noted in a significant series of entries in Josephine's diary:

August 22nd   Mr Arnold and Willie came to us
30th   Papa went to Manor Hamilton to shoot with the Huttons,—Joe and George Griffin dined at Mr Littles—I rode with Mr Arnold—Books Mr Arnold recommended—Conversations with Goethe, Life of Schiller.
Aug 31st   Joe, Mr Arnold, Willy and George rode to the mountain—went beating after while Mr A and George fished.
Sept 1st   Mr Arnold and Joe went to Enniskillen a rainy day.
Sept 2nd Mr Arnold, Willy, George G and Pow [Thomasina's family nickname] went by boat to Crone.

Sept 4th   After Mass, Pow and I walked with Mr Arnold towards Lough Erne, it rained all the time, Papa returned at night.

Sept 5th   Papa, Mr A Willie and George went out to course. Mr Arnold and Willie left us at 30c, I wish we could have kept them.

Sept 9th   Heard from Mr Arnold, Resolved against—D.V.

Sept 21st   Broke resolve.

Sept 23rd   Wishes vain as resolves as if power will and even inclination to follow the right were dead.

The final entries are explicit enough to suggest that Josephine, who was 30, had fallen in love with Tom, or believed she had. Whatever her feelings, she never betrayed them, though she and Tom developed a tender, mostly epistolary, friendship.

At University College, Tom Arnold plunged enthusiastically into his duties as Professor of English; he found his students were very young— none of them over 17—and not very well informed. He had discussed with Newman proposals for a course in English Literature, as part of a degree in the Humanities. Newman approved his ideas, but was keen to see the inclusion of essays and periodical literature, particularly the writings of Addison: 'on whom I doted at the age of 15. I only say this, to show his power still of affecting untaught minds.' But not many of the untaught minds of Dublin would be young Newmans; as perhaps he acknowledges when he says, 'I have some compunction in leaving out the novelists, yet who can get boys seriously to read them?' Newman sardonically warns Arnold to be aware of their delicate situation in Ireland: 'but if you go into an *English subject matter*, in opposition to *literature*, the Irish will think it hard that the English rebellion or civil war has the precedence of the raid of Fergus Mac Diormad into Munster in revenge for the dun cow which was stolen from the pastures of his great uncle Thrady in the second century before the Christian era'.[24]

Some of the time Arnold must, like many teachers of literature, have been only one jump ahead of his students. As he told Newman later in the year, 'Though my knowledge is meagre enough now of course I can be constantly adding to it, and I think I see my way in the course of a year or two to the production of a text-book on the subject-matter of my professorship; a thing which seems to me much wanted.'[25] Arnold was right; and though he proposed far more schemes than he ever accomplished, the text-book did eventually see the light and proved useful and popular. But first Arnold needed to have his appointment confirmed, and here Archbishop Cullen was predictably obstructive. He claimed that the university could not afford the post, and that a Professor of English Literature was not necessary, since anyone could do that kind of teaching (an argument that has rumbled on ever since the establishment of English in universities). Newman patiently but firmly replied that no new funds would be involved, since Arnold was replacing MacCarthy; Cullen may have thought this a bad exchange, since Arnold was English and MacCarthy was Irish, even if a former Young Irelander. Although Cullen tried to act as if he had sole authority, decisions had to be ratified by a committee comprising the four archbishops, and when they met in the autumn they approved of Arnold's appointment to an established post.

The long delay in knowing about his future had been understandably trying to Arnold. He was probably not reassured by a bland, non-committal letter from Cullen which told him that as his petition had been put in Dr Newman's hands, the archbishop was sure it would be properly managed, and that no complication would arise from it. So things were best left as they were and Tom should not give himself any trouble about what had been done.[26] He was still on leave with half-pay from Tasmania, and in August 1857 he applied to the Legislative Council there for a further extension of six months without pay; it is as though he were reluctant to sever links completely with his former employer before his future in Ireland was assured.[27] There was, too, his continual anxiety about his stammer, which came and went in the manner of such nervous disorders. Worrying about the stammer may well have made it worse. After his position had finally been approved, Newman wrote from Birmingham to a colleague in Dublin: 'I had been feeling very much for Arnold's anxieties, and (if I may say it) had only been this morning praying for him. He has a great many troubles of various kinds, I doubt not, which he alone can know. I think it affects his spirits, if I judge from his manner.'[28] As Newman goes on to discuss, Arnold's troubles came from lack of money, and various schemes were suggested to increase his income by finding him extra tutoring. And there were additional domestic tensions, resulting from the unhealed rift with Julia about his change of religion, and her dislike of living in a Catholic city. The signs were appearing that she had become a nagger, and was not a competent housekeeper. Tom may also have been worried that Julia was once more pregnant; another child, Lucy, was born the next year, followed in 1860 by Francis.

His state of mind would not have been helped by a letter from Matthew, written on 28 December 1857. It is affectionate in tone, and compliments Tom on the breadth of his reading and his interests: 'How

refreshing it is to meet with anyone who knows anything about any literary matter.' But after a page or so of pleasant discussion of literature,
Matthew concludes waspishly: 'in literary matters we may still have strong
sympathy. Là, vous ne vous êtes pas cramponné à une légende morte.
Admire my politeness in having recourse to French to say an uncivil thing
. . . '.[29] Matthew subsequently remarked to his mother, with studied
understatement, 'In a letter to him I touched in one sentence on his
change of religious profession—which it is possible he may not have
liked.'[30]

On a visit to London, probably in 1857, Tom was reunited with
Clough. He and Clough and Matthew dined at Verrey's in Regent Street,
where Matthew found occasion to irritate the earnest Clough:

He talked copiously and brilliantly about all manner of things, and, *inter alia*, mentioned some work of Voltaire with high praise. Clough objected that it was licen-
tious. He, with a wave of the hand, intimated that such considerations had very
little weight with him. 'Well, you don't think any the better of yourself for that, do
you', swiftly retorted Clough.[31]

At the end of 1857 Newman left Ireland, more or less for good, and
Tom Arnold was bereft of his mentor and support. Newman had wanted
to give up the rectorship after the three years for which he had originally
consented—in fact, by 1857 it was six years since he had first arrived in
the country—but he had been persuaded to stay on for a further year in
an unsatisfactory compromise, as 'non-resident rector', which would enable him to return to Birmingham, as the Oratory Fathers had been urging him to do. In order for this implausible scheme to have any chance of
success, a vice-rector would need to be appointed, to run the college on a
day-to-day basis. The bishops were very slow to appoint someone to this
position, and when they eventually did he promptly died. For all his deep
differences with Newman, Cullen did not want him to leave, since his
name and distinction were so much an asset to the university. Cullen always resented Newman's frequent absences in Birmingham, and one can
see his reasons; his suggested solution was for the Oratory to be transferred to Dublin, though he can hardly have welcomed a further influx of
Englishmen. It was certainly not an idea that Newman or the Oratorians
would have found acceptable.

Like other English converts in Ireland, such as Newman before him
and Fr Gerard Hopkins SJ thirty years later, Arnold found that he had
religion in common with the Irish and very little else. He had grown up in

an environment permeated by the beliefs and practice of the Church of England; in the smaller and larger Anglican theocracies of Dr Arnold's household and Rugby School; and in a university that was staffed and run by clergymen and was, in effect, an adjunct of the Established Church. Questions of belief apart, the Church of England represented what Coleridge called a 'clerisy', which placed an educated man in every village. Arnold discovered, with a degree of culture-shock, that the Catholic Church in Ireland was very different. There the Church educated the sons of the poor for the priesthood; in Arnold's words, 'the poorest cottier can look forward to making his son a priest'. In a letter to Clough he remarked of the Catholic University, 'the real secret of our comparative ill-success is, I believe to be found in the peculiar character of the Irish priesthood, and in the intellectual superiority of the Protestants . . . the Irish priesthood, taken as a body, are not *gentlemen*, while the Protestant clergy are, and all the political and social consequences that stem from that one fact, you will instantly perceive.'[32] Arnold was beginning to learn something about Irish culture and society.

Back in Birmingham, Newman was trying to run the university at long range, and was increasingly concerned at the failure of the bishops to appoint a vice-rector. At the same time, he was engaged in a new educational enterprise, where he would have an altogether freer hand. This was to establish, alongside the Oratory, a Catholic public school, modelled on the existing English establishments, that would prepare students for the Catholic University, if that institution survived. Newman decided that he would like Tom Arnold to teach at the school, and in the spring of 1858, while it was still only in the planning stage, offered him the post of second master to teach Classics, at a stipend of 300 pounds a year. This could be described as an attempt at poaching; or, in modern jargon, as the redeployment of resources. Arnold declined, with regrets. He acknowledged that the pay was a lot more then he earned in Dublin; but there he had a good deal of free time, and was hoping for more pupils to boost his salary. Casting about for further reasons for declining, he mentions that he has just bought a quantity of furniture and would have to sell it at a loss if he transferred himself and his family to England. More convincingly, he says, 'I feel that the University *may* come to something after all, if we all put our shoulders to the wheel; that it is a "carrière ouverte", and that it is worth submitting to much privation, even on the mere chance that our hopes may one day be realized.'[33] Arnold was, indeed, seriously committed to education, beyond his professional involvement with Classical and

English literature. He helped to launch a programme of evening lectures for the young men of Dublin, which he described as 'answering nearly to the Working Men's College in London', and which were well attended. Newman was disinclined to take 'no' for an answer, though he respected Arnold's reasons, and accepted them for the time being.

Meanwhile, Arnold had accepted a post as 'extern tutor' to St Patrick's House, a student residence. In the summer vacation of 1858 he was at Fox How, where he was reunited with Mary and met Clough again. Clough tended to drop his friends if their ideas diverged too much from his, but he preserved his former warm relation with Tom Arnold, even though he was now a Catholic. Mary wrote in her autobiography:

I can recall one or two golden days, at long intervals, when my father came for me, with 'Mr Clough', and the two old friends, who, after nine years' separation [eleven, in fact] had recently met again, walked up the Sweden Bridge lane into the heart of Scandale Fell, while I, paying no more attention to them, than they— after a first ten minutes—did to me, went wandering and skipping, and dreaming by myself. In those days every rock along the mountain lane, every boggy patch, every stretch of silken, flower-sown grass, every bend of the wild stream, and all its sounds, whether it chattered gently over stony shallows, or leapt full-throated into deep pools, swimming with foam—were to me the never-ending joys of 'a land of pure delight' . . . I might quite safely explore these enchanted spots under male eyes, since they took no account, mercifully, of a child's boots and stockings—male tongues besides being safely busy with books and politics.[34]

In September Clough, still at Ambleside, gave a succinct account of Tom to Charles Eliot Norton: 'Tom Arnold, who turned Roman Catholic out in Van Diemen's Land is here—or rather was, till this morning. He is employed in the Catholic University at Dublin, of which Newman is the nominal Rector though he is but little there: most of his time is spent at the Oratory at Birmingham. The University as yet does not seem to be a success.'[35] In October, Tom wrote to Clough looking back on their meetings with pleasure and saying how much he valued their continued friendship. At about this time, Clough lent him 100 pounds. Originally Tom proposed to pay interest at 5 per cent on the loan, which would be repaid in two years. However, Clough would take only 4 per cent, though the repayments continued for many years; in 1862 Tom told Clough's widow that he hoped to repay the capital within a year or so, but fifteen years later he was still paying her the interest. In December 1858 Clough sent him a chatty letter from his desk in the Education Department, discussing books and asking: 'What do you read now? English literature for your

class or classics for your pupils?'[36] In the months to come Tom and
Clough were corresponding about a joint project, a series of 'Lives of the
Poets', to carry on from the point where Johnson left off. Unfortunately,
but not at all surprisingly, given the capacity of both of them to devise
schemes and then abandon them, no more was heard of it.

In November Newman was back in Dublin for his last public act as
rector, a lecture to the Medical Faculty on 'Christianity and Medical
Science'. Many people wanted to see him, and Arnold had only a few brief
glimpses of him. Newman was under renewed pressure not to leave.
Cullen seems to have been in a state of outright denial about Newman's
resignation, telling him that it would be necessary for him to spend much
more time in residence. The professors of the university signed an
address organized by Ornsby, begging Newman to remain associated
with it. Arnold told Newman that he had agreed with every word, but had
declined to sign: 'chiefly because I thought that you must know your own
affairs best, and that if you were really bent upon resigning, it must be
because you felt and knew it to be the right thing for you to do . . . '.[37]
Newman was indeed bent upon resigning, and did so, crossing the Irish
Sea for the last time in his life. Even so, it was several more months before
the bishops formally accepted his resignation. Soon after his return to
England Newman mordantly observed, 'As to the University, I really fear
that at least some persons already begin, like Frankenstein, to be scared at
their own monster.'[38]

Arnold's own affairs encountered a setback, since the tutorship at St
Patrick's House was required by the new dean for someone else, and he
was deprived of it. He told Newman, 'it is rather afflicting to find the
ground thus sinking from under one, but God's will be done'. Newman
meanwhile had renewed his offer of a mastership at the Oratory School,
and Arnold was tempted by the stipend of 300 pounds. But he slipped
into his prevaricatory mode and asked for a week to think about it. He
confided to Newman that there was a chance of a Catholic being
appointed to an examinership of schools by the Board of Education and
he wanted to give himself the possibility of getting it, faint though that
might be. Though Tom Arnold liked teaching, he had set his sights on the
kind of work as an inspector which he had done in Tasmania, and which
Matthew was carrying out with distinction. It would not be surprising if
Tom felt a certain envy of his brother's steady and secure professional advancement (not to mention his growing literary reputation), but if he did
there is no trace of it in his correspondence.

In December 1858 Tom and Julia were in England, spending Christmas with his sister Mary and her husband, the Revd J. S. Hiley, at Woodhouse Hall in Leicestershire. On 28 December Tom, on his way back to Dublin, called on Newman at the Oratory in Birmingham, perhaps to find out more about the school. He was still hoping for an inspectorship, and in the end once more decided against accepting Newman's offer. Back in Dublin he wrote to Julia, who was unwell and had stayed on at Woodhouse, strongly recommending what he described as a 'blue pill' for her ailments. He forwarded a letter from her father in Tasmania, and tells her about the antics of their little sons, Theodore and Arthur, and Fury the dog. He reflects adversely on Thomas Scratton, secretary of the university—'How Newman ever came to appoint him, is the mystery to me.'

Tom's hopes of an inspectorship were dashed, and in March 1859 he tells Clough, 'If you ever hear of a berth in the public service which might be suitable for me, and for which an application would have any chance of being successful, I know you will not forget me. I am ground down nearly to starvation pitch where I am, having—contrariwise to Sam Weller—"plenty to do and little to get".'[39] The intention of the previous year, to stay on and help the University to survive, had weakened, following Newman's final departure and the discouragements of his own life. A few weeks later he wrote to Clough with the sad news that his brother William, whom he had not seen for many years, had died on the way home from India. In June Arnold is again in correspondence with Clough about a possible change of employment, and is now in an uncertain mood, suggesting that the 'starvation pitch' of his life in Dublin might, after all, be not quite so bad:

The pay is but small—£200 a year; but as a good deal of my time is left at my disposal, I am able to take private pupils and so help out my income to some degree. It would not therefore be worth my while to make a move unless I could obtain in England a permanent position with a salary of not less than £300 a year. Indeed were it not for the uncertainty which hangs over the prospects of the University, it might seem imprudent to give up what I have, except for the sake of a much greater difference of income that what I have mentioned, but the fact of a situation's being *permanent* would I think make the step expedient.[40]

There is no doubt that Arnold was not really paid enough to live on, and that 300 pounds—the salary that had been offered at the Oratory School—would have made a lot of difference to him. But his feelings about his situation fluctuated from near-despair to strong hopes of getting something better.

III

One consideration was that the free time which Arnold admitted his professorial post gave him allowed him to make extensive forays into higher journalism. In New Zealand and Tasmania he had contributed to the local press; he had a fluent pen, had read widely, and was interested in many subjects. In Ireland he turned to periodical journalism; it was the age of the great Victorian reviews, the substantial quarterlies that disseminated knowledge and prompted debate among the tiny but influential segment of the population that took ideas seriously. The quarterlies were rather forbidding in format; the level of discussion was, as a rule, impressively high, though the amount of space available to contributors was an invitation to prolixity. Most of what they published is now remembered only by scholars, but they provided a platform for famous analyses of Victorian culture from Ruskin and Matthew Arnold and other sages. In order to raise the intellectual level of English Catholics, a quarterly reflecting Catholic ideas and interests had been launched by Cardinal Wiseman. This was the *Dublin Review*; it was started in Dublin and then transferred to London, but kept the original name. In 1857 Arnold became a contributor, perhaps making use of the brief contact he had had with Wiseman when he arrived in London. He published a long review-article called 'Filibusters in Nicaragua', a study of recent events in that country, discussing a number of recent books, including one in French and one in Spanish. There had been no sign of any previous interest on Arnold's part in this area, but he draws on the books to provide an informative and readable narrative, describing a recent civil war in Nicaragua, when an American adventurer called William Walker seized power with the support of the US government. Eventually Walker was defeated by the Nicaraguan people, with help from the neighbouring republics, as Arnold describes in vigorous prose. He interpreted the episode as an attempt by the slave-owning states of the South to extend their influence and to spread Protestantism. (In perspective it looks like one more instance of the United States' perennial wish to maintain hegemony in the hemisphere.)

At the Catholic University Newman started *Atlantis*, a review which was intended to provide a showcase for the scholarly talents he had assembled. Arnold, reverting to his Classical training, contributed an article to the first number in 1858 called 'The Genius of Alcibiades', a solid but dull study of the Athenian statesman. Newman had been keen to include something by Arnold, and had paid him in advance, but confessed himself disappointed in his contribution: 'It has so little point.'[41] Matthew Arnold was a regular contributor to *Fraser's Magazine*, and in 1861 he interested the editor, James Anthony Froude, in an article that Tom had proposed on New Zealand. When it arrived, Matthew passed on the word that it was not altogether what Froude had hoped for: 'too little about New Zealand and the society there, and too much about your own feelings'.[42] It seems as if there was to have been a second instalment, and Matthew urged him to make it less subjective. Tom's 'Reminiscences of New Zealand' appeared in the August number, but there were no further instalments. It may have been too personal for Froude's taste, but it remains an interesting account of Tom Arnold's time in the colony, standing between the immediate responses of his correspondence at the time and the more remote memories in *Passages in a Wandering Life*. Tom also had hopes of breaking into the *Edinburgh*, the great Whig review where his father had made his onslaught on the Oxford Malignants. He asked Clough if he knew who was editing it and if he thought Tom would have any chance of them taking a study of Walter Scott he had written.

Most of Tom's journalistic work, though, was contributed to *The Rambler*, a Catholic bi-monthly. It had been founded in 1848 by John Moore Capes, a convert clergyman, as a focus for the post-Tractarian converts, many of them Oxford graduates with intellectual interests and academic attainments. Like the *Dublin Review*, it hoped to improve the quality of Catholic discourse, but unlike Wiseman's magazine, which was conservative in tone, reflecting his own background and temperament, *The Rambler*—the title was a weak echo of Samuel Johnson's magazine of that name—was liberal and open-minded. After its launch it had a number of owners and appeared in a variety of formats; in 1859 it was owned jointly by Frederick Capes, the founder's brother, Sir John Acton, and Richard Simpson, another convert clergyman, who was acting as editor. The Catholic bishops were increasingly hostile to *The Rambler*, finding cause to question its orthodoxy and its loyalty. There was great objection to an article that claimed that St Augustine had contributed to the spirit of Jansenism (though that is now generally accepted by theologians), and annoyance that the magazine had criticized the bishops' decision not to co-operate with the Royal Commission on education. Richard Simpson was particularly *non grata*; as a Catholic layman he continued the speculative interest in theology he had developed as an Anglican minister; the bishops thought that laymen had no place writing on theological matters. Simpson made matters worse by his witty, iconoclastic, style. The bishops had a good many problems to contend with; it was only a few years since the re-establishment of the Catholic hierarchy, which had been widely condemned as an act of 'papal agression', and anti-Catholic prejudice was widespread. They were practical men with pastoral priorities, educated in seminaries rather than universities, and like their Irish counterparts had no great conviction of the desirability or need of free intellectual activity. Their patience gave out and they declared that *The Rambler* would be subject to ecclesiastical censure unless Simpson gave up the editorship. He agreed to do so, and in order to fill the gap, Newman, with great reluctance, temporarily took on the post.

While he was acting in this capacity he received a note from Tom Arnold, asking if he would accept a 'short paper' on John Stuart Mill's *On Liberty*, which had been recently published. Newman passed the letter on to Acton with the annotation, 'I suspect Arnold would not write without pay. His name would be good. I declined his offer, as being too late.'[43] By the autumn of 1859 Newman had stepped down and Acton had become editor, though the bishops regarded him with almost as much suspicion as Simpson, who continued to serve as sub-editor. Although Newman had originally declined Arnold's offer of a review of Mill, he now recommended him to Acton: the remark that Arnold's name was good and that he would expect to be paid were recurring motifs in his career. Acton had not liked Arnold's essay on Alcibiades, but he was willing to take him on. Indeed, he wrote to Arnold warmly inviting him to contribute a review of Mill's book, adding that the magazine had great need of the help of friends.[44] Simpson was agreeable: 'let us have Arnold by all means; it is a good name, & the man is worth a trial'.[45] Later Simpson expressed great irritation with Arnold when he delivered his copy so late that he nearly missed the issue for which it was intended.

Nevertheless, Acton expressed hopes for frequent contributions from Arnold,[46] who went on to write regularly for *The Rambler* and its successor, *The Home and Foreign Review*. His acquaintance with Sir John Acton enlarged his horizons but took him rather out of his intellectual depth. Lord Acton, as he later became, is now remembered as a magisterial, remote, and heavily bearded figure, famous for his aphorism that all power tends to corrupt. But in the 1850s he was clean-shaven and youthful in appearance. He was a cosmopolitan, off the scale of familiar Victorian types, though he might have made a memorable minor character in a novel of the period. He came from an old Catholic family, and was one of the few cradle-Catholics to play any part in the intellectual life of his time. His paternal grandfather had been prime minister of Naples, and Acton inherited his father's baronetcy when he was 3 years old. An uncle, Cardinal Acton, had been an ornament of the papal court. His mother was German, daughter of the Duke of Dalberg, though her preferred language was French. As a Catholic, Acton could not attend an English university, and his higher education took place in Munich, where he was the student and intellectual apprentice of the theologian and historian Ignaz von Döllinger. In the words of his biographer, David Matthew, Acton was 'an English gentleman brought up on German scholarship'. In 1859, when he took over *The Rambler*, he was still only 25; he was wealthy, formidably intellectual, fluent in several langauges, learned beyond his years, and no respecter of persons, clerical or lay. He betrayed, at times, a trace of aristocratic *morgue*, and comes across as a spiky, chilly, and rather lonely individual. His Catholicism, which was inherited and habitual and reinforced by the South German milieu where he spent much of his time, had a different resonance from that of the English converts. His quasi-Gallican attitudes made him resist papal claims to infallibility. Simpson, who at that time was his only close associate, shared, unusually for a convert, Acton's sense of the nature of Catholicism. The ideal that they tried to express in *The Rambler* was that the idea of the primacy of conscience should extend to the primacy of truth in historical and other intellectual enquiries: the historian must try to uncover the truth even when it is embarrassing for the institutional church. The bishops were deeply suspicious; in Rome Blessed Pio Nono was lamenting the advance of modern ideas and infidelity, and was facing the loss of the papal lands to the forces of United Italy. It was not a climate in which Acton's liberal Catholicism could flourish; in fact, it was a century ahead of its time, an attempt to enact the attitudes of the Second Vatican Council before the First had taken place.

Tom Arnold's long, thoughtful essay on Mill's book was hardly the 'short paper' that he had proposed to Newman. The first part came out in the November 1859 issue, and the remainder in the March 1860 issue. He writes about Mill with sympathy and understanding, whilst noting the areas of incompatibility between his approach and Christian belief. Mill, he remarks, seems to think that most opinions are false and need to be examined rather than meditated upon. He pragmatically agrees with Mill in being opposed to the censorship of ideas, since suppression does more harm than good, and he cites Milton's *Areopagitica* in support. Arnold describes coercion as an educational instrument which Western Europe has outgrown, whilst defending the right of the Church in appropriate cases to apply spiritual coercion, such as excommunication. He notes that Mill's doctrines could help to dissipate the intolerance that imposed disabilities on Catholics in society. Arnold's essay was published over the initial 'A', which deceived some readers, such as Mary Gladstone, who assumed in her posthumous edition of Acton's letters that he had written it; Arnold's ideas seemed close enough to Acton's to make the notion plausible. Having found a foothold in *The Rambler*, Arnold unearthed his article on Scott, which had not appeared in the *Edinburgh Review* or anywhere else. In a studiedly off-hand way he wrote to Acton: 'Should you ever, like some newspaper editors, be at a loss for "copy", I have an article lying by me which would perhaps serve to stop a gap; it is on Sir Walter Scott, and would cover between 30 and 40 pages of the *Rambler*.'[47] Acton accepted the article, but was equally off-hand about it, remarking to Simpson, 'Arnold's Scott will I suppose be lightish reading . . .';[48] he also took the opportunity, in his precociously learned fashion, to tell Arnold a few facts about Scott that he had not known. Arnold responded with respectful gratitude, but when he received proofs he displayed the unexpected firmness that intermittently marked his tentative movement through life. He saw they were marked up to appear in two instalments; he emphatically told Acton that it was not suitable for such a division, and that he would rather wait until the article could come out as a whole. He evidently got his way, and without having to wait very long, for it appeared as a single contribution in the May 1860 number.

Acton liked it well enough to suggest that he should write more on Scott, emphasizing the historical dimension of the novels. This he did not do, though he did pick up another of Acton's suggestions. It materialized as an article, published in two parts without apparent objection on his part, called 'The Negro Race and its Destiny', which appeared in the July and September issues. It represents yet another new direction in his journalistic writing, though his hostility to the slave-owning states of the USA was first expressed in his article on Nicaragua. This essay is, in effect, an extended review of a German book in the emerging science of anthropology. It displays Arnold's journalistic abililty to sustain a narrative and apparently master a subject from a single source. Arnold's attitudes would be called racist now, but were moderate for those days. He cannot see any absolute objection in principle to slavery, but dislikes it in practice, particularly as it was currently practised in the American South; he believes that the lot of slaves is better in the colonies of Catholic countries such as Cuba and Brazil. He hopes to see the end of slavery, but more by a process of gradual manumission than by instant abolition. He was writing the year before the outbreak of the Civil War in America, which he foresaw: 'I cannot see how slavery with them can end otherwise than in some tremendous catastrophe.'[49] Arnold denies any essential inferiority in the Negro race, but regards them as backward and needing help to develop: 'The Christian Church may hope gradually to raise the Negro race out of the depths of impurity and superstition in which they are plunged.' This article had an embarrassing aftermath for Arnold; Acton had lent him the book on which it was based, and two years later he had to confess that he had lost it, or at least, that it had disappeared from his shelves.

The remarkable variety of Arnold's subjects reflects the range of his intellectual curiosity and of his interests; it shows, too, the self-confidence with which he was ready to write about so many different things, even while he was expressing doubts about his competence to do so. In this respect he was part of the high Victorian culture that looked for a degree of relaxed polymathy in pundits and commentators. One thinks, for instance, of Walter Bagehot, economist, banker, constitutionalist, and literary critic; or George Henry Lewes, novelist, biographer, physiologist, and philosopher. The concept of field-work was yet to emerge, so Arnold did not hesitate to write at length about countries he had never visited, just on the basis of reading about them. This attitude persisted until the end of the century, when Sir James Frazer produced a massive and influential work of anthropology without stirring from the confines of a library.

There were, though, two articles in *The Rambler* where Arnold wrote about things of direct personal concern. In 'The Catholic University of Ireland' in the May 1860 issue, he engages in anonymous reflections on the troubled state of the institution that employed him. Apart from the medical faculty it was not prospering; the number of students remained static, a rector had still not been appointed to replace Newman, and the British government would not grant a charter to recognize the university's degrees. The Catholic University was supposed to be a Louvain for the English-speaking world, but it was in a much weaker state than the Belgian university. Arnold points out that Louvain has an energetic and

1. Dr Thomas Arnold. A painting by Thomas Phillips, 1839

2. Matthew Arnold, late 1860s

3. Tom Arnold. A daguerreotype made shortly before
his departure for New Zealand in 1847

4. Julia Sorell. A watercolour by Thomas Wainewright, *c.*1847

5. Sir William Denison, when Lieutenant Governor of Van Diemen's Land

6. Arthur Hugh Clough. A drawing by Samuel Rowse, 1860

7. 'The main road, New Town, with the coach Perseverance.' A painting by Henry Gritten, 1857, showing the white house in which Tom and Julia Arnold lived from 1850 to 1853

8. Fox How, Westmorland

9. Sir John Acton, *c.*1858

11. Tom Arnold, 1870s

10. John Henry Newman, 1870s

12. Josephine Benison with her niece Katie, early 1880s

13. Tom Arnold, 1890s

14. Mary Augusta
Ward. A painting by
Julian Russell, 1889

15. Tom Arnold's daughter, Julia Huxley, with
a grandchild (probably Trevenen, *b*. 1889)

16. Tom Arnold's grandson, Aldous Huxley,
b. 1894

committed rector, Mgr de Ram, who holds the position permanently, whereas in Dublin 'a man of genius was only lent for a time, and then snatched away'. Newman was very ready to be snatched away when the time came, though if Dublin had been more like Louvain he might well have contrived to stay. The other article, 'The Irish Church', appeared in the March 1861 issue. It engages in a hostile comparison of the privileged position of the established Protestant Church in Ireland compared with that of the Catholic Church, the religion of the great majority of the people. One passage, unusually scathing for the mild Arnold, is drawn from his direct experience of life in Dublin:

The singular spectacle of the two ancient cathedrals of Dublin, Christchurch and St Patrick's, rising in the midst of a dense Catholic population, by whose ancestors they were reared and used, but barricaded and barred during the week, and only opened on Sundays to a flirting, tittering, gossiping Protestant crowd, who resort thither as to a public promenade, anthems by Stevenson being simply substituted for waltzes by Labitsky, is to a newcomer not the least astounding.

The congregation whom Arnold describes so unkindly were the flock of Archbishop Whately, who was a welcome regular guest of Mrs Arnold at Fox How. It was as well that his article, like most contributions to *The Rambler*, appeared anonymously. Polemics apart, he argues that the Church of Ireland's possession of pre-Reformation ecclesiastical remains is illegitimate and that they should be restored to the Catholic population. Acton was not happy with this article and took it upon himself to make changes. He told Simpson:

The article is very loose in thought and words, and carelessly got together as to facts. I have boldly interpolated and altered, so as to fit it for an editorial. Some points are very good as to the present position of the Catholic clergy, but I have broken the edge of his argument from the analogy of confiscations abroad, and put in at the end what is the key stone of the question, that the right to the property lies not with the people but with the Church. He neither knows the history of Ireland nor anything of public law, and calls peasants and shopkeepers a proletariate![50]

Acton told Newman that Arnold's paper had been 'very revolutionary at first', no doubt referring to the idea that ecclesiastical property should be handed over directly to the people. Arnold accepted Acton's other changes but tried to resist the major alteration:

to make a direct claim upon the ecclesiastical property 'for the Catholic Church' would be the sure way to fill the general English mind with a stubborn determination never to give it up. And I must own that I do not think such a claim sustainable. If, because the Catholic Church once had the property, it ought to be restored in Ireland, it follows that it ought to be also restored in England. Yet what English Catholic would seriously think of such a Quixotic enterprise, as an agitation for the restitution of the property of the Church of England to the modern representatives of its former owners.[51]

Arnold was arguing pragmatically; as a former Anglican he had a strong sense of what kind of approach was likely to succeed. Acton, an exotic figure in English culture, took a more absolute stance: stolen property should be restored to its original owners. In Ireland the Catholics were a large majority, and in England they were a tiny minority, so the two positions were far from parallel. Acton claimed that there was no time to make further changes following Arnold's objection—to whom he sent an effusive letter of apology—and the article appeared with the alteration in place.

Relations remained amicable. *The Rambler* paid 2 guineas per thousand words and Arnold was glad of the money. On one occasion he had to tell Acton, 'You forgot to send the cheque: excuse my reminding you of it, but I am like one of Pope's Grub Street authors, in a state of great impecuniosity.'[52] Arnold had made efforts to assist Acton by ascertaining if the magazine could achieve a greater circulation in Ireland, but it was too English in tone and too independent in its attitude to ecclesiastical authority to attain very much of an Irish readership. The cultural gap that had defeated Newman was still yawning. Not that Acton and Simpson were finding their path easy in England; *The Rambler* was increasingly attacked by the Catholic hierarchy for its alleged heterodoxy and disloyalty, and Cardinal Wiseman was making representations in Rome which were expected to lead to a condemnation on high. The editors had for some time considered, on practical grounds, turning *The Rambler* into a quarterly, which would make it more like the other reviews of the age. The change would also make it possible to claim that the offensive publication no longer existed and so could not be censured; it was, at least, a way of buying time.

Writing for *The Rambler* gave Arnold a platform for his ideas, and marginally helped his finances, which continually needed reinforcement. He conceived a scheme for opening his own student house and received a handsome letter of support from Newman; but it went the way of so many of his schemes. In September 1859 Tom was once more at Fox

How; Clough was there, and Matthew and his wife and children. Tom enjoyed sailing on the lake with Mary, and impressed on Anne Clough, the headmistress of her school, and on his mother and his sister Fan, the necessity of the little girl taking plenty of exercise. This may have been because of a need to release her animal spirits, for she was notoriously hot-tempered. Tom's concern shows that though he was an erratic parent he was not totally neglectful; but the fact that he passed on the address of the school to Julia when Mary had already been there many months suggests that her mother was in no hurry to write to her. The girl had good reason to feel neglected.

In November Clough wrote to Tom, thanking him for the 2 pounds half-yearly interest he has paid, and adds, 'I heard from somebody that you had a young Portuguey prince in hand. I hope he will pay you well.'[53] This Portuguese count was one of the exotic 'decoy ducks' that the university cherished in the hope of attracting other wealthy foreign Catholics. The young count was staying in Arnold's house, and in fact cost him his Christmas holiday in England, since he had only just arrived and Arnold did not want to leave him to his own devices. Julia went without him to stay, once more, with Mary Hiley in Leicestershire; according to Janet Trevelyan, Mary was Julia's closest friend in the Arnold clan, though their meetings cannot have been frequent. A letter that Tom wrote to Julia on 26 December 1859 provides one of the very few surviving direct insights into the depths and difficulties of their marriage at that time:

My thoughts were often with you yesterday dearest: God grant that this Christmas time may be a time of new birth in the hearts of us all. I cannot you know speak out freely to you; you would tell me it was cant; and perhaps it might be, so hard is it to give exact expression to the inner thought, and so great the temptation to use stereotyped forms of speech which are near at hand. Again, the constant system of repression to which you compel me cramps and stiffens my very thoughts ... My dearest Julia do not let anything which I have said pain you; when I say I love you most dearly I do not think I lie; at any rate I know that I love nobody else; and if as you often say, from coldness of nature I am incapable of true love, or if I lie, as I rather think, under a kind of enchantment,—either way I am rather to be pitied than to be blamed.[54]

Tom's painfully direct words show that though it was a marriage where the partners were very liable to make one another unhappy, they were far from indifferent to each other: a kind of love endured, even though it was, for him, 'a kind of enchantment'.

In 1860 their sixth surviving child was born, named Francis. Arnold hung on at the Catholic University, though, as he reported to Newman, 'Our affairs are in a sad way, and could not well be otherwise'; a new rector to succeed Newman had not yet been appointed and the college was virtually leaderless. Nevertheless, in April Newman is agreeably surprised to learn that Arnold and another professor have had an increase of salary; according to an editorial note to Newman's letter in the Oxford edition it was an increase of 100 pounds, which would have brought Arnold's salary up to the 300 pounds that he told Clough was the minimum he needed in order to consider a move. But Arnold does not refer to this increase (assuming the report was correct) and his financial situation went on being difficult. A growing family and mounting debts, together with Julia's ineffectual housekeeping, would soon have mopped up the extra money, if he ever received it. Newman still had hopes of attracting Arnold to his school; Acton told Simpson, 'I find Newman is very fond of Arnold, and expects that someday he will settle at Edgbaston.'[55]

Writing to Newman in July, Arnold raises other personal matters. He refers to the state of his spiritual life and how he has come to prefer the lives of the saints to all other reading:

I cannot find the true hero—the true sage—such as even the natural mind represents these characters to itself, anywhere else depicted. People speak of Wordsworth as a *sage*; but he was only so in *words*; I, who knew him well, remember that in the daily walk of life he was far from having that calmness, that mastery over self and outward things, which are involved in the idea that the word conveys.[56]

He raises a problem that has worried him ever since he became a Catholic: the propriety of attending family prayers in a Protestant household. He has been told by his confessor that it would certainly be forbidden in Ireland, but that practice might be different in England. He is about to go to Fox How on his annual visit; up to now he has attended family prayers without joining in. It would be painful to have to absent himself, but he would if it were required, and he wants Newman's advice. The tormented scrupulosity was characteristic, though there is no doubt about the answer he hopes for; we do not know what Newman advised. A few months later Arnold raised another matter with him: the lawfulness, for a Catholic, of using hymns by Protestants in the bringing up of children. He pertinently remarks, 'The extreme unsuitableness of most English Catholic hymns to the capacity—and their powerlessness to reach the feelings—of young children, are matters of which I have long been convinced.'[57] Arnold may not have got much satisfaction on that point; it is only fairly recently that Catholic hymnals have included 'Protestant' hymns, acknowledging the superiority of their words and music.

Tom was at Fox How in August 1860; once more without Julia, though his mother had a photograph taken of the 9-year-old Mary to send her; Tom said: 'The hair was put in a net as you desired; and Fan and I took some trouble with her *get up* generally, and I think you will on the whole be satisfied with the result.'[58] One gets the sense that while Tom, in his way, tried to be a dutiful father, Julia preferred her daughter at a distance. Back in Dublin Tom heard there was another chance of an inspectorate, as one of the very few Catholic inspectors was on the point of resigning. The Clougho-Matthean axis did what it could for him. On 25 August Clough wrote to Matthew from the Education Office: 'Marshall has resigned—so let Tom bestir himself. I only heard last night but I believe it has been a fait accompli for two or three days. I fear the L.P. [Lord President] has some one ready.' Matthew forwarded Clough's note to Tom, with a covering letter: 'You had better, I think, apply instantly for the place: and use what influence you can. Could you get Ld. Carlisle to write to Ld. Granville for you?' Matthew goes on to engage in general reflections about the problems of living on a low income which, though true, would have been neither necessary nor welcome to Tom at this juncture. He concludes with some brotherly nagging: 'But perhaps, my dear Tom, it is one of your few weaknesses, that you *cannot* look your position in the face, and *force* yourself, and others, to adapt themselves to it.'[59]

One sees what Matthew means, but Tom was not the man to act in this proto-Nietzschean fashion; he was prepared to take steps in his own interests, but he was easily discouraged, and liked to enlist the aid of others. Influence was still necessary in the pursuit of official posts, and Tom made his own attempt to lobby Lord Granville, the Lord President of the Council, who was responsible for educational matters, not via Lord Carlisle, but by applying to Acton, Granville's stepson; he asked Acton if he might use his influence with Granville, referring to his experience as a school inspector and head of educational services in Tasmania. He is once more in a despondent mood: 'with my large family, the income which I derive from the Catholic University is something like starvation. Things might and would be different, were the institution administered differently; but as it is, everything languishes—my fortunes along with the rest.'[60] The job went to someone else, who was perhaps already lined up for it, as Clough had feared.

The following year Tom was entertaining hopes of another public appointment, though not, it seems, in the educational sphere. In May 1861 Matthew told his mother, in the tone of irritable concern that he tended to use about Tom:

I think it very doubtful if Tom does right in not sticking to his University, now it seems likely to do better. I don't believe he will get the Factory Inspectorship: if he got it I doubt whether it would be worth so much to him as his University place may be, if the institution rights itself, and his trying to leave it may damage him with the authorities there, if he does not succeed . . .[61]

Trying to help Tom was becoming a wearying business.

Clough died in Florence on 13 November 1861, when he was not quite 43 years of age. Unfortunately, no record survives of Tom Arnold's response to this shattering event; he had known Clough from their school-days and regarded him as his closest friend. Matthew commemorated him in the great pastoral elegy 'Thyrsis', which exquisitely evokes the wanderings of the Clougho-Mattheans in the countryside around Oxford:

> Where are the mowers, who, as the tiny swell
> Of our boat passing heaved the river-grass,
> Stood with suspended scythe to see us pass? -
> They all are gone, and thou art gone as well!
> ll. 27–30

Some weeks later Tom wrote to Clough's widow enclosing some of his letters. In 1863 she consulted him about the edition of her late husband's literary remains that she was compiling. Arnold promised to contribute a memoir of his friend, but failed to deliver it. He finally made amends, thirty-five years later, when he published his memories of Clough.

Newman went on being concerned about Arnold's situation in the languishing Catholic University. In November 1861 he remarks to Robert Ornsby, 'How *he* stays I cannot comprehend (*you* have almost naturalized yourself in Ireland)—I believe they have increased his salary—but it seems wonderful to me with his connections that he does not get something better. I say to myself, here are men losing their best years for nothing!'[62] But Fate, or Divine Providence, was about to play a hand, which would enable Arnold to leave Ireland and Newman to fulfil his desire to get him to the Oratory School. The unlikely occasion was an industrial dispute (as it would not then have been termed).

The Oratory School had opened in 1859, with Fr Nicholas Darnell as headmaster, and was regarded as a success. But, as Wilfrid Ward put it:

One severe trial, however, it did undergo in 1861—a trial which brought out all the determination and force in action which Newman could show on occasion. The masters protested—at Christmas 1861—against the very special position accorded by Newman to Mrs Wootten, the matron, and demanded that she should be removed. Newman resolutely declined, and they represented that if he persisted they would all have to resign. On the exact rights and wrongs of the dispute it is hard now to form a judgment. But the crisis, as I have said, brought all Newman's energies into play. Father Darnell resigned on December 27, and the other masters on the 29th. Ambrose St John was at once despatched by Newman to Dublin to secure Arnold as leading classical Master, and Newman set to work to find without delay other competent masters to replace those who were gone.[63]

Tom Arnold, meanwhile, was in London, where he had gone to see the publisher Longman about his *Manual of English Literature*, which was to come out later in the year. He stayed with Matthew at his house in Chester Square. The household was stricken with illness, but Matthew was happy to see him; he wrote to his mother, 'Dear old Tom's visit in the midst of all this was a great pleasure, as he takes things very easily and placidly, and, for himself, is never exigeant. I think he enjoyed himself very much indeed—he thoroughly likes London, and is much occupied with his new Manual. I should not wonder if it really brought him some money.'[64] Tom did, indeed, have a considerable capacity to enjoy life, when he was not worrying about money; and, one is tempted to add, when he was away from Julia.

CHAPTER 6

Birmingham

I

Newman took advantage of the crisis with the striking schoolmasters to advance his long-standing plan to get Tom Arnold into the school. He handled it skilfully. When Fr St John went to Dublin early in January 1862 he took with him a letter addressed to Archbishop Cullen, respectfully asking if Newman could borrow one of the professors of the Catholic University to help out in the present emergency 'for a month or two'. This letter seems not to have been presented, and subsequent negotiations were conducted with Mgr Bartholomew Woodlock, who after a long interval had succeeded Newman as rector. An entry in Newman's diary, dated 6 January but probably written later, says that Fr St John had 'secured Arnold'. He had got the university to agree to lend him for three months, but Arnold himself was still in England, at Matthew's. He was about to leave when he received a telegram from Newman asking him to call at the Oratory on his way back to Ireland, and did so on 7 January. Newman made him an offer and Arnold accepted it; he would be paid 150 pounds for a term's work, though out of this he would have to pay a substitute to cover his teaching in Dublin. Newman had originally thought that Arnold would come by himself for the term and live in the Oratory without charge. Now, after discussing it with him, he proposed that if Arnold wished to bring his family with him the Oratory could supply, rent-free, a four-bedroomed house in Edgbaston. Arnold asked for time to consider this offer, and took several days over it; Julia may well have resisted re-entering Newman's territory. Eventually, he wrote on 16 January accepting the offer of a house, adding 'Mrs Arnold will probably join me at Birmingham after paying one or two visits'.[1] In fact, Julia went to Fox How with her younger children, staying with Arnold's mother and sister, and remained there for several weeks.

At the end of January Arnold came to Birmingham accompanied by his three elder sons and a servant; Mary was still in her boarding school.

Arnold moved into the house at 6 Vicarage Road, Edgbaston, where he found the climate very trying. He shared the common Victorian belief that climate was dependent on local topography, and could vary greatly in adjacent areas. Thus, Mark Pattison claimed in his *Memoirs* that Littlemore and Oxford, though no more than 4 miles apart, had quite different climates. Like Ruskin in his house overlooking Coniston Water, brooding about the smoke that blew up the lake from the foundries of Barrow-in-Furness, 20 miles away, Arnold resented the intrusions of industrialism: 'The worst wind was that from the north-west, which blew perseveringly for a great part of spring and early summer, and not only was exceedingly cold, but brought smoke and abominable vapours from the neighbouring "Black Country" over the unhappy suburb.'[2]

Arnold's position in the school was senior Classics master, but he was also 'first master', which made him in effect second-in-command to the head, Fr St John, and the senior layman on the staff. As when Arnold had first gone to Dublin, five years earlier, Newman was delighted to have him, for his abilities, which Newman now knew more about, and for his famous name, with its high public-relations value: 'We have, I am thankful to say, weathered this great storm; and hope that, in having the son of Dr Arnold for our first master, we shall have gained more than we have lost . . .'[3] Newman was already writing as though Arnold was to be a fixture, and he did not disguise his wish to keep him; a few days later, on 26 January, when he had been in the school for a few days, Newman wrote, 'Arnold is throwing himself into his work famously. I hope we shall be able to keep him.'[4] But Arnold was still under the impression that his stay would be temporary; indeed, in his initial discussions with Newman he had insisted that he had to be back in Dublin by the middle of April, as the lease on his house in Kingstown expired at the end of that month and he would have to find somewhere else to live. Meanwhile his lectures in Dublin were being given, for a consideration, by Peter Le Page Renouf, the Professor of Ancient History and Languages, who was enough of a polymath to take on English Literature if required. Julia still showed no signs of moving to Edgbaston, and at the end of Feburary Arnold paid a flying weekend visit to Fox How to see her and the children and his mother.

Newman continued negotiating with Woodlock about Arnold's future. He had a valuable item on the table, the university church in St Stephen's Green, next to the college, which he had commissioned. It had been built from Newman's own resources (the surplus of the funds contributed by his supporters when he had been sued for criminal libel by a rascally ex-priest, Giacinto Achilli), and designed by the Professor of Fine Art, John Hungerford Pollen. The university now wished to acquire the church. There was more involved than a simple exchange, but after a mutually satisfactory financial settlement the university got the church and the Oratory School got Arnold. On 7 March Newman wrote to Woodlock, 'Arnold told me yesterday that he had gained your consent to his resigning his professorship.' Presumably Arnold could have resigned in any case, but Newman was at pains to keep good relations with the university. In his letter to Woodlock he throws out an ingenious but impractical thought about how Arnold could continue an association with the university: 'I suppose it is an absurd suggestion but if you wanted a *non-resident Anglo-saxon* Professor, as you have a Celtic, he is quite up with it, and could come to Dublin, as others have, to give a course of lectures now and then, without professorial pay.'[5] The proposal was not likely to work and was not taken up, but it showed that Arnold was already proficient in the Anglo-Saxon studies that culminated in his edition of *Beowulf*.

On 10 March Arnold wrote to Thomas Collinson, his old friend from New Zealand days, whom he had not seen for some time:

I came over from Dublin ... towards the end of January with three months' leave of absence from the Catholic University. I have been hard at work since I came, assisting to reorganize the school; and recently Dr Newman has made me an offer which would place me in a position so much more advantageous in point of salary than that which I hold at Dublin that I have decided on accepting it ...[6]

He remarks, 'I have been living here *en garçon* for some time, but I am quite tired of it, and I am glad to say my wife, who is at Fox How, joins me tomorrow.' It looks as if Julia had resolved to stay at Fox How for the whole of Arnold's temporary stay in Edgbaston, and only decided to join him when the job became permanent.

How far teaching at the Oratory School was so much more advantageous financially than lecturing at the Catholic University is uncertain. In January, when Newman was already reflecting on the possibility of getting Arnold a permanent appointment he had noted, 'I would offer Arnold 350 pounds per annum.' In his earlier attempts to attract him he had offered 300 pounds. If Arnold had found either of these sums a substantial improvement on what he was getting in Dublin, the suggestion, referred to in the previous chapter, that he was already receiving 300 pounds must be incorrect. In fact, Newman remarked later in the year that he had heard that 'Arnold said to the Rector that he would stop in Dublin, if he had £50 more *secured* to him, in addition to £200; and he could not get it.'[7] It looks as if he had received 200 pounds throughout his time in Dublin, and in comparison the Oratory was paying a good deal more, though the salary was still low for a middle-class man with a large family. Julia joined Tom in Edgbaston and promptly became pregnant; one wonders if her voluntary separation from her husband for over two months might have been intended by her as a contraceptive measure. Their seventh surviving child, Julia, known as 'Judy' in the family, was born in December 1862.

Although the previous year Matthew had thought Tom would be better off staying at the Catholic University and hoping for better days, he now expressed satisfaction at the move, telling their mother: 'The news about Tom is excellent. Jane seems rather uneasy about the solidity of the school, but I am certain it is a thousand times more solid than the Catholic University. And dear old Tom will have a position he truly likes and a position that will more and more interest him.'[8] Matthew had disapproved of Tom's moves in the past, and would do so again, but on this occasion he seems to have thought that his brother was doing the right thing; or, that if it was not, there was little point in saying so, as Tom always did as he intended once he had made his mind up.

In April Arnold was briefly back in Ireland to wind up his affairs, and the family moved from No. 6 to No. 7 Vicarage Road in Edgbaston; Arnold found the new house badly drained and otherwise inconvenient. Meanwhile, he was putting the finishing touches to his *Manual of English Literature* before it went to press, and preparing an article for Acton's new *Home and Foreign Review*. In August the family were holidaying at Fox How. A letter to Acton apologizing for not meeting a deadline gives a charming account of life there, and reflects the scholar's impatience with domestic and social pressures:

I find it is of no use trying to get my article ready for tomorrow; this mountain sojourn is too much against me. My father built a house in the valley, nearly thirty years ago, which my mother still inhabits; every one here knows me, or of me, and I know almost everybody; and old maids ask one to tea, and brothers, sisters, aunts, nephews, nieces, in short every sprig on the tree of consanguinity, are always forming plans for walks on Loughrigg, or picnics on Windermere, or this or that expedition; and it is vain to think of not being drawn into the vortex. On Wednesday however we return to Birmingham, and there will be an entire change of scene; my leisure will be complete, for the school does not meet till the 10th prox...[9]

On this visit to Ambleside Arnold wrote to Blanche Clough, apologizing for being in arrears with the payments of interest on the 100 pound loan that her late husband had made him some years before. He says that he will make up these payments when he returns to Birmingham, and hopes to repay the bulk of the principal in the following year. This was an aspiration that Arnold was unable to fulfil, and he went on repaying the interest for many years to come.

At the Oratory, Arnold was in close contact with Newman, and saw much more of him than he had in Dublin, where they had overlapped for less than a year. In his autobiography he presents an affectionate memory of Newman in the quasi-monastic setting of the Oratory:

The debate being over, the Superior led the way to the recreation-room, where usually a bright fire was burning. Here restraint was laid aside; fathers and guests gathered round the fire, on the left side of which was Newman's chair, and conversation rose and fell just as in an Oxford common-room. Recreation time, if I remember right, lasted for three-quarters of an hour. Newman was always cheerful, and, if not talkative, *abordable*, and ready to talk.[10]

But for all his *gentilezza*, Newman could be a tough employer, with a sharp eye for detail, particularly financial. In September 1862 Arnold asked if he could have two of the boys at the school as lodgers in his house, as their father wished. Newman was inclined to turn down the request as the school would lose money by it, and have less control over the boys in question. He remarked tartly, 'Arnold has a large salary *on the ground* that he had not pupils to make money by. If he becomes a lodging house keeper, he should have a smaller salary.'[11] From Newman's point of view, the school was paying Arnold a large salary, out of limited resources; but despite his initial enthusiasm he was not finding it large enough, given Julia's poor housekeeping and his continually growing family. An austere celibate clergyman and a philoprogenitive paterfamilias inevitably saw things in a different light. Newman must have wondered at times if, in a cost-benefit analysis, Arnold's academic attainments and distinguished name were worth the expense he involved.

Relations remained friendly, though, and in October Arnold presented Newman with a copy of the *Manual of English Literature*, just published by Longman. It was the fruit of his years of teaching at the Catholic University, and is an early example of a genre intended for students that has become endlessly replicated since the growth of English Literature as an academic subject. The book is divided into two sections, Historical and Critical, reflecting a fundamental division in approaches to the discipline. Arnold uses 'literature' in the latter-day sense of writing with a particular aesthetic and imaginative quality, rather than in the older (and still current) one of anything written, though the earlier chapters of the book are mainly about intellectual history. He covers a great deal of ground in a flowing narrative that is always readable if sometimes superficial. The account of prose writing attempts to say something about oratory, philosophy, historiography, and theology, as well as more specifically literary writing. This is an ambitious endeavour, though it reflects Arnold's own wide-ranging interests, and represents the kind of activity that early professors of English were expected to engage in. He gets things wrong at times, as when he refers to the author of *Piers Plowman* as 'Robert' Langland, reproducing an error by the eighteenth-century literary historian Thomas Warton. In places he seems hard put to it to know what to say, as when he refers to Jane Austen as the 'beautiful and too short-lived authoress'. He gives a lot of space to Wordsworth, whom he had known, but devotes only two sentences to Keats. He says nothing at all about Blake, whose posthumous fame had not yet been established by Swinburne's praise and W. M. Rossetti's edition. Coming on to living writers, Arnold refers warmly but coyly to Dickens, without actually naming him.

In Arnold's analysis of what he calls 'Fictitious Narratives' there is an interesting anticipation of a classic of twentieth-century critical theory, Northrop Frye's *Anatomy of Criticism*. Like Frye, Arnold has a clear sense of generic distinctions, and he illustrates them with a flow-diagram. He begins with a distinction between 'Romances' and 'Stories of Common Life'. The former are divided between 'mock' and 'serious' examples. The latter branch down into 'Novels', and 'Stories of Adventure', as in Defoe. The 'Novels' then divide into works 'of the past', as in Scott, and 'of the present', which are further sub-divided into novels of 'High Life', as in Richardson, 'Middle Life' as in Austen, and 'Low Life', as in Smollett. Arnold's model possesses the interest and the limitations of Frye's schemata; at the very least it shows an approach to literature that is analytical and systematic rather than merely impressionistic.

An early and very interested reader was Matthew, who wrote to Tom from the Athenaeum on 20 October:

I have received your note and your book, and both with great pleasure. The book of course I have not had time to read but I have turned over the leaves and read here and there—of course I shall read it steadily hereafter. Your division into a historical and a critical part does not exactly, on a transient sight of it take my fancy; but I have no doubt you had good reasons for it. I liked your preface extremely, and one or two things I read as I turned over the pages of what comes after. But what did strike me was that the book looked promising as a manual; solid, well-arranged, not too preachy, full of facts; indeed as I looked through the treatise on metres a thrill of apprehension went through me as I fancied its contents vomited forth upon me by thousands of students in training-schools; so exactly is it the sort of thing these intellectual ghouls love to alight upon and batten to their hearts' content, with the design of throwing it up again at a public examination. But if it ever gets into circulation in the haunts of the British ghoul your fortune is made; I shall introduce it wherever I can, and I shall watch the reviews' treatment of it with the greatest interest . . .[12]

Matthew's vivacious account of regurgitation as a pedagogic technique still strikes a chord.

Acton was sent a copy of the book. He said he liked it, but offered a number of criticisms, including a complaint that it said nothing about Samuel Rogers, who had died a few years before. Though now largely forgotten, Rogers was one of the most admired and popular poets of the early nineteenth century. Arnold's response was submissive, even obsequious: 'It was certainly an oversight to make no mention of Rogers, but it shall be rectified in the second edition. My knowledge of the subject is really so inadequate, that I have probably erred both in the points you particularize, and in many others . . .'.[13] The note of humility is overdone, but it is typical of Arnold that it should nevertheless be accompanied by the confidence that his book would go into another edition. The reviews were mixed. Those in the *London Review* and the *Saturday Review* were very favourable, but they were followed by savagely hostile ones in the *Guardian* and the *Examiner*, the latter described it as 'one of the poorest of its sort, lifeless in classifications, undigested, tasteless'. Matthew was worried by these dismissals, remarking to his sister Fan, 'I only hope he does not get any blows out of dislike to me.'[14] But regardless of reviews, the *Manual* was a long-term success; there was, as Matthew had anticipated, a steady demand for it, and it ran into six more revised editions before the end of the century. It would have earned Tom some money, even if, inevitably, not enough.

Matthew continued to express slightly nagging solicitude to, and for, his brother. Although he had been pleased that Tom had moved to the Oratory School and seemed happy there, a few months later he was urging him to consider returning to Australia. He sang the praises of Queensland—'You know there is a nest of very good Oxford men there'—where the climate was fine and the living, by all accounts, was easy; school inspectors were needed, and there were opportunities for investing money at an outstanding return. But Tom, for the time being, had no desire to return to the Antipodes. In March 1863 Matthew told Tom that he had seen their old Rugby and Oxford friend Walrond, who was highly placed in the Civil Service Commission, and there was a chance of Tom getting a part-time examinership for the Indian Civil Service. Matthew ended his letter with a touching reflection, where the elegiac note of his poetry creeps into the normally brisk prose of his correspondence: 'My dear old boy—how I should like to see you. I sometimes think, if I was very rich! then one of my first actions would be to set you free, so that you might be as of old and we might be together as of old. But the past never returns—all we can do is not to let its memory die out of us.'[15] Tom asked Acton if he could put in a good word for him with the Civil Service Commissioners, and on 20 April he was pleased to announce that he had been appointed an examiner.

Newman continued to think highly of Arnold and to be very satisfied with his work at the Oratory School, once he had been dissuaded from taking on extra pupils as lodgers. Yet he was in principle prepared to let Arnold go in the interests of a higher cause. Provisional plans were under discussion to open a Catholic hall or private college at Oxford, to enable Catholic undergraduates to enter the university without endangering their faith. This initiative reflected a growing conviction that the university in Dublin was never going to attract Catholics from other parts of the British Isles. In June 1863 Newman wrote to William Monsell, an Irish Liberal MP, who had been associated with the Catholic University and was now interested in the new project, outlining the plan and reflecting on who might be a suitable person to launch it:

I will tell you who I think would be the best man of all, (*but I had rather you did not mention this* just now, while all is in nubibus)—He would be a *great* loss to us, for he is one of our own men, but for so great an object we would spare him. I have no *proof* he would do for a *large* society, but for a free and easy quasi Private Tutor or Head of a Lodging House, he would be perfection, and that is *Arnold*. His name is good, his connections good—he is a perfect gentleman in his manners and bearing towards young men and boys; though *perhaps* not a good disciplinarian. He is, as a Catholic, liberal to a wonderful extent—yet with a simple faith and spontaneous devoutness which are most edifying. But you must make it worth his while. *We* give him as much as £400 a year and his children's teaching—and don't think it enough for him.[16]

Newman gives a concise character sketch of Arnold, drawing on the elusive but potent concept of the 'gentleman', which once had so much resonance but is now likely to provoke incomprehension or hostility. He elsewhere described Arnold as having trouble with discipline and being better with the cleverer pupils; in other words, he was by temperament more of a don than a schoolmaster, though he liked to teach. The Oxford scheme failed to take off; the bishops were unenthusiastic about it, and Henry Manning, shortly to be made Archbishop of Westminster, was wedded to the idea of a separate Catholic University in England. So, indeed, was his bitter intellectual opponent, Acton, who was prepared to give land for a university in Shropshire, and to provide access to his large personal library. In the event nothing happened, and Catholics were not permitted by the Church to enter English universities until the end of the nineteenth century (though they still did so, Acton's son being one of them). Tom Arnold had discussed the Oxford proposal with Newman, and cautiously favoured it, but it is not clear if he knew that Newman envisaged him as heading it.

Newman's letter referred to Arnold getting 400 pounds a year, which suggests that he may have had an increase since he was appointed the previous year; it was twice what he had been earning in Dublin, but was still, as Newman acknowledged, 'not enough'. Arnold, with his growing family, would have agreed. Newman refers to Arnold's children getting a free education at the Oratory, but that, of course, applied only to his older sons. Mary was at boarding school and spending her vacations at Fox How with her grandmother and aunt. Her Uncle Matthew remarked in a letter to her father, 'How astonishingly cheap Miss Davies's school is, for modern times—at least to be a good school, which I believe it is.'[17] If Miss Davies's school in Shropshire, which Mary attended, was cheap it was because she was taken on at a reduced rate, as a kind of charity girl, and it appears to have been a pretty bad school, where Mary was unhappy.[18] Matthew's remark, though complacent and ill-informed, belies Sutherland's claim that, 'Uncle Matt seems not to have registered Mary's independent existence until many years later.'[19] In fact, when she was 12 she was at a dinner in Matthew's house in Chester Square for his son Tom's birthday, and made a very good impression: 'her behaviour and "deportment" were quite excellent, and I have been using her as an example ever since'.[20] Having been neglected by her parents, Mary saw more of them after their return from Ireland. When she was about 13 she was taken by her father to visit Arthur Stanley, who had recently been appointed Dean of Westminster. She had known him as a small girl at Fox How, when she recalled bracing herself 'in a mixture of delight and fear' for the disconcerting questions he fired at her, such as 'Where did Henry the Fourth die?':

But memory leaps forward to a day four or five years later, when my father and I invaded the high dark room in the old Deanery, and the Dean standing at his reading-desk. He looks round—sees 'Tom', and the child with him. His charming face breaks into a broad smile; he remembers instantly, though it is some years since he and 'little Mary' met. He holds out both his hands to me—

'Come and see the place where Henry the Fourth died!'

And off we ran together to the Jerusalem Chamber.[21]

She remembered 'the great and to me mysterious figure of Newman haunting the streets of Edgbaston', though she was not encouraged, perhaps not permitted, to meet him. Her mother would have presented him as a baleful figure in the life of the family. Many years later Mary did meet Newman, recently made a cardinal, at a great reception for him in Oxford: 'As my turn came to shake hands, I recalled my father to him and the Edgbaston days. His face lit up—almost mischievously. "Are you the little girl I sometimes remember seeing—in the distance?" he said to me, with a smile and a look that only he and I understood.'[22]

William, the oldest son, did well at the Oratory School, though Julia found it difficult to rejoice in his success. She wrote to Tom from Fox How when she was staying there:

I was very glad to hear of Willy's having done so well in the examination of his class, although I must confess the thought of *our son* being examined by Dr Newman had carried a pang to my heart. Your mother I found felt it in the same way; she said (when I read out to her that part of your letter) with her eyes full of tears, 'Oh! to think of *his* grandson, *dearest Tom's son*, being examined by Dr Newman.'[23]

Devotion to Dr Arnold's memory meant keeping alive his battles against the Tractarians. After the family returned to England Julia made regular visits to Fox How, where she found the sturdy Protestantism of her in-laws a restorative after the papistry of Edgbaston. At the same time, she was temperamentally rather at odds with the Arnolds, if we are to believe her granddaughter: 'Julia's temptations—to extravagance in money matters and to passionate outbursts of temper—were not Arnold temptations, and she often felt herself dispproved of in spite of much outward affection and kindness.'[24] Janet Trevelyan, we have to remember, was not even born at that time, and her accounts have been filtered through the novelistic consciousness of her mother, Mary Ward. But there are letters which Julia wrote to Tom from Fox How showing intensity of depression, and something of a Calvinistic sense of reprobation: 'The feeling grows upon me that I am one of those unhappy people whom *God has abandoned*, and it is the effect of this feeling I am sure which causes me to behave as I often do. Oh! it is an awful thing to *despair* about one's future state.'[25]

On a later occasion, in January 1865, Julia wrote a distressed and distressing letter to Tom from Fox How, affirming her love for him and her dissatisfaction with her difficult daughter, Mary, then aged 13:

I think it will end in her doing as she likes. I cannot say that I shall be sorry when she is well off. *She is very hard to bear with.* I am so heartily tired of this kind of life . . . I am not feeling well or in good spirits. I quite long to be with you again, you are worth your whole family put together, in my eyes at all events . . . Do not think me ill-natured or that there has been anything in the slightest degree disagreeable, but I must unburden myself to you or I should explode.[26]

Nevertheless, Julia remained sufficiently attached to the Arnolds and to Fox How to express a wish to be buried at Ambleside.

II

The first issue of Acton's *Home and Foreign Review* came out in the summer of 1862 and Arnold was associated with it from the beginning. Although in one sense a successor to *The Rambler*, with the same editor and the same Catholic character, it represented a new start, as a quarterly rather than a bi-monthly, and its Catholic aspects were less explicit:

'It is no longer a Catholic review,' wrote Simpson, 'but a review whose conductors happen to be Catholics; it challenges notice no longer as representing Bishops and Priests, but as a literary rival of the old reviews'. Simpson did not deny the essentially Catholic character of the *Home and Foreign*; but it had passed from the narrow field of Catholic journalism, represented by the *The Tablet*, the *Weekly Register* and the *Dublin*, to the wider ranges of the great English reviews, the *Quarterly*, the *Edinburgh* and the *Westminster*. It sought an audience which was not exclusively Catholic. One of its foremost objects, Acton said, was 'by instructing

English readers generally concerning Catholic ideas, and by familiarizing Catholics with the facts and thoughts of the world around them, gradually to break down some of those obstacles to an understanding at least which are not founded on purely religious grounds'.[27]

Each number of the *Home and Foreign* contained an impressively large and wide-ranging set of reviews of recent books on many subjects, published in England and abroad. Acton wrote many of these himself, and his European interests and contacts enabled the magazine to publish well-informed accounts of international affairs. Acton invited Arnold to contribute regular reviews of new books on Classical subjects, in addition to longer articles. As the *Home and Foreign* paid 5 pounds a sheet there was a distinct financial incentive.[28] Arnold pointed out that his work at the Oratory School and for the Civil Service Commission gave him less free time than he would like, but he cautiously accepted Acton's proposal:

I think I can undertake the department you offer me (which I understand to be 'the literary and political history of the Greek and Roman world, including French and German works on the subject') if it be understood that the 20 or 24 works which I am to review during the year, need not all be solid digested publications, but may include occasional monographs or 'opuscules' of a less formidable character . . .[29]

These short notices are not listed in the Wellesley Index of Victorian Periodicals and cannot be easily identified.

In the October issue Arnold published 'Hayti', an essay on the Caribbean Negro republic which continued in a more particular form interests that he first set out in his *Rambler* essay on the Negro race; they had perhaps originated with a Haitian woman he had known in New Zealand. The article gives a historical account of the founder of Haiti, Toussaint L'Ouverture, and looks at the disappointing later development of the country. Arnold is opposed to slavery, but believes that black rule needs to be strengthened by white immigration. His philosophical interest in slavery is indicated in a proposal that he made to Acton for a further article on Caribbean topics (which was apparently not written): 'I should compare the historic course taken by Spain in regard to slavery with that taken by England, tracing up each to the moral philosophy from which it ultimately springs, in the one case to the teaching of Victoria, Soto, Suarez etc, in the other to that of the Quakers and other religious philanthropists in England.'[30] Arnold's next contribution was a review-article on a book about the Jesuit 'Apostle to the Indies', St Francis Xavier; it was by a

Protestant and took an unfavourable view of Xavier's missionary activities; Newman had encouraged Arnold to review it. At Arnold's request, Acton added a lengthy conclusion on the difference between standards in Xavier's day and those of the nineteenth century.

In his next article, published in April 1863, Arnold turned to another small, little-known nation, in this case Albania. Like the account of Haiti, this chairbound travelogue was based on books borrowed from Acton's large personal library. After he had finished it, Arnold confessed to Acton that his 'Albania' was very dull.[31]

The next (and last) two articles that Arnold published in the *Home and Foreign* took him back to one of his central interests, Anglo-Saxon history and culture. Writing to Acton on 3 June 1863, he makes a proposal for an article on boundaries, an essay in what would now be called 'liminality'. Arnold advances it with the enthusiasm of someone with a fresh bee in his bonnet: 'It would be a "theory of boundaries", applied to the actual history and circumstances of the English counties. All geographical treatises deal with the *statics* only of political geography; my object would be to deal with the dynamics—to lay bare the forces by the joint conflicting operation of which such a city assumed such a form, such a city arose in such a region.' If there is a suggestion of Mr Casaubon about this ambitious proposal, there is also a hint of Marx—of whom Arnold had probably never heard—setting out the iron laws of history. Arnold concludes with a characteristic combination of confidence and self-doubt: 'I should like to try my hand upon this subject, though I do not believe I shall be able to exhibit adequately the idea which I have formed in my mind. But perhaps you will think that it would not be a subject of much general interest.'[32] Acton liked the idea; when the work was in progress, he remarked, 'I read nine good but severe pages of Arnold on English Boundaries, which will be original, and soon ready.'[33] The completed article, 'The Formation of the English Counties' appeared in October 1863. It provides a speculative study of the spread of Anglo-Saxon culture in England, and is intellectually bolder than most of Tom's scholarly writing.

It was followed by 'The Colonization of Northumbria', in April 1864, in the last issue of the *Home and Foreign* to appear. It is a more conventionally antiquarian study. Matthew found it 'fractuous reading', and offered various particular criticisms, but was encouraging overall:

The vicissitudes in the North of England and the changings of rulership are clearly marked—I have learnt a good deal I did not know before—though that, you will say, I might easily do . . . The remark on what is indicated by the names Scotland & England respectively is striking and ingenious. The bit from Bede about the sparrow noble, worthy of Homer, and as you say instructive as to the then mode of living. The article is too gründlich to be lost in a review: something extensive and complete might with advantage be done on the subject . . .[34]

As a contributor, Arnold came to know Acton well, and conducted an active correspondence with him. He was a regular recipient of parcels of books borrowed from Acton's library (on one occasion Acton offered to lend Matthew a set of Heine; the offer was declined, with effusive gratitude, as he had found the books elsewhere). They met from time to time, and Arnold was a guest at Acton's country house, Aldenham. But he never lost a certain constraint and unease in his dealings with him. He was usually ready to defer to Acton's views, and after several years of acquaintance still awkwardly opened his letters, 'My Dear Sir John Acton' (in contrast to Simpson's crisp, collegial, 'Dear Acton'). Nothing in his earlier experience—in the Arnold household, in Australasia, in Dublin— had prepared him for someone as exotic as this learned and opinionated young aristocrat.

The first issue of the *Home and Foreign* was well received, by Catholic journals as well as the national press. But the Catholic bishops, who had attempted to suppress *The Rambler* for its heterodox tendencies, were intensely suspicious of what they saw as an old offender in new garments. One of them said that 'he had not come across a more dangerous heretic than Acton since Pelagius'.[35] A fresh cause of offence was soon discovered. Cardinal Wiseman claimed that the *Review* had misrepresented remarks he was alleged to have made at a meeting of bishops in Rome, and had, in effect, circulated a false report and made a personal attack on him. He assumed that he could expect nothing better, given the earlier history of Acton's enterprise: 'under another name, the absence for years of all reserve or reverence in its treatment of persons or things deemed sacred'.[36] One of Acton's offences was his disinclination to take bishops with too much seriousness; in the South German milieu where he had spent much of his life, bishops were a form of middle-ranking civil servant, and worthy of a comparable degree of respect. In this as in other matters, he was out of tune with the assertive, Ultramontanist Catholicism of mid-Victorian England, which was ready to reverence the bishops as successors of the Apostles. The cardinal's attack was answered in a moderate rejoinder in the *Home and Review*, affirming the journal's loyalty to the Catholic Church, and its overriding concern with discovering and proclaiming the truth, even when it was unwelcome. But opposition was being stoked in conservative quarters, notably the *Dublin Review*, edited by the dogmatic reactionary W. G. Ward.

Newman's initial attitude to the *Home and Foreign* was at first cautiously favourable, though he never really trusted Acton, and still less Simpson. But by the second issue he too had found something to annoy him; predictably, it was by Simpson. In regard to Acton's publications, Simpson improbably combined the functions of prop and loose cannon. He gave every kind of editorial support, did much of the donkey-work, and was in effect joint editor for much of the time. All this was done unofficially, since it was politically desirable in dealings with the hierarchy to be able to say that the suspect Simpson had no official connection with the reviews; he had even ceased to be one of the proprietors. Yet when Simpson got a pen in his hand he was hard to restrain, as even Acton felt. His taste for advanced theological speculation went down badly, particularly coming from a layman (albeit a former clergyman), and he made matters worse by a provocative, witty, light-hearted style which could be seen as mocking sacred persons and causes. The contrast between Simpson's *esprit* and Acton's weighty though sometimes sardonic manner gives their collected correspondence a distinctive and attractive flavour. In his public writings Simpson's tone recalled Matthew Arnold's, and could give a comparable offence (the two men seem never to have met, despite the Tom Arnold connection).

In the October 1862 number Simpson published an article (unsigned, as the contributions usually were) called 'Döllinger on Heathenism and Judaism'. It was a review of a new book by Acton's Munich mentor, and it began with a free-wheeling discussion, only loosely connected with what followed, on the relations between primitive religion and the Book of Genesis. These remarks provoked Newman into what he called a '*sfogo*', a release of steam. He wrote to Arnold from Deal, where he was on holiday, about the new issue: 'I am so put out with one article in it, that I cannot talk of the others.' He then set down several pages of detailed analysis and rebuttal of what Simpson had written on Genesis. The fluctuating curve of Newman's attitude to the *Home and Foreign Review* had drooped sharply.[37] Arnold was taken aback by the vehemence and bulk of Newman's communication, but he responded in urbane and conciliatory terms:

I had not looked at the article on the first chapter of Genesis before receiving your note—for which many thanks—but on looking over it now in connexion with your comments I certainly agree with you in the opinion you have formed of it. Its insertion in the first place seems incompatible with the announcement on p.518 that 'a secular sphere alone remains' for the Review, which therefore 'cannot enter on the domains of ecclesiastical government or of faith'. But further my feeling about such hazy speculations is, and has always been I think, much the same as yours.

Arnold ends his letter by asking if Newman would wish him to pass it, or a copy, on to Acton; he also refers to another communication, concerning Wiseman's attack on Acton. Newman had there remarked, 'Now the Cardinal has accused the Rambler of treachery to the cause of faith. I think it the duty of one who has occasion to notice this charge made against him, to be *indignant*.'[38] Acton had a fine sense of the value of contemptuous silence, but Arnold agreed with Newman, tactically at least: 'I feel the force of what you say as to the absence of "indignation". Is it the German atmosphere in which Acton lives moves and has his being, that is accountable for this?'[39] Arnold had nicely shared Newman's indignation without prejudicing his own connection with the *Review*.

He sent a copy of Newman's letter to Acton, with a comment of his own that the offending article was just like *Essays and Reviews*, the notorious volume by Anglican radicals which the Church of England had officially declared to be heretical. However, after Acton had, intellectually speaking, leant on him he relented; Acton told Simpson, 'I have, in Arnold's opinion, sufficiently answered the critique of your article.'[40] Others were less convinced: another contributor, William Monsell, resolved not to write any more for the *Home and Foreign*. He told Newman, 'I fear that Acton will get deeper and deeper into the mire—His ideas of respectful submissiveness are not those we are accustomed to in these countries.'[41] Arnold kept up his connection with the *Review*, but the recent dispute had made him uneasy, as he shows in a letter to Acton. It is incomplete and lacks a date, but James Bertram is surely correct in placing it in late 1862:

As far as we laymen are concerned, no doubt the cause of free speech and freedom of intellectual movement is too sacred, and has been too shamefully trodden under foot in Catholic countries in times past, to allow of our being debarred from the prosecution of legitimate inquries under any circumstances likely to arise. Still I must say that these episcopal censures make a very painful impression on me—as I am sure they must on you—and I do most earnestly hope that for the future no just occasion for them will be afforded. The Home and Foreign has declared that 'a secular sphere alone remains for it', that it 'cannot enter on the domains of ecclesiastical government or of faith'; and if these self-imposed prohibitions are observed, one cannot see how any serious difficulty can arise.[42]

The *Review* continued to be highly regarded as a contribution to the intellectual life of the nation. After Newman's *sfogo* over Simpson's article the curve of his esteem rose and he found much to admire in the magazine.

Acton's brand of liberal Catholicism was heading for trouble. In the autumn of 1863 he attended a conference of Catholic scholars and intellectuals in Munich, sponsored and chaired by Döllinger. They professed their loyalty to the Pope and received his blessing by telegram. Acton was encouraged by the proceedings, writing afterwards in the *Review* that the congress 'will enable the Catholic writers of Germany to vindicate the Church from the reproach that faith is inimical to freedom, that we are hampered in our investigations, that we acknowledge a power which may prevent the publicity of truth, or impose untruths on our belief'. But these were not ideas that went down well in Rome. Pius IX, after his early liberalism had been shaken out of him by the Roman revolution of 1848, had become authoritarian and reactionary. He was alarmed by the spread of modernity and infidelity, and feared the loss of the papal lands to the forces of united Italy. (The Pope's threatened temporal power was a burning and divisive issue in the Church at that time.) He saw the need to run a tight ship, with Rome firmly grasping the wheel, and found the debates at Munich subversive of ecclesiastical order. A papal brief to the Archbishop of Munich implicitly condemned Döllinger and explictly condemned the conclusions of the conference; Catholic thinkers and scholars, it insisted, were required to submit not just to established dogmatic definitions but to the decisions of Roman congregations. The 'Munich Brief', as it was called, was sent in December but not published until March 1864.

Acton read it with bitter disappointment and an instant understanding of its implications. He could contrive, for a time, to finesse the English bishops, but he could not hope to resist denunciations from Rome. As he told Simpson, the principles set out in the Munich Brief were not compatible with the ideals of intellectual freedom which inspired the *Review*, but to have defied papal authority would have invited condemnation and deprived it of any claim to represent Catholic opinion. The doctrines of the Brief were not unfamiliar, but the aggressive tone and the will to enforce obedience were new and unwelcome. The only course of action open to Acton was to wind up the *Review*. Simpson agreed, and the last issue came out in April 1864. Newman expressed his regrets and sympathy in a letter to Acton: 'I am grieved at your news. The Review seemed to me improving, number after number, both in religious character and in literary excellence. It had gained a high place among the periodicals of the day, and that, in a singularly short time.' Newman attempted to add a consolatory note: 'But good may come out of this disappointment. There is life, and increasing life in the English Catholic body; and, if there is life, there must be re-action. It seems impossible that active and sensible men can remain still under the dull tyranny of Manning and Ward.'[43]

Matthew Arnold, too, was unhappy at 'the extinction, so much to be regretted, of the *Home and Foreign Review*; perhaps in no organ of opinion in this country was there so much knowledge, so much play of mind; but these could not save it. The *Dublin Review* subordinates play of mind to the practical business of Roman Catholicism and lives.'[44] The end of the year brought a further blow to liberal Catholicism with the papal encyclical *Quanta Cura* and the attached 'Syllabus of Errors', with its notorious final proposition that it is wrong to think that the Church could or should reconcile itself to progress, liberalism, and modern civilization. In Owen Chadwick's words, 'No sentence ever did more to dig a chasm between the pope and modern European society.'[45] Even without these blasts from Rome, the future of the *Review* must have been uncertain, at least as a publication with both a national and a Catholic aspect. As far as the former was concerned, it was highly regarded, for the reasons that Newman and Matthew Arnold indicated. But it aroused more hostility than support among Catholic readers, particularly those who identified with the conservatism of Ward and Manning, and it was losing subscribers. Once again, Acton's venture was in a century before its time. If the *Review* had survived it would have had a hard time after Acton's enemy Manning became Archbishop of Westminster in 1865. After unsuccessful attempts at bringing out a new review, Acton did what Newman had been advising him to do, and abandoned periodical journalism for historical scholarship, to which he was temperamentally better suited. His work in this field led, many years later, to his appointment to the Regius Chair of Modern History at Cambridge. He continued to resist excessive Roman claims, and particularly the growing movement for the definition of papal infallibility, which came to a head at the Vatican Council in 1870. Acton and Döllinger worked actively behind the scenes at the council to prevent the definition. They were unsuccessful, and there came a parting of the ways.

Döllinger left the Catholic Church; Acton never did so, though he was harried by Manning and narrowly missed excommunication. He gave up public Catholic activity, whilst preserving intact his belief and devotional life. After Cardinal Manning's death in 1892 he was invited by Manning's successor to take part in public Catholic events, and did so from time to time.

Acton was 30 years of age when the last number of the *Home and Foreign Review* appeared, and it went out with dignity and style. He gave his reasons for discontinuing it in an editorial article, 'Conflicts with Rome', which, against normal practice, was signed. And scrupulously adhering to the principle *audi alteram partem*, he printed the whole of the Pope's Munich Brief in the original Latin. Other contributions included Tom Arnold's 'The Colonization of Northumbria', and 'Asceticism among Mahometan Nations', by W. G. Palgrave; this was a 'communicated' article, which meant that the editors did not necessarily agree with its ideas. Arnold had known Palgrave at Oxford and in 1849 he derisively remarked in a letter from New Zealand that Palgrave had been 'goose enough to turn Roman Catholic'. Palgrave became a Jesuit, and an expert on Arabic and Muslim matters, and served as a missionary in Syria and Arabia. He resumed contact with Arnold when he was visiting London in 1864 and expressed a wish to meet Acton; Arnold tried unsuccessfully to arrange a meeting, but Acton accepted Palgrave's article for publication in the *Review*. Arnold described him as 'a good and clever man, but a little flighty, I think'.[46] Simpson found Palgrave's article appealed to his taste for theological speculation, telling Acton, 'It would be good to print it, if possible, in order to say that we had a Jesuit writing such a theory of religion as he opens with—a theory which certainly goes beyond any Catholic theory I have yet seen in fundamental inconsistency with any absolute revelation.'[47] Palgrave is a cloudy writer, but his approach looks radically syncretistic: 'Infinite as are the forms, immense the divergences between Paganism, Judaism, Christianity and Mahometanism, and again between their countless sections and sub-sections, aberrations or developments, orthodoxies or heresies, they have all as the subject-matter of such multiform variety one common field of action—the human race.' Such thoughts might have caused trouble to the *Review* if they had not been buried in the last number. Though Arnold found Palgrave 'flighty', their acquaintance continued.

III

The year 1864 was, Arnold remarked in his autobiography, 'one of constant change and movement'.[48] The previous September, after visiting Acton at Aldenham Park, he was laid low by lumbago for three weeks, which involved a period of recuperation at Great Malvern. He had not long been back at work when in December he was struck down by scarlet fever, otherwise scarletina, which was a much more serious disorder in the nineteenth century than it is now. Arnold recalls:

My wife took absolute command of the household; the children were all sent to Fox How, that they might be out of the way of infection; one of the servants who showed signs of sickening for the fever was transferred to the hospital; the other servant, for some reason that I now forget, was absent from duty; and in that bitter winter my wife, who all the time was nursing me most carefully, rose on several mornings before dawn, lighted the kitchen fire, and met all the household calls of the day.[49]

This illness meant more than the inconvenience to the school of Arnold's absence from teaching. Its infectious nature would have alarmed the parents of the boys if there had been any chance of it spreading through the school. Newman took no chances, and as a precaution Arnold was asked to remain away for a suitable period after he had apparently recovered. Early in January 1864 Fr St John happened to meet Julia Arnold and, as Newman put it, 'from effusion of heart, expressed to her his hope that Arnold should not return till Easter'. The clear implication was that Arnold would be on full pay for the term; Newman said that St John had said too much: 'you must undo it as far as this—viz to say that we must provide a substitute, when we shall pay £50 out of Arnold's £133'.[50] St John told Arnold of this arrangement, and provoked a vehement reaction. He wrote to Newman strongly protesting against it: he did not accept the need for so long an absence, and saw himself as subjected to an unjust reduction of income (though he had acquiesced in a similar deduction to pay a substitute when he had arrived from Dublin two years before). The customarily mild and hesitant Arnold developed an impressive head of anger, even a touch of paranoia, in the concluding paragraph of his letter:

I must return once more to the proposal of making this large deduction from my salary. I am afraid there is some further meaning behind it. I am told that even in the case of lawyers' or merchants' clerks, who may happen to fall ill, their employers never think of mulcting them of any portion of their salary, unless in the case of individuals whom they may think not worth keeping, to whom they intimate in this way their estimate of the value of their services. If such is the opinion which the Fathers of the Oratory entertain respecting my services at the school, I only beg that I may be distinctly informed of it, and I will take the most effectual steps I can to relieve them of my presence at the earliest possible period. In all sober seriousness I have formed a totally different estimate myself of the value of those services, and people outside, I have reason to think, would generally agree with me. However, if, to put the matter very plainly, it is thought at the Oratory that I am a bad bargain, and get more salary than I am worth, I have only to beg that this may be intimated to me, and I shall then know what to do.[51]

Newman must have been shaken by this unexpected outburst. He discussed Arnold's letter with the congregation of the Oratory, and in a kindly response indicated a climb-down: 'We will cheerfully give you your full salary for Lent Term as you wish . . . As to your suspicion that we have an arrière pensée, I do not know how we have deserved it. What have I done to be visited with so unkind a suspicion? . . . I am conscious to myself that my wish that you should be free from work till Easter was inspired by the purest desire of acting considerately towards you.'[52] In his reply Arnold acknowledged that he had been hasty: 'Your kind language makes my serious vein seem almost absurd. But men with large families, who are dependent on their salaries, are always extremely touchy, and I think justifiably so, on the subject of reduction of pay . . . The concluding portion of my letter I am quite willing to withdraw, perhaps it was inspired by an irritability resulting from illness.'[53] It might also, one suspects, have been written under pressure from Julia, and conveyed some of her rage at what she would have seen as Newman's double-dealing. Arnold is still unhappy about the way Newman and St John made their proposal that he should take a long leave of absence, but he is basically conciliatory. He even concedes that he is willing to have some of his pay diverted to a substitute, if an independent medical adviser deemed that a long absence was necessary. The matter had been settled amicably, and Newman turned his attention to writing the rejoinder to Charles Kingsley that was to become the *Apologia Pro Vita Sua*. But Tom's petulant suggestion that perhaps he was a 'bad bargain' for the Oratory had repercussions.

Arnold took a period of leave, though a shorter one than was originally proposed. On 19 January the family moved to lodgings at Clifton, near Bristol. He later wrote, 'I could not have supposed it possible that an interval of only 120 miles of southing, and about 300 feet of diminished elevation above the sea, could cause such an extraordinary difference of climate. In a few days I felt like a new man . . .'[54] Bristol is, in fact, only a little more than 80 miles from Birmingham, but no doubt the distance seemed greater to Arnold in his restored state. Early in February he wrote to Acton about a review of Longfellow he was writing, and added that he was quite well enough to resume work but the doctors and parents jointly insisted on keeping him in quarantine for some time to come.[55] He occupied himself in Bristol in visiting the old churches of the city, and later wrote an article about them, which was published in *Fraser's Magazine* in 1866. By the end of February he was back in Edgbaston, after spending a night or two with Matthew in London. It was a little while before he heard that the *Home and Foreign* was to be wound up; on 17 March he wrote to Acton with a proposal for fresh contributions, including a review of a new book of poems by his old friend John Campbell Shairp. Writing soon afterwards, Arnold refers to the 'extinction of the Review', but does not comment further.

The restoration of Tom's health was accompanied by troubles within the family. The 7-year-old Arthur broke his thigh-bone and was laid up for several weeks, and the house was burgled; Julia told Josephine, 'every morsel of clothing belonging to either my husband or myself was stolen as well as every trinket we possessed'.[56] Then in May Tom succumbed to an attack of measles, which kept him at home for a week. In August Matthew and his family were on holiday in Llandudno, North Wales, where Tom joined them for a few days, much to Matthew's satisfaction. He always took pleasure in Tom's company; 'dear old Tom', as he usually referred to him, with the predictability of a piece of epic diction (though many other things were also 'dear old' in Matthew's habitual idiolect). The brothers went hill-walking together; Matthew told his sister Fan, 'The poetry of the Celtic race and its names of places quite overpowers me, and it will be long before Tom forgets the line, "Hear from thy grave, great Taliessin, hear!"—from Gray's Bard, of which I gave him the benefit some hundred times a day on our excursions.'[57] Matthew came to feel that Wales, with its rich cultural associations, was superior to the Lake District which he had come to know so well. The fruit of these impressions was to appear three years later in *The Study of Celtic Literature*. Meanwhile, his walks with Tom had given him a painful blister. Tom left Llandudno on 11 August. It had been planned that he would return the following week with the rest of his family, but Julia vetoed the idea.

Matthew told his mother with barely repressed irritation but commendable restraint:

> ... last night we had a line from him to say that he and Julia were alarmed at the dearness of Llandudno, and had decided to go to Clifton: it is evident Julia takes him there and that he himself would much rather come here as the climate of Clifton at this season is as bad and oppressive as that of Llandudno is good and fortifying and will do Mary no good at all, whereas this would have been just the thing for her. Flu [as Matthew's wife, Frances Lucy, was known in the family] had been indefatigible looking for lodgings for them, but luckily had not actually engaged anything. Dear old Tom and I should have had some more walks and I regret his not coming exceedingly; and they will probably pay just as much at Clifton as they would have paid here, only they will certainly get better rooms for their money.[58]

Matthew had himself commented on the high cost of living in Llandudno, and such considerations would always weigh with the impoverished Tom Arnolds. But Julia had made friends in Clifton whom she wished to see. We do not know whether Tom found the climate of Clifton in summer as bad as Matthew claimed, or whether it still kept the attractions he had found there in the winter. However, he finally did something about the unhealthy house in Edgbaston; he was convinced that its bad drainage and the unwholesome climate of the area had been a factor in his recent illnesses. That summer the family moved to Harborne, which Tom called 'a breezy village', a mile or two away. Before school reopened Tom and his son Will crossed to Ireland, to make another visit to the Benisons, with whom he had kept in touch, mainly by his correspondence with Josephine.

Soon after the autumn term began Arnold embarked on some dangerous reading, in the form of the recent report of the Public Schools Commission. It showed, with a wealth of figures, that at a school such as Rugby a master of his status and qualifications would be distinctly better off than he was at the Oratory. He drew the obvious conclusion and with the faux-naif directness that characterized him on occasion, he respectfully asked Newman for 'a considerable addition to my salary from the commencement of next year . . .'. Newman was not disposed to be very accommodating to this blunt request. He still thought highly of Arnold as a teacher, but with increasing reservations. In August he had replied to a letter from Sir John Simeon, who had complained that his son was not doing as well in his studies as he might. Newman acknowledged that there was a problem with the whole class that the boy was in:

It arose, as I think, from their having since Easter, got under Mr Arnold—who is *above* them—I think he has been teaching them higher things, and has not so much attended to their grammar, and I must see to this when the new term begins. I say this to you (if you please) *in confidence*. Arnold is a very superior man—but he ought not to have little boys—no one comes near him without gaining from him—but he is what his father was—he opens a boy's mind—he gives him a great deal of information—but he thinks we may take it for granted that a boy knows grammar.[59]

The flurry of dashes indicates a certain perturbation of mind on Newman's part. He was facing a recurring problem in pedagogic life: that the inspired teacher who opens minds and enlarges horizons may not be so good at the nuts and bolts of teaching, the passing of examinations, and the satisfying of paying parents. A growing sense that Arnold was too good for much of the day-to-day work of the school and impatience over his frequent absences because of illness during the past year were leading him to the conclusion that Arnold was not the asset he had once seemed to be, was expensive, and could be regarded as expendable.

Newman replied to Arnold's request with feline politeness: 'I do not at all wonder that you should rate your services more highly than we seem to do by the salary with which we acknowledge them; nor do we complain of your thinking it right to look at the question simply from your own point of view, and not at all from ours.' He pointed out that the Oratory School, which was running at a loss, was not Rugby, which had large endowments and resources, and there was, unfortunately, no prospect of an increase in Arnold's salary. He concluded with a reference to the letter Arnold had sent during his illness earlier in the year, when they were in dispute about his salary: 'Moreover, your letter suggests to us that you have an idea of relinquishing your connection with us, an idea to which you gave expression in a letter which you wrote to us last Christmas [January, in fact].'[60] There was in fact no such suggestion in Arnold's letter, but it shows the way Newman's mind was working, and he may have put this remark in as a challenge. If so, Arnold rose to it in his reply written two days later, on 10 October 1864: 'As I find that there is no prospect (even, apparently, though the school should increase) of a rise in my salary, I must look forward to the close of my connexion with the school; for a man with growing burdens cannot permanently reconcile himself to a position which admits of no improvement.'[61] He goes on to say that he is making plans but they will take some time to mature, and he will give Newman due notice when they do; meanwhile, he will contine to give of his best to the school. Newman took these vague observations as a definite offer to re-sign, and put Arnold's letter before the Congregation of the Oratory. He wrote to him on 3 November: 'The event of your leaving us is so serious that you will not be surprised that, in order to meet it, we wish very much to fix the date of it. Shall we say at Easter next, that is, Palm Sunday April 9.'[62] It was a sharp and chilly response, with no exhortations to Arnold to think again. Once more, Newman was proving himself a tough employer. Arnold protested in his reply that he had made no such firm decision, merely considered future possibilities. He was being unworldly; any em-ployer faced with such a muffled threat would have reacted like the Oratory. Newman, having decided that Arnold was no longer a clear asset to the school, and believing, perhaps, that *ces pères de familles sont capable de tout*, had outmanœuvred him. Arnold sensed something of the truth in his aggrieved rejoinder, 'It is evident therefore that you and the congregation wish me away; and this wish, when I recall the circumstances under which my services were engaged in 1862, causes me, I must own, some sur-prise.'[63] Once the decision was made, relations between Arnold and Newman were perfectly civil, and when he left the school he received what he acknowledged was a generous financial settlement.

Matthew thought that Tom had acted irresponsibly, and told him so:

I certainly think that your saying to them, on their refusing the augmenting of your salary, that you must 'look forward to the terminating your connexion with the Oratory' was stark madness unless you were prepared for their treating it as a resignation, if they chose; your being prepared for this ought to have depended on what strings you had to your bow. In your position you could not, you cannot have, many: so I think you should have held on like grim death.[64]

Tom was evidently putting forward ideas about his future, which Matthew dismissed as impractical (we do not know what they were as, un-like Tom, he did not keep his brother's letters). Matthew returned to the idea that Tom should take a place in the education service of Queensland; Tom may not have had many strings to his bow, but Matthew had a few he could pull—the governor and the two chief ministers of the colony were friends of his from Oxford days. At first Tom seems to have liked the idea, or so Matthew thought, but then he turned to other possibilities, which provoked a sharp outburst of fraternal plain-speaking: 'My dear Tom, it seems hard to say so but there is no kindness in saying anything but the truth—in the educational line you have *used up* your advantages as Papa's son. They got you your appointment in Van Diemen's Land; they got your employments with the Catholics since your return; but situated as you are, they can do no more at present.'[65] A day or so later he writes to Tom, with continuing irritation at his unrealistic aspirations: 'You seem to have no notion whatever of the real state of the case as to the feeling about the employment of Catholics in educational matters, or in any matters where it is supposed that religion in the smallest degree comes in! *You had not the faintest chance*, being a Catholic, of being appointed one of the ordinary assistant Commissioners.'[66] After spending several years in the Catholic environments of Dublin and Edgbaston, Tom was having to face the pervasive anti-Catholicism of English national culture. Matthew continues with a significant comment: 'If you cease to be a Catholic, this objection to your employment will cease; but it will die away very gradually, and only through the exercise of great discretion on your part.'[67] This remark, and Matthew's earlier comment to his mother, 'his detachment from the Catholics seems complete',[68] are the first signs of a new crisis on Tom Arnold's part: dissatisfaction, not just with the Oratory that would not pay him enough, but with the Catholic belief that had brought him there in the first place.

Tom may have weakly acquiesced in Matthew's plan to ship him off to Queensland (a disinterested proposal on Matthew's part, since he always enjoyed Tom's company, which he would lose) but he changed his mind before long. His real intention was to go to Oxford and set up as a freelance tutor. Matthew was dismissive about it: 'you have not the *drive* that makes and keeps that sort of connexion, and a deal pleasanter you are for not having it; however, you have it not. The life, too, is a most unpleasant one, and I suspect Julia would find it detestable.'[69] Nevertheless, Tom had the help and encouragement of the influential Arthur Stanley, Dean of Westminster, who until the previous year had been professor of Ecclesiastical History in Oxford, and had many valuable contacts in the university. Writing to Stanley in April 1865, Arnold pursues his intention of going to Oxford and embarking on a new career, without entirely ruling out the Queensland proposal, although he says that he does not want to emigrate and 'my wife feels the most extreme distaste for it'.[70] In opting to be a tutor rather than a schoolmaster, Arnold was perhaps influenced by his father's ideals. Dr Arnold had written in 1831:

The misery of private tuition seems to me to consist in this, that men enter upon it as a means to some further end—are always impatient for the time when they may lay it aside; whereas, if you enter upon it as heartily as your life's business, as a man enters upon any other profession, you are not then in danger of grudging every hour you give to it, and thinking of how much privacy and how much society it is robbing you. But you take to it as a matter of course, making it your material occupation, and devote your time to it, and then you find that it is in itself full of interest, and keeps life's current fresh and wholesome by bringing you in perpetual contact with all the spring of youthful liveliness.[71]

Arnold's period of notice at the Oratory School ended in April 1865; he had previously attempted, without success, to continue in his post until the end of the school year in July. This attempt suggests that he was in no hurry to leave, and possibly regretted having to do so. Om 20 April he travelled to Oxford to lay the foundations of his new career, leaving his wife and family in their house in Wellington Road, Harborne. The previous day he had called on Newman to say goodbye, only to find that he would be away until the end of the week, so he made his farewells in a letter. Newman sent him a friendly reply on 23 April; most of it was about a memorandum Arnold had forwarded to Newman from Stanley, taking issue with remarks about the Oxford liberals in the *Apologia Pro Vita Sua*. Newman goes on to tell Arnold that he has a cheque ready for him, and concludes: 'There is a *shameful* report here that "you have quite given up Catholicism, but that you did not wish it known at the Oratory, until you had left". As it will hurt us, unless I am prompt about it, I will ask your leave to contradict it on your authority.'[72] Tom had told Matthew about the changes in his religious attitudes but had otherwise kept quiet about them. Julia, though, discovered them and started spreading the news around, just as she had in Hobart when Tom was on the point of becoming a Catholic. Fr St John had reported to Newman that Julia was saying that her husband had quite given up Catholicism but did not wish it to be known until he had left Birmingham. Newman did not necessarily believe the report; indeed, he wished Arnold to contradict it. His immediate concern was less with Tom Arnold's spiritual state than with the potential damage the report could do to the school.

Arnold's reply was not calculated to reassure him: 'The report about me which you mention is false, and you have my authority to contradict it. But I fear I must pain you by saying that I cannot guarantee where, or in what form of opinions, the course of thought may eventually lead me.'[73] Newman's reply has not survived, but on 2 May Arnold wrote from Oxford, responding with grateful thanks for the cheque it enclosed—'though I am certainly conscious of having tried to do my duty, I never could have, and never did, expect that what I did should be met in such a generous spirit, so much more than met, I may indeed say'—but

saying nothing more about his crisis of belief. Then, on 4 June, Newman
wrote to Arnold telling him that he had heard on good evidence that he
no longer accepted the infallibility of the Church:

Though it is so short a time since you told me to say on your authority that you
had no intention of giving up Catholicism as soon as you left Birmingham, I fear
my informant is not mistaken. Do not suppose I write these lines to trouble you
with controversy, or to exact an answer—but I cannot bear to let you go from the
one fountain of grace and spiritual strength, without saying a word, not of
farewell, for well it cannot be so to direct your course, but to express my deep
sorrowfulness at hearing the news. I will not believe that you have not found
strength and comfort in Masses and Sacraments, and I do not think you will find
the like elsewhere. Nor shall I easily be led to believe that the time will not come
when you will acknowledge this yourself, and will return to the Faith which you
are leaving. Meanwhile, as you have for some weeks been in my prayers with reference to these sad waverings of faith, so shall you be still.[74]

Newman's distress and disappointment are evident and understandable,
though he was right about the longer term prospect.

In his reply to Newman, Arnold indicates a depressed and confused
state of mind. He thanks Newman for his kind thoughts, but feels he does
not deserve them: 'As I look back, to whatever part of my past life I turn
my eyes, shame and confusion of face are the result of my reflections. No
party or school has ever been the better for my adhesion, and probably
never will.' On the matter of Catholicism, he acknowledges, 'yes, it is true
that I can no longer believe in a permanent and living infallibility in the
Church. I tried hard to believe it for a long time, in spite of the objections
that constantly presented themselves, but at last I broke down.' Arnold
concludes his letter with a contradictory response to a widely circulated
newspaper report that he had returned to the Church of England: 'It is
not true, for I have never taken any overt step whatever since I have been
here, and never attended an Anglican service except University sermons.
Still I do not think of contradicting it, because I look forward, if I stay
here, to taking my master's which, I suppose may be called in one sense
"returning to the Church of England".'[75] For Arnold to take his MA, as
he did before long, meant unambiguously embracing Anglicanism, since
under the religious tests still in force that step required adherence to the
Thirty-nine Articles. Arnold was expressing the confusion that had made
him consider taking a job in Australia whilst not wanting to emigrate.
But in January 1866 he told another correspondent, 'I returned to the

communion in which I was brought up; not doubting still that man must live by faith, and not by sight . . .'.[76]

Arnold could not bring himself to call on Newman when he was back in Birmingham winding up his affairs, fearing that he might be unwelcome, and it was several years before they met again. But, happily, their relationship was not altogether severed. After he had been in Oxford for some months Arnold wrote to Newman with a pleasant account of men and events in the university, which aroused Newman's nostalgic interest, as he indicated in his reply. Despite his distress at Arnold's loss of faith, Newman took some satisfaction in the saving of money his departure meant; he told James Hope-Scott: 'It is a great relief to us (pecuniarily) to have parted with Arnold. He, poor fellow, went because we could not give him *more*. He will not allow he has joined the Protestant Church.'[77] In Catholic eyes Arnold had become a Protestant by reverting to Anglicanism, though he was reluctant to admit it; the definition depends on one's position in the wide spectrum of Anglican attitudes.

The reasons for Arnold's change of direction, or loss of faith, remain as puzzling now as they were to Newman at the time. He clearly resented the failure by the Oratory to increase his pay, and the way in which he had been eased out of his job, but those disappointments would not have been sufficient to shake a strong faith, though they might have further undermined one which was already weakening. Arnold's later attempts to explain the change are misleading, and contradicted by such contemporary evidence as is available. In 1888 he wrote to General Collinson, with whom he had resumed contact after a long interval, filling him in with the events of his life: 'Towards the end of 1864 a sort of cloud settled down over my mind; perhaps a long continuation of ill health had something to do with it. I gradually lost faith in things unseen altogether; nothing but science and its methods commended itself to me. In this state I remained many months.'[78] This makes it seem that Arnold had experienced a familiar Victorian loss of religious faith in the face of scientific materialism. It is flatly contradicted by the conviction he had expressed in 1866, quoted above, that 'man must live by faith, and not by sight'. Arnold had changed religion, not abandoned it. Again, in his autobiography, he wrote: 'In the course of 1864 the Oratorians began to think that I was drifting towards Liberalism, and gradually growing out of sympathy with them and their aims.'[79] He had communicated his shifts in belief to Matthew, but until Julia started spreading the news around, there was no suspicion of them at the Oratory. Newman remarked in June 1865, 'As to Arnold we had no suspicion of any thing till Easter for he was just what he had been all along.'[80] Arnold was again rewriting this troubled phase of his life.

The 'Liberalism' to which Arnold referred was a problematical term. In Continental politics, a 'Liberal' was liable to be anti-clerical, even anti-religious. But in Britain the Liberal Party drew in many Catholics, such as Acton, who was for some years a largely absentee Liberal MP for an Irish constituency, and was later a close associate and warm admirer of Gladstone. Tom Arnold acknowledged that his own politics were broadly Liberal. In a religious context, Newman, in his Anglican days, had battled against the liberalism of Dr Arnold; and as a Catholic he would have rejected such a label. But his style of religious thinking can appropriately be called liberal, in contrast to the rigidity of Ward and Manning. Writing in praise of Arnold in 1863, Newman had said, 'He is, as a Catholic, liberal to a wonderful extent—yet with a simple faith and spontaneous devoutness, which are most edifying.'[81]

Arnold's account of the Oratorians' suspicion of his 'liberalism' appears to have no foundation. He refers to a particular incident which he saw as crystallizing his growing difficulties at the Oratory. He gave a boy in his highest form an extra prize in the shape of Döllinger's book *The Church and the Churches*; but Newman and Fr St John would not permit the boy to have it. Döllinger's book, based on a series of lectures he had given in Munich on the vexed question of the temporal power of the papacy, had aroused much interest in Germany and sold widely there. Acton had reviewed the German edition, respectfully and at great length, in *The Rambler*. There was never any suggestion that it was a heterodox work; indeed, Acton told Simpson in 1862 that Döllinger's book had 'been approved by the Pope—personally'.[82] Newman had met and respected Döllinger; early in 1864 he wrote, 'The more I know of Döllinger's views (I mean in his German works) the more I find I agree with him.'[83] (Newman's parenthesis is curious, since he could not read German; Arthur Stanley once remarked that if he had, the course of nineteenth-century religious history might have been different.) The letter in which Newman wrote this reflects his unease with the growing authoritarianism of the Roman authorities; it was alarmingly confirmed by the publication soon afterwards of the Munich Brief, which implicitly condemned Döllinger, notwithstanding the Pope's reported earlier approval of his *Kirche und Kirchen*. The Munich Brief showed that the Roman authorities were pulling down the shutters, confirmed at the end of the year by *Quanta Cura* and the Syllabus of Errors. If Newman and St John refused to let Arnold's pupil keep Döllinger's book, it was likely to have been on political rather than doctrinal grounds; if Döllinger was now *persona non grata* in Rome, it would be unwise for the Oratory to be freely distributing his works. It was an ignoble but prudential move in the new and harsh climate.

It is this climate, I believe, that was responsible for Arnold's crisis of faith. Although a man of considerable learning, unlike Acton and Simpson he was not theologically educated. Like many post-Tractarian converts he came to the Catholic Church because it embodied spiritual authority, ultimately deriving from the Apostle Peter, who was deemed to be the first Pope; he was not inclined to make distinctions and qualifications about the nature of that authority, how it was exercised, in what circumstances, and with what limitations. If that authority seemed to be applied in an arbitrary and repressive manner, a likely reaction would be to reject it altogether, rather than, as Newman and Acton did, distinguish between the ultimate Petrine authority and the particular bureaucratic structures that claimed to speak in its name. Acton, with his theological knowledge and his familiarity with Continental Catholic traditions that resisted extreme Roman claims, resolved to oppose the doctrine of papal infallibility enthusiastically advanced by Ultramontanes such as W. G. Ward, who claimed that he would like to read a new infallible definition in *The Times* each morning. What strengthened Acton's resolve was likely to confuse and disorientate Arnold. A further factor was Arnold's acquaintance with the Jesuit Fr Palgrave, who was already noticeably heterodox in his religious ideas, which was what Arnold may have meant when he described him as 'flighty'; Palgrave, I suspect, influenced Arnold and contributed to his intellectual distress. It would have been deepened when *Quanta Cura* and the Syllabus of Errors were published at the end of 1864.

There is supporting evidence in Newman's correspondence. In June 1865 he remarked on Arnold's defection in a letter to Fr Henry Coleridge, SJ (the convert brother of the Arnolds' Oxford friend John Duke Coleridge): 'he told Mr Palgrave that he could not receive the infallibility of the Church, and was in the same boat with him'.[84] Following *Quanta Cura* and the Syllabus, Palgrave left the Jesuits and abandoned Catholicism at about the same time as Arnold. He then worked for many years in the diplomatic service, using his knowledge of Arabic life and culture; like Arnold, he returned to Catholicism in later years. Newman was well aware of the effect that the tightening of the Ultramontane screw would have on liberal-minded converts. He strongly dissented from a claim by

Ward that 'The recent Encyclical and Syllabus are, beyond question, the Church's infallible utterance', adding 'My reason is, charity to a number of persons, chiefly laymen, whom such doctrine will hurry in the direction of Arnold. There must be a stop put to such extravagances.'[85]

Although Newman and Arnold no longer met, they kept in touch, and Arnold wrote at intervals. In 1868, writing to his friend Maria Giberne, Newman gave an overview of his protégé's life, character, and domestic situation:

He is a very good amiable fellow, but weak and henpecked. His wife is a Xantippe. From Australia, before he was received there, she sent me two abusive letters, and vowed he never should be a Catholic. When he was received there, she threw a brick through the Church window. When I gave him a professorship at Dublin she was still unmitigated—and when he came to Edgbaston, she used to nag, nag, nag him, till he almost lost his senses. She preached against Catholicism to her children and made them unmanageable. Tho' we gave him a large salary, she took care to make him feel he had nothing, and was out at elbows. He did not take enough to eat and drink—and got ill. Then came Protestant friends and talked to him. Moreover, I always thought he had been badly instructed and did not know his religion . . . Then he left us and went to Oxford, *not allowing* he was a Protestant—nor is he. He is a non-practising Catholic, if he is anything. Very friendly still, and interested in our matters. He was very religious, when with us— used to delight to be before the Blessed Sacrament etc etc. And now there is nothing bitter in him; he takes pleasure in Catholic matters. I fear he *never* has had *faith*.[86]

Julia's abusive letters would still have rankled, but Newman gives a persuasive account of Arnold's temperament and family life. He may be right in saying that Arnold had been badly instructed before his conversion, but at that time converts were admitted to the Church with very little formality or instruction, like the hero of Newman's own novel, *Loss and Gain*. He was going too far in claiming that Arnold had never had faith; it was certainly not what he thought when he was in frequent contact with him; in 1861, for instance, he had described him as 'both a zealous Catholic, and an able large-minded man'. But Newman was perceptive in calling him a non-practising Catholic after his defection, notwithstanding his regular appearance at Anglican worship at the church of St Philip and St James in North Oxford.

CHAPTER 7

Oxford Again

I

Tom Arnold quickly made use of his privileges as a life member of the Oxford Union. Writing to Julia on its notepaper on 22 April 1865, soon after his arrival, he remarked on the fact that the Union supplied him with free stationery and a term's postage at a greatly reduced rate. He wondered why undergraduates should willingly contribute to let old members, who paid nothing, enjoy such resources. But he briskly concluded, 'However I did the same when I was an undergraduate, so I "take the good the Gods provide" and say nothing.' He mentions his friendly reception from the Oxford establishment, or at least a leading member of its liberal faction. Benjamin Jowett, not yet Master of Balliol but confidently biding his time, had invited him to breakfast that morning, but Jowett had had a sleepless night, and Arnold found him rather dull. A few days later he attended an evening event at Jowett's, which he described to Julia as a 'strange gathering'. The most distinguished guest was Robert Browning, whom Jowett was busily cultivating (Browning reciprocated Jowett's attentions, in the hope of getting his son into Balliol, but in the end the boy went to Christ Church). Arnold and Browning exchanged recollections of their common friend Alfred Domett. Among the other guests were the sculptor Thomas Woolner, J. W. Colenso, the notoriously heretical Bishop of Natal, Frank Palgrave and his ex-Jesuit brother Gifford, and Mrs Mark Pattison, the vivacious and learned young wife of the Rector of Lincoln, who was not present himself. Arnold also breakfasted with another academic worthy, Edward Hawkins, the Provost of Oriel, who had launched his father on his career at Rugby, and whom he had not seen for nineteen years.

On Sunday 30 April, still uncertain in his religious allegiances, Arnold set off down the High Street to hear Mass in the little Catholic chapel at St Clement's. But seeing a crowd turning into St Mary's, he recalled that Mark Pattison was delivering a university sermon and thought he might be more worth hearing than the priest at St Clement's. Pattison was notorious as one of the contributors to the heterodox *Essays and Reviews*. He had once been a Tractarian, but now he was Broad Church at its broadest and loosest, and would soon cease to be regarded as a Christian at all. Arnold enjoyed the sermon, which he described as 'a most *remarkable* one', and could have easily listened to another half-hour of it. But it was more like a philosophical discourse on education than a sermon in the conventional sense. Christ and the Apostles were not mentioned, and Arnold imagined that the High Church and orthodox party would have been scandalized by it. That evening in a vein of, as he put it, 'in for a penny, in for a pound', he heard another and very different university sermon, this time delivered by an admired leader of the High Church party, Henry Liddon. The church was packed, 'the ladies mustered in overwhelming force'. He described Liddon as 'a dark black haired little man— short straight stubby hair—and with that singular shining glistening appearance about his sallow complexion which one so often sees in dissenting ministers, and which the devotees no doubt consider a mark of election'. Liddon's sermon was 'an impassioned strain of apologetic argument for the truth of the resurrection, and of the church doctrine generally'. The tone was earnest and devout, though there were sarcastic sallies at the liberal and rationalizing party. The sermon lasted 1 hour and 20 minutes, which Arnold thought was too long.[1]

Religion kept impinging on his life, and not only in the embarrassed process of leaving Newman and the Oratory. He was pleased that the headmaster of Rugby was prepared to take his son William into the school at a favourable rate, though disconcerted to hear that the boy would henceforth be brought up as a Protestant. Arnold could no longer regard himself as a Catholic, but he was reluctant to be thought of as a Protestant.

His eldest daughter, treated with her parents' customary neglect, was not told of her father's retreat from Rome. Away at her boarding school, the 14-year-old Mary learned the news several weeks later from a press report. As an ardent adolescent Evangelical, she was overjoyed, writing to her mother, 'My darling Mother how thankful you must be. One feels as if one could do nothing but thank Him.'[2] She was happy at the prospect of living in a household that was not divided by difference of religion; and she was very excited by Oxford. Long afterwards she recalled arriving for the summer vacation of 1865:

I see a deserted Oxford street, and a hansom coming up it—myself and my father inside it. I was returning from school, for the holidays. When I had last seen my people, they were living near Birmingham. I now found them at Oxford, and I remember the thrill of excitement with which I looked from side to side as we neared the colleges. For I knew well, even at fourteen, that this was 'no mean city'. As we drove up Beaumont Street we saw what was then 'new Balliol' in front of us, and a jutting window. 'There lives the arch-heretic!' said my father. It was a window in Mr Jowett's rooms.[3]

Mary's memory must have been at fault. For some months Tom Arnold lived in lodgings at 77 George Street, while Julia and the younger children remained in the house at Edgbaston, where he returned for the summer. They were not all together in Oxford until they moved into a rented house in St Giles early in October. Mary may have been thinking of a Christmas visit, or even have been a year out, confusing 1865 and 1866. Her parents still required her to return to her boarding school until she was 16. It is as if they were determined to keep her at arm's length for as long as possible; Julia had previously told Tom how difficult she found her daughter, who had inherited her hot temper, and they may have been genuinely apprehensive about having an intellectual and wilful teenage girl permanently about the place.

Tom's wife and daughter may have been overjoyed at his retreat from Rome, but his Catholic friend Josephine Benison was deeply distressed. He had given her the news in a letter dated 5 July 1865, setting out the reasons much as he had given them to Newman, but in a tortuous statement that is both self-tormenting and self-justifying:

It was because I had come reluctantly to the conviction that the claim of the Catholic Church to the exclusive possession of religious truth was unfounded, and to the further conviction—closely connected with the former, that the supposition of an infallible authority, permanently residing in the church, was a dream. It pains me very much to say this to you, because I know how it will grieve you, and how it will alter and lower your opinion of me. Nevertheless I am conscious to myself of having all my life through followed after and embraced what seemed to me the highest truth attainable, and though there must of course be some great defect in my nature somewhere, otherwise I could not have presented such an example of mutability, to the grief of the few and the scorn of the many, yet I do not in my conscience believe that these movements, whether we suppose them to be backward or forward, render me less deserving of what little esteem my friends have at any time been pleased to honour me with, I could laugh at and satirize myself with as much gusto as he who condemns me most, and as for endeavouring to argue the question and make myself out right, I am too well aware of how ridiculous is the position of him who unsays one year half of what he has said the year previous, to think of attempting it.[4]

In contrast, Josephine's reply on 10 July is direct and dignified. She does not attempt to hide her pain and bewilderment at his move, writing both as a committed Catholic and as someone who was probably in love with him, but she tries to avoid reproaches:

Yesterday in our little Chapel I could hardly keep back my tears, as I thought how not quite ten months ago you knelt beside us there, and now—it is like no other sorrow I have ever known. Only a Catholic who in the poorest weakest way has realized what the Mass, and the Sacraments are, can tell what it is to grieve for those who of their own deliberate choice forsake them. Was it not very soon to decide in such a weighty matter? but doubtless there were wise and holy friends to plead with you, how can they have failed? It all looks such a troubled mystery, years of sacrifice for the faith, daily wearing cares, borne I used to think, with heroic patience.

But for all her distress, Josephine wished their friendship to continue; she tells Tom that he will be as welcome as ever at Slieve Russell: 'My personal regard must remain unchanged, you can understand this, and yet see too, how the bitter has crept up and lain down close beside the sweet in our friendship, please God it will not be so always. I should be so miserable if I did not hope.'[5]

Josephine had told Tom that she found the tone of his letter 'hard and cold'. In his reply he says he is sorry to have given that impression:

I am sure such were not the feelings with which it was written, but there is in me a sort of instinctive shrinking (I know it is a piece of pusillanimity, but I cannot help it) from being blamed or condemned, and when I anticipate this, something prompts me to coil myself up, so to speak, and harden myself against attack. But your letter shows me that when I feared that I did not quite understand you. Let us then still be friends; the common ground between two human beings is of infinite extent, if only the springs of affection and the courses of thought be kept open.[6]

The friendship between Tom and Josephine continued, in one form or another, until his death. In his first letter Tom had begun, 'My dear Miss Bension', but thereafter he picked up the familiar form his wife had used, and began 'My dear Josephine'; it was no doubt easy for him to regard her as a favourite niece. Her letters, though, always began, 'My dear Mr Arnold'. Tom in effect took over the correspondence that his wife had begun; there are no signs that Julia objected, and he always ended his letters to Josephine by saying that Julia sent her love. The letters show an affectionate friendship that was clearly valuable to both of them; they discuss family matters, politics, the state of Ireland, recent books, and religion. Indeed, Tom seems to have used the correspondence with Josephine as a way of keeping in touch with Catholic thought and practice.

He felt guilty about not having made a proper farewell to Newman when he left Edgbaston and he was at pains to keep in touch. In November 1865 he sent Newman a chatty letter about people and events in Oxford, which was greatly appreciated. Arnold had remarked that 'Dr Hawkins is still at Oriel, as of course you know, and is far from having lost his vigour. I hear that some defect of temper prevents him, as a general rule, from getting on well with the tutors of the college, and that a decline in its popularity and academical reputation has been the result.'[7] Commenting, Newman, who had clashed with Hawkins long ago as a fellow of Oriel, let off a *sfogo*:

What you said of Hawkins made me muse. I suspect he is just what he was. It is not defect of temper, unless he has altered with age, but a determination to reduce the tutor's work to the mechanical carrying out of a paper system, allowing no free judgment or action to those who have the real work; this it is which has ruined the prospects of the college, and that for more than thirty years.[8]

In November Tom wrote to Blanche Clough with the half-yearly interest on Arthur's loan. He told her, 'I have a good many pupils, and like the dear old place exceedingly. Need I say that a good many things here conspire often to remind me of one who is gone? whose breakfast party at Oriel on the Sunday morning was then one of the most interesting events of my life.'[9] Mary remarked on how at home her father was in Oxford: 'Historical scholarship was his destined field; he found his happiness in it through all the troubles of life. And the return to Oxford, to its memories, its libraries, its stately, imperishable beauty, was delightful to him.'[10] But whatever the attractions of scholarship and libraries, Arnold had gone to Oxford to support his family by working as a tutor; if he told Mrs Clough that he had a good many pupils, he certainly needed them. Despite the opposition of Matthew and Theodore Walrond to his move, the work was there if one looked for it. The Oxford University Act of 1854 had ordered the university and the colleges to put their house in order, and to take the business of higher education more seriously. Undergraduates were no longer divided between the minority of 'reading men', who were destined for the Church (and occasionally, in addition, for lives devoted to independent scholarship) and the majority of wealthy gilded youth, who found plenty to divert them whilst putting in a bare minimum of study. Entrants to the university were still drawn from a very narrow social group: male, upper or upper middle class, and products of public schools. But they now wanted more from their education than was once the case, and had a wider range of goals, including law, public administration, and journalism. A combination of university reform and the interests of students produced pressure for more things to be taught than the traditional Classical syllabus. And in all areas, more teaching was needed. The practice of allowing college fellows to teach or not, as they felt inclined, was no longer supportable. The fellows needed to be reinforced by tutors, who were either employed by the colleges, or freelances like Tom Arnold. Freelances, or 'coaches' as they were more bluntly known, could make a reasonable living, according to their talents, energy, and range of contacts; Stefan Collini quotes figures indicating that, allowing for these variable factors, they earned between 250 pounds and 800 pounds a year.[11]

In his autobiography Arnold refers to himself as preparing young men for university life—'the pupils who were sent to me were prepared for entering different colleges with fair success'—and also to teaching undergraduates and taking them on long-vacation reading parties.[12] He seems to have got off to a good start with the work; in fact, he was doing well enough for his customary castle-building to take a concrete form. He decided to build a large house for himself and his family, where students could board and be tutored. This plan represented in some respects a throwback to the medieval system where students lived in lodging-houses presided over by a Master of Arts, which developed into the collegiate system of Oxford and Cambridge. In fact, the Oxford University Act permitted Masters of Arts to open private halls for non-collegiate undergraduates, in a virtual revival of the medieval practice.[13] This innovation never caught on, but Arnold may have been influenced by it. His house on the Banbury Road was designed by John Gibbs in the Gothic style that was rapidly covering North Oxford; it still stands, in a considerably enlarged form, as the Evangelical training college, Wycliffe Hall. But it was a good size even in its original form, with fourteen bedrooms.[14] In May 1867, Matthew, about to visit Oxford to give one of his lectures as Professor of Poetry, sardonically told his brother, 'I shall have but a few hours in Oxford, but of course I shall come and look at the palace you are building and the site of the forest which you have destroyed.'[15] The following month Tom reported to Mary, 'The house makes continued but slow progress. The hall really looks very handsome for its size.'[16] By early 1868 the family were installed in the house, which Arnold called 'Laleham', after the Middlesex village where he had been born and where his father had set up his first school. Although North Oxford was expanding rapidly, 'Laleham, The Parks', was still a sufficient postal address.

On the face of it the family was now united in religion, and worshipped at the new North Oxford church of St Philip and St James. Julia could join her husband in the formal occasions that she had taken no part in when they lived in papist Dublin and Edgbaston. There was, for instance, an enjoyable visit to Commemoration day at Rugby, where they found their son William looking well and very brown. They sat down to a luncheon for eighty guests; Julia was taken in to it by Baron Bunsen's son, Henry; the Bishop of London had asked to be introduced to her and was very cordial; at least, for him, Tom remarked, 'for he has a cold manner'. He met Stanley and caught sight of many men he had not seen for years. 'The speeches followed immediately, and were much the same as these delectable exhibitions are everywhere; and then, after ices in the school house garden, we had to return at once.'[17] They were unable to stay for the dinner in the evening; Tom heard from Theodore Walrond that Matthew had been expected but had not shown up. Julia took to Oxford life happily; she was finally part of the 'clerico-professional' level of English society that she had aspired to in her early years, as opposed to the soldiers, officials, and settlers of colonial Tasmania. In the memoir that Tom wrote for their children after her death, he recalled, stiffly but admiringly: 'She accommodated herself wonderfully to the atmosphere of the place, and became, as you know, a valued & congenial member of the university society.'[18] Julia liked Oxford so much that she refused ever to leave it.

The Arnolds' latest child, Ethel, had been born in 1864. Matthew commented briskly, 'I am very glad it is a girl, and all well. And now, for Heaven's sake, don't have any more.'[19] Some oblique comments in *Culture and Anarchy* suggest that Matthew favoured birth control.[20] He and his wife, Fanny Lucy, had had six children, only three of whom survived into adult life. Tom did not take Matthew's advice; another and final child was still-born in 1868. Of the older children, William and Theodore were away at school, but in 1867 Mary joined the household after her long exile in unsatisfactory boarding schools.

II

Oxford was a liberating experience for Mary. She loved the old buildings, the smell of libraries, the presence of learned men. She was soon taken up by the Pattisons, a strange and noticeable couple. Mark Pattison, the Rector of Lincoln, was a characteristically Victorian polymath and a difficult man to get on with. As a young Tractarian clergyman he had been very close to Newman. After Newman left the Church of England, Pattison abandoned his former views and lost his religious faith, or at least anything resembling its traditional form, though he continued to revere Newman. He wrote a life of Milton, and edited the poetry of Milton and Pope. His major area of interest was the intellectual history of the Renaissance, where he accumulated learning and was slow to publish. Pattison was an unhappy man, whose *Memoirs* must be one of the most lowering works of autobiographical writing in literature. As he there records, he was disappointed of his hopes of the rectorship when one of the fellows of Lincoln changed his vote at the last minute. It eventually came his way, second time round, in 1861. By then Pattison was bitter and disaffected with Oxford. He had spent time in Germany studying the university system there and was convinced that the pursuit of pure scholarship on the German model was the proper end of academic life, rather than the production of young Christian gentlemen who had a sufficient acquaintance with the Classics.

As a fellow of the college Pattison had not been permitted to marry; as rector he could, and he hastened to take advantage of this facility. In September 1861, when he was nearly 48, he married Emily Francis Strong, twenty-seven years his junior. Francis, as she was usually known, was golden-haired and very pretty; she was also clever and intellectually ambitious. She was a talented artist who became a scholarly art historian, whose several works, written much later in life, on French art, architecture, and design in the eighteenth century were standard authorities. She learned about scholarly method from her husband; it was perhaps the only thing they had in common. It has been regularly asserted, and just as regularly denied, that George Eliot had the Pattisons in mind in the marriage of Mr Casaubon and Dorothea Brooke in *Middlemarch*. The Pattisons' marriage was a predictable disaster, which in the end broke down painfully, but when Mary got to know them they were still presenting a united front to the world, of poignant and picturesque contrasts. They each had reasons to take an interest in her. Pattison liked young girls, especially when they had intellectual interests. Francis, only eleven years older, perhaps regarded the bright, aspiring girl in the protective and encouraging manner of a big sister.

Mary preserved romantic memories of Mrs Pattison: 'I remember my first sight of a college garden lying cool and shaded between grey college walls, and on the grass a figure that held me fascinated—a lady in a green brocade dress, with a belt and chatelaine of Russian silver, who was playing croquet, then a novelty in Oxford, and seemed to me, as I watched her, a perfect model of grace and vivacity.'[21] The young Henry James, who was taken to lunch with them in 1869, gave a sharp account of the Pattisons:

The Rector is a dessicated old scholar, torpid even to incivility with too much learning; but his wife is of quite another fashion—very young (about 28) very pretty, very clever, very charming and very conscious of it all. She is I believe highly emancipated and I defy an English-woman to be emancipated except coldly and wantonly. As a spectacle the thing had its points: the dark rich, scholastic old dining room in the college court—the languid old rector and his pretty little wife in a riding-habit, talking slang.[22]

Mrs Pattison provided Mary with a model of the accomplished and emancipated woman, while the rector provided her with instruction, encouraging her aspirations towards learning and the life of the mind. He set her on an extraordinary and opportunistic fast-track towards scholarship, telling her she ought to settle on a particular subject and find out everything she could about it. She decided on early Spanish life and literature, which no-one in Oxford knew very much about. There was the little matter of learning the language first; then Pattison obtained for her the remarkable privilege of access to the stacks of the Bodleian. She had never been to Spain and listened enraptured when George Eliot, on a visit, talked about her travels there. She rapidly and precociously mastered enough of the subject to write what John Sutherland describes as two pedestrian articles on early Spanish subjects, which were published in *Macmillan's Magazine* in 1871–2; the prestige of the Arnold name may have helped them on their way. She was well regarded enough for the university occasionally to employ her as an examiner on Spanish subjects. Mary later acknowledged that Pattison's advice, though well intentioned, was mistaken, and that she would have been better off extending her general education. In any event, her real ambition was to become a novelist.

Mary's friendship with the Pattisons, and her reputation as a serious researcher, meant that she was noticed and respected in university circles. On a personal level, Mrs Pattison's emancipated turn of mind and the rector's caustic scepticism undermined her Evangelical faith and turned her into a devout agnostic, like so many of her intellectual contemporaries. The seeds had been sown that were to burgeon in *Robert Elsmere*. In that novel she portrays Pattison as Roger Wendover, a learned and polemical unbeliever, whose harsh, abrupt manner conceals a desolate, unhappy temperament. (The account of Wendover's situation—certainly not of his ideas—as a wealthy country gentleman and private scholar with a large library, may have been drawn from what Mary knew of Acton.)

Mary's intellectual interests, and the company she was keeping, made her unwilling, perhaps unable, to fill the traditional role of the eldest daughter in a large family, of acting as an adjutant mother to the younger children. John Sutherland suggests that the Arnolds determined to marry her off as soon as possible. That may be so, but Mary did not need any urging. At the age of 19 she got engaged to Humphry Ward, a fellow and tutor of Brasenose. Tom Arnold gave his consent to the marriage, having questioned Humphry about his prospects and, in particular, his state of health (though Humphry was to outlive his wife). He told his mother, 'I have already warned her in the strongest words I could find, how absolutely it is her duty to postpone literature and everything else to the paramount duty of keeping a straight and unindebted household; and as she is conscientious, I have not much fear of her, though I know she will make mistakes.'[23] Mary accepted as much of this advice as she found convenient; she had no intention of 'postponing literature'. As he wrote it, Tom would have reflected wryly that his own household was anything but unindebted. Humphry may have talked up his own prospects to his future father-in-law. Although the rule against fellows of colleges being married was declining it was still in force at Brasenose, and Humphry had to give up his fellowship, but he was able to retain the post of tutor. He augmented his earnings with journalistic work, but he was never well off. Humphry and Mary were married by Arthur Stanley in April 1872, two months before her twenty-first birthday. They bought a large house in Bradmore Road, near where Humphry's friend and Brasenose colleague, Walter Pater, lived with his sisters. A version of him appears in *Robert Elsmere*.

Humphry Ward was the right husband for Mary; he was a quiet recessive man, who gave his wife the support she needed in her career and otherwise let her get on with it. In electing to write under his name she preserved it for posterity, even though no-one now knows very much else about him. Disappearing under a husband's name is objectionable to modern eyes, but Mary perhaps had good reasons to prefer that name to her father's distinguished one, for the Arnolds had been neglectful parents. Their difficult oldest daughter was now off their hands, though living not far away; in fact, she had not been on them for very long. One imagines a certain sense of relief on their part.

III

Family concerns and domestic worries did not keep Tom Arnold from writing. *The Home and Foreign Review*, which had provided a regular home for his articles, was now no more; but he contributed 'Recent Novel Writing' to the January 1866 number of *Macmillan's Magazine*. It looks at and dismisses a fairly small number of recent productions, all now long forgotten. Arnold is mainly concerned to engage in general reflections on the way novels are produced and received. He insists on the need for critical standards in assessing current fiction: 'Criticism should not spare conceit or folly, though arrived at a second edition, nor let nonsense pass, though circulating in its fiftieth thousand.' He is concerned at the growth of the reading classes, whose taste is low and undemanding: 'Those who launch upon the book-sea with no better previous training than the greater number of our middle-class schools supply, will be deterred by no amount of bad taste, bad English, and literary crudity, from reading what is suited to the barbarous condition of their intelligence.' It is evident that Arnold had read and studied his brother Matthew's recently published essay, 'The Function of Criticism at the Present Time'. In places, he echoes Matthew's expression as well as his ideas: 'Still, on the whole it may be boldly maintained that novels minister to culture.' The essay concludes rather lamely with a plea that novels should reflect the best that has been thought and said, and that good writing should drive out bad. At the end, Arnold invokes Goethe and 'the greatest novel that literature can show'—*Wilhelm Meister*. Matthew told Tom that he liked the essay, as well he might, given that it was permeated with his ideas, but disagreed about *Wilhelm Meister*, which 'does not seem to me to deserve, as a novel, so much praise as you give it: it is as a repository of thoughts and observations that it is so valuable'.[24] But Tom had long been devoted to Goethe's novel, and identified with its hero.

Once he was settled in Oxford, he became keenly interested in the debates and divisions about the nature and purpose of university education which had been set off by the reforms imposed by the state; in 1868 he told Acton, 'I am thinking of writing something on the subject of faculty organization here; you know we have no such thing, and the teaching of the place is really in a scandalous condition.'[25] A long essay on the subject finally emerged, and after appearing in two instalments in the *Dark Blue Magazine* it was published as a pamphlet in 1872 under the title of *The Revival of the Faculties at Oxford*. It is a thoughtful, trenchant, piece of writing, which, to an extent unusual in Arnold, is directed at an immediate contemporary issue. He has reservations about some of the reforms, and gives a qualified welcome to others. He regrets the diminution of regional scholarships, which brought poor talented boys into the university, and believes that the new system of completely open scholarships may benefit those who hold them rather than the university or the country, and prove a means of subsidizing idleness. He approves of the extension of the curriculum beyond the Classics and Mathematics, and the setting up of new schools such as Law, Modern History, Physical Science, and Theology. They have had good effects, but they exist more for examinations and competitive results rather than the pursuit of learning. Here Arnold comes to the crux of his argument: 'Oxford is unquestionably *not* a seat of the highest learning—a school of the most advanced science.' Arnold is here using 'science' in the sense of *Wissenschaft*, and his essay is driven by a sense that academically speaking things are done better in Germany: 'the German student looks forward to professorial lectures, the Oxford student to examinations and class-lists'. Arnold had not seen German universities in action for himself, but he was influenced and impressed by recent accounts from those who had, notably his brother's *Schools and Universities on the Continent* and Mark Pattison's *Suggestions on Academical Organization*, which he called a 'thoughtful and attractive essay', though he disagreed with some of Pattison's ideas, such as the proposal that colleges should become centres for studying specific disciplines.

Arnold puts forward a number of propositions. The first, extending the principle of the Oxford University Act, is that the ultimate control of universities should be in the hands of the state rather than the Church. The second is that in a serious university the model of teaching and learning should be professor and student, rather than tutor and pupil. His third proposal is that power in Oxford should be shifted from the colleges to the faculties; a revival of faculties teaching specific disciplines—in some ways a return to the medieval model—would make Oxford more like a German university. He makes exasperated satirical thrusts at hallowed Oxonian ideals: 'We call for scientific analysis, for profound research into the causes and conditions of phenomena, and from his fools' paradise on the top of Mont Blanc or the Devil's Peak, the first-class man and fellow of his college, radiant and self-satisfied, invites us to marvel at his athletic performances.' It is the lack of scientific analysis and the spirit of re-search, Arnold believes, that has led to the failures of the English ruling class, such as the muddles and breakdowns in the Crimean War. He is engaging in a controversy that rumbles on to this day.

Though the sharper minds in Oxford were convinced that more re-form was needed, there were deep divisions about the direction it should take. Jowett believed that teaching the young was the principal business of the university, and that the pursuit of learning for its own sake was likely to become sterile. Jowett's conviction had practical results in the generations of keen and able young men who emerged from Balliol to engage in public service, in Britain or the Empire. Pattison, though he had long been a college tutor, was less and less interested in teaching, and more concerned with research and learning. (He was not a simple reac-tionary, though; he believed, perhaps influenced by his scholarly wife, that women should have access to higher education.) Despite their differ-ences, Jowett and Pattison were united in opposing the High Church party, who were fighting a rearguard action to preserve Oxford as an Anglican theocracy. In the current debates Arnold sided with Pattison; in opposing Jowett's belief in the primacy of teaching he was also going against a hallowed ideal of his father's. *The Revival of the Faculties at Oxford* is a serious discussion of important subjects (some of them remain so), but it also indicated a shift in his opinions.

He engaged in more run-of-the mill productions. His *Manual of English Literature* went into further revised editions, and he produced a spin-off from it called *Chaucer to Wordsworth: A Short History of English Literature from the Earliest Times to the Present Day*; he had some difficulty in finding a pub-lisher, but it finally appeared in 1870. For the schools market he edited selections of Addison's *Spectator* papers and of Pope's poetry. He ac-knowledged that he had somewhat bowdlerized the poems so as to remove anything inappropriate for the eyes of young readers, but empha-sized that he would not dream of tampering with the text in an edition intended for adults. Oxford gave Arnold the opportunity to do the work he was increasingly drawn to, which fitted Pattison's ideal of rigorous scholarship: editing manuscripts. In his daughter's words, 'To look at the endless piles of his notebooks is to realise how hard, how incessantly he worked. Historical scholarship was his destined field; he found his happiness in it through all the troubles of life.'[26] In 1869–71 the Clarendon Press published his *Selected English Works of John Wiclif, edited from original Mss*, a substantial work in three volumes. He was also an Anglo-Saxon scholar; as early as 1866 Acton told Richard Simpson, 'Among the people one knows I think Arnold most likely to know of the latest performances in Saxon studies.'[27] Arnold would have had no difficulty in learning Anglo-Saxon, since he was an accomplished linguist who could read the principal Romance and Germanic languages and speak some of them. He also had to train himself in paleography. Arnold's primary contribution to Anglo-Saxon studies was his edition of *Beowulf*, with notes and a running translation, made from the unique fire-damaged Cotton manuscript in the British Museum. It took him several years to prepare and was finally published in 1876. Arnold was unlike earlier Anglo-Saxon scholars in being self-taught and having studied only in England. Previous translators of *Beowulf*, Benjamin Thorpe and J. M. Kemble, had worked in, respectively, Denmark and Germany, Kemble as a pupil of the great philologist Jacob Grimm. Arnold's authority as an expert on *Beowulf* was acknowledged by a subsequent translator: 'Beside his translation Mr Thomas Arnold published in 1898 a small but valuable volume entitled *Notes on Beowulf*. This, and his translation, and the translation by J. R. Clark Hall represent, perhaps, the high-water-mark among English scholars in the study of the poem.'[28]

After their marriage Mary and Humphry Ward offered Tom a generous reverse wedding present by offering to fund him on a foreign holiday, or, on a narrower definition, a trip to examine manuscripts in French libraries. He happily accepted, as he did most good things that were put before him, and spent August 1872 on his first Continental visit since 1846, when he had travelled in Europe with Edward Whately. At Rheims he observed the hated Prussians still occupying the town, then travelled south to Besançon, and on to Switzerland and Northern Italy, where he met Matthew and his wife and son Dick, who were touring; Matthew introduced him to another English traveller, the keen mountaineer Leslie Stephen.

IV

As his daughter said, scholarly work in libraries provided Arnold with relief from the troubles of life, and so did the foreign travel that she and her husband had provided. But the troubles were still there, most of them to do with money. He had gambled on his future success in setting up in Oxford as a tutor, and then in building Laleham. In order to put up what Matthew facetiously called the 'palace', and later the 'barrack', on the Banbury Road Tom had taken out a mortgage backed by his share in a family trust fund. The Arnolds were not a wealthy family—Matthew and Tom had depended on scholarships to go to Oxford—and Dr Arnold, conscious of this, had taken out a large insurance policy on his life; after his early death the proceeds were placed in trust for his family. One of the trustees was Tom's brother-in-law William Forster, Liberal MP for Bradford, who became his unofficial financial adviser. His letters to Tom reflect his personal generosity and benevolent concern. Forster and his wife, Jane, were better off than the rest of the family and they did what they could to help. In 1862, for instance, Forster, in his role as trustee, had agreed to pay him 180 pounds out of the fund; but added that he and Jane would like to pay him this sum themselves, in order to preserve his patrimony. In 1864 Tom was applying for more money; Forster remarked it was sad that he should have to diminish still further his portion in his father's property, but he was willing to draw it from the trust, hopefully enquiring if 250 pounds would clear all debts. Alas, Tom's debts would not be cleared for a very long time, though not for want of trying and help from others. Later he took to borrowing sums from the fund rather than withdrawing them outright, which meant that interest as well as repayments had to be ensured.

A letter from Forster dated 7 July 1868 shows that Tom's project was running into difficulties, saying that he was sincerely sorry to hear that the number of pupils had declined, but hoped they would soon pick up again. Forster continued, with characteristic generosity, that he would like to pay the interest on the money Tom had borrowed from the trust account and that he should not trouble about payments of interest or repayments of capital until he had a house full of pupils.[29] In a letter written later that month, Matthew remarks 'I have been grieved to hear of your anxieties about pupils' and says that he will do what he can to find them. Matthew had never approved of the move to Oxford and the building of Laleham.[30] In 1866, still thinking that a return to the Antipodes would be

Tom's best course, he had held out hopes that his brother could become Professor of Classics at Sydney. He told his mother that Tom had agreed to the idea; but Tom, especially where Matthew was concerned, was inclined to agree to things that he did not really want, for the sake of a quiet life. In any event, this plan collapsed when the appointing panel heard that Tom had previously been obliged to leave Australia on becoming a Roman Catholic; a bitter irony, given that he now ceased to be one.[31] But there is no evidence that Tom seriously wanted to return to Australia. Matthew liked to exercise his skills at networking and string-pulling, but he was never able to achieve anything concrete for his brother.

Forster's forbearance was great but not boundless, and later in 1868 he adopted a crisper tone; after estimating the amount that Tom had drawn from the fund, he went on to ask how much was for building and how much for furniture; how much Tom had borrowed for a mortgage and at what rate of interest. On 2 November he wrote that Tom could have a further advance of 700 pounds if his brothers guaranteed the interest. He went on to ask, ominously, whether it was a good idea for Tom to remain in Oxford, at least in his present house. Laleham had only been completed for a year, and already the castle in the air was looking like a white elephant on the ground. This was no surprise to Matthew; in March 1869 he told Tom, 'You know I think the house and the pupils a horrid risk and bore altogether and should be glad to see you rid of it—but as long as you have it I do all I can to get pupils for you.'[32] A large influx of pupils would have helped Tom's position but it would not have transformed it, given Julia's inadequacies as a housekeeper. In June 1869 Forster wrote about fresh plans to put Tom on a better financial footing, raised the possibility of a second mortgage, and added that he was sure his wife would help by applying close domestic economies. Forster was being politely but unrealistically hopeful. Most careers were closed to middle-class Victorian women, but they were expected to make a success of the one that was open to them, of running a household, and Julia does not seem to have been up to it. Mary was very conscious of her mother's deficiencies. John Sutherland in his biography is, I think, rather too ready to extract biographical information from her novels, but a passage he quotes from her late novel, *Lady Connie*, has the ring of remembered experience. In this book Mrs Hooper 'was the most wasteful of managers; sevants came and went interminably; and while money oozed away, there was neither comfort nor luxury to show for it. As the girls grew up, they learnt to dread the sound of the front doorbell, which so often meant an angry tradesman.'[33] One sees why Mary was so eager to escape into marriage.

In April 1872, soon after the wedding, which must have placed a particular strain on the family finances, Tom sent Julia something of an ultimatum:

I intend to try to raise some money, as I do not see any possibility of going on till June without it, but before doing so I wish to come to an understanding with you. It is necessary that I should have some promise from you to the effect of that which I enclose; otherwise whatever temporary relief I may obtain will only end, as has been the case before, in involving me still deeper. Your cleverness and expertness in a great deal that concerns the management of a household are well-known, and could not easily be surpassed; but for keeping accounts and balancing income against exenditure, you have no turn whatever; and it is this which makes it desirable, really quite as much for your sake as for mine, that you should give the undertaking which I require . . .[34]

He raises the possibility, if things do not improve, that the house will have to be sold, 'the final result of which operation would be to place us all homeless and bare before the world, with an occupation gone, and perhaps £100 to the good . . .'. Tom felt it necessary on occasion to act the part of the irate paterfamilias, but his bark was worse than his bite, and beneath the quasi-legal language there were currents of self-pity and melodrama.

Matthew had no doubts that Tom should get rid of the house and find another way of living. He was not the only one who thought so; he reported to his mother that after he had dined in Balliol, Jowett, now Master, told him, 'how anxious he and Tom's friends were that he should get something to free him from the necessity of pupils—that he was getting too old for pupils, and that they would more and more drop off from him'.[35] Jowett's point was well taken. Tom was now approaching 50 and had an anomalous position of being in, but not of, Oxford, other than as a resident Master of Arts. Most tutors, or coaches, were young graduates, doing the work until something better came along, though a few were older men, fellows of colleges, who needed extra money or else had an inordinate taste for teaching. At Tom's age there was clearly no future in it, and Jowett's remark suggests that he was becoming something of an embarrassment in the university. Tom's financial position remained critical, though collapse was somehow avoided for the time being. He had intellectual as well as material reasons for seeking a change. When he arrived in Oxford in 1865 he had been inspired by his father's convictions that tutoring the young was an entirely worthy life's work. But at Oxford he had both embraced textual scholarship and been influenced by Pattison's arguments that the end of academic life is learning, not teaching generations of young people in what he contemptuously called a 'boarding-house university'; Arnold was still commmitted, though, to earning his living by doing just that. There is a significant sub-text in *The Revival of the Faculties at Oxford*. He is dismissive of the kind of superficial young men with First-class degrees who become college fellows without making any contribution to scholarship. His ideal is the professor on the German model, who is the master of a subject, which he wants to impart to students; whereas a tutor's main concern is with his pupil and his attainments and capabilities. It remains a basic division in the philosophy of higher education; Tom Arnold's misfortune was to have to earn his living on one side of the divide, whilst being intellectually committed to the other.

Matthew, though he sometimes sounded like a bully and a busybody, was deeply attached to his brother and genuine in his attempts to find more suitable employment for him. Early in 1875 Matthew discovered that there was likely to be a post going as an assistant charity commissioner and believed that with the right support there was a good chance that Tom could get it. Although in his writings Matthew was the apostle of sweetness and light, who believed that the reformer should not get too involved with the machinery of day-to-day decision-making, he showed a keen political sense in the business of lobying support: 'not too many Jews Turks Infidels and Heretics for your recommenders . . .'. He became rather carried away at the prospect:

I am delighted at seeing what I really think is a chance for you. You will get rid of that barrack, and live in a small house on the pleasant side of London—Dulwich or somewhere—where you can get advantages for the children, access to the Museum, &c, &c. You will go about a good deal, which you won't dislike. Keep the Anglo Saxon going—everything else may be suffered to drop. But we must not be too sanguine.[36]

Matthew *was* being too sanguine. As well as his affection and good will, he probably felt embarrassment at his brother's lack of prospects and increasing difficulties at Oxford. It would have been better all round if Tom could have been installed in some respectable as well as adequately remunerative profession. What Tom thought of the proposal we do not know, but he may have welcomed it. Public employment then was not highly demanding of time, indeed would seem to us to be conducted on a part-time basis. Matthew, after spending the mornings in the Education Department, would sit and write in the Athenaeum throughout the afternoon. Testimonials from influential people came in on Tom's behalf; Matthew managed to see them and thought them very satisfactory, though he wryly remarked that Arthur Stanley had praised Tom at his own expense: 'without the qualities which excite so much alarm in his brother M.'. Sir James Hill, the chief charity commissioner, was reported to be favourable.

Others plucked at strings on Tom's behalf. In Oxford, C. L. Dodgson, Anglican deacon and lecturer in Mathematics at Christ Church, better known to the world as Lewis Carroll, was a friend of the Arnolds and an admirer of their youngest daughters, Julia and Ethel. He had some influential acquaintances, among them Lord Salisbury, to whom he wrote on 31 January 1875, giving a graphic account of Tom's situation, including bad drains:

Mr Tom Arnold, son of the late Dr Arnold, has been working for years in Oxford as a private tutor (chiefly preparing youths for Oxford) and has a large house for boarding his pupils, which he has up to this time kept fairly full. With that, and some literary work, in editing, etc. (as he is a man of considerable attainments) he has succeeded in supporting his family. Now the business seems to have deserted him, partly by changes such as certificates being taken in lieu of the Little-Go examinations, and partly because such alarming reports are about as to the sanitary condition of his part of Oxford. The house has emptied and he is obliged to get rid of it, and acting under the advice of friends, is a candidate for the post of 'Assistant Charity Commissioner'. I understand that the Commissioners appoint, and that they consult with the President and Vice-President of the Privy Council. He has, I believe, sent in excellent testimonials, but if you could further his object by a word to any of the persons named, you would, I am sure, be aiding a most worthy man.[37]

Matters hung fire for several months, until in October came the dismaying news that Sir James Hill had suddenly died. Though the idea of meritocracy, of a career open to all talents, was taking root, public employment was still in large measure a matter of personal influence and patronage, as it had been when Matthew and Tom had been found government jobs in the 1840s. Matthew acknowledged to Tom that Hill's death had been '*most* unlucky for us' but said he would not despair. Writing to Julia, he was franker, describing Hill's death as 'a dreadful misfortune' for Tom's prospects. He seemed to imply that Julia had talked too freely about them, and he had perhaps done so himself:

I must say my dear Julia, that if it had not been for the stir caused by premature rejoicings over our success, for the alarm then given to Sir James Hill's mind, and for the check thus caused to the whole project, Tom would in my opinion have been appointed and safe long before Sir James Hill's death. However the rejoicing and talking were very natural, unluckily though they turned out for us.

Matthew was responding to a letter from Julia and he concluded: 'I did not mention to Tom that you had written to me. I cannot tell you how sorry I feel for you; for you even more than for him, for he has a singular placidity, I think, which deadens the sting of worry for him.'[38] The whole episode could have made a bitter short story in the naturalistic mode.

Though that door had slammed shut, there was the possibility that another one might open, hinted at in Matthew's injunction to Tom to keep up the Anglo-Saxon. In December 1874, before the possible job at the Charity Commission had come up, he told Tom, 'what I wish for you is a post with a certain income, and the Anglo Saxon professorship can alone give you that'. The Rawlinson Chair of Anglo-Saxon had been launched in 1795, funded with an endowment from the eccentric antiquarian and collector Richard Rawlinson, who had died forty years before. His will was so complicated by peculiar restrictions and exclusions it had taken that long to get the legal position cleared up and the professorship off the ground. In the late seventeenth and early eighteenth centuries Oxford had been a flourishing centre for Anglo-Saxon studies, associated with scholars such as Humfrey Wanley, William Elstob, his learned sister Elizabeth, known as the 'Saxon nymph', and Edward Thwaites. By the time the first Rawlinson Professor was appointed the spirit of those pioneers had been lost and the study of Anglo-Saxon was not flourishing in the university. Under the terms of Rawlinson's bequest the professor was to serve for five years only (and every fifth professor had to be a St John's man). Eventually that restriction was overturned and in 1858 Joseph Bosworth, who was already nearly 70, was appointed Rawlinson Professor for life; retirement does not seem to have been envisaged, or at least not prescribed. By the mid-1870s he was not expected to live very much longer and speculation about a successor was arising. By then a new, scientific philology had emerged, in contrast to the amiable antiquarianism that had dominated earlier Anglo-Saxon studies. The Rawlinson Professor was supposed to cover not only Anglo-Saxon but the early forms of other Germanic languages and their associated cultures, which were the focus of increasing scholarly attention. Friedrich Max Müller, an expatriate German scholar, had been professor of Modern Languages at Oxford and in 1868 became professor of Comparative Philology; some years before he had crossed swords with Tom Arnold in the columns of the *Times* on an etymological point, and had politely sent him off the field by his superior philological knowledge. He embodied, if anyone did, Mark Pattison's ideal of rigorous scholarship on Germanic lines.

V

Disappointed of the post at the Charity Commission, Tom Arnold now set his sights on the professorship of Anglo-Saxon. He was completing his edition of *Beowulf* and was justified in thinking he was well qualified for the post when it fell vacant. He had suggested in his pamphlet on the re-organization of the faculties that it is a finer thing to be a professor than a tutor, and as a professor his life would be totally transformed for the better. Oxford professors were well paid, so his financial difficulties would be resolved. He would have a high status in the academic community, in which Julia would share. And he would have time and opportunity to devote himself to scholarship. It was a prospect to dream about and to strive for. Longman accepted his *Beowulf* and Tom hoped that Bosworth would live long enough for his edition to appear and make an impact, though Julia was concerned that the work of preparing it for the press would strain his eyes. But Tom Arnold's crisis over employment became caught up in a larger convulsion, the third of the spiritual crises that he had undergone at approximately ten-year intervals, and which, like the previous ones, resulted in his physical displacement.

Arnold's son William wrote after his father's death, 'From first to last religion was to him the central thing in life.'[39] After his abandonment of Dr Arnold's Broad Church Anglicanism, his wanderings in heterodoxy, and his years as a Catholic, Arnold's return to the Anglican fold looked like a homecoming, and was a cause of rejoicing to Julia and Mary and of satisfaction to the academic community. But Tom was never entirely sure that he was at home there. Nor was Newman, who wrote of him in 1868, 'He is a non-practising Catholic if he is anything. Very friendly still, and interested in our matters.'[40] Newman and Arnold kept in touch; Newman sent him a collection of his poems, and wrote a note of condolence when Mrs Arnold senior died, in 1873. This was more than simple friendliness. Newman suspected that Arnold had not seen the last of the Catholic Church; so, probably, did Arnold. It is true that his edition of the proto-Protestant Wycliffe suggested an allegiance to the Anglican Via Media; in his introduction to the third volume he remarked of the Reformation, 'it is no wonder if no more mercy was shown to the monks and friars, than they had shown to the Lollards. So little did Englishmen, till the civil war of the seventeenth century, understand that spirit of compromise and gradual change, which, since that epoch, has been the main preservative of our national institutions.'[41] But in 1868, when he was studying Pattison's *Suggestions on Academical Organization*, a book he admired and was influenced by, Arnold wrote to Acton objecting to Pattison's charge that Catholic higher education was an impossibility and asking Acton for contrary evidence from his experience of Continental universities.[42] Arnold was drawing closer to Catholicism; travelling once more in France in 1874 he visited Lourdes, already a famous shrine of Marian devotion, and was impressed by what he saw.[43] It was evident throughout his correspondence with Josephine that he saw her as a private lifeline to the religion he had apparently abandoned. The year after his departure he was sharing ecumenical speculations with her:

The time perhaps may arrive fore-planned in the eternal counsels, when all who believe in the One Saving name will again be united in the same communion, as of old; nor should I be unwilling to believe that the chair of Peter, then as formerly, will emerge from the waters as the centre and rallying point of a re-united Christendom; but that day is yet far off; you and I will not live to see it, no, nor our children's children . . .[44]

The sentiments would have sounded familiar and acceptable after the Second Vatican Council to Catholics who were concerned to further Christian unity, but following his return to the Church Tom would probably have found them, in the spirit of those days, too vague and accommodating. On 30 August 1868 he ended a letter to Josephine, 'do not cease to pray for me, I am sure your prayers have done me good in time past. In spirit and desire I am not far from you, but duty to others holds me fast at present. Do not allude to this when you write; some prejudices seem invincible, and to avoid arousing them, unless bound to do so, is the better course.'[45]

Julia was becoming anxious about Tom's possible backsliding, and his grandchildren have passed on bits of family lore. Janet Trevelyan reported:

> But now and then Julia would stop suddenly in her household tasks, hearing ominous sounds from Tom's study. Was it the chanting of a Latin hymn? She put the fear behind her and passed on . . . Tom Arnold was growing restless again in the mid-seventies, and when he went with his younger children to church at St Philip's, they would nudge each other to hear him muttering again under his breath the Latin prayers of long ago.[46]

These accounts may be apocryphal, but the anti-papist *frisson* sounds authentic. Julian Huxley, evidently fascinated by his grandmother's capacity for violent displays, wrote, 'He liked to keep in touch with his Catholic friends, preferably when his wife was not present. On one occasion she had gone to London, but returned earlier than expected, to find her husband entertaining two priests to dinner. Legend has it that she flew into a great tantrum, and the party broke up under a shower of plates.'[47] The hot-tempered Julia would have been capable of it.

Mary Ward refers to 'a kind of nostalgia, which grew and grew till it took him back to the Catholic haven in 1876, never to wander more'.[48] But there was more rational conviction in the decision than his daughter allows for. Arnold may have come to believe that leaving the Catholic Church was not only a mistake, but an unnecessary mistake. Acton had disliked *Quanta Cura* and the Syllabus of Errors quite as much as Arnold, and he had responded by closing the *Home and Foreign Review*, since they had made its position impossible, but he had never faltered in his commitment to Catholicism. Tom remarked in a letter to Josphine, 'you, and Sir John Acton . . . represent a system of thought and practice in which reason and feeling are reconciled'.[49] Whatever the idea of the 'infallibility of the Church' meant—which had driven Arnold out of it in 1865—it certainly did not involve assenting to every pronouncement that came from Rome. A further factor in Arnold's timing may be, as Meriol Trevor has suggested, the publication in 1875 of Newman's *Letter to the Duke of Norfolk*, which made a studiedly moderate interpretation of the infallibility decree of the First Vatican Council (itself a good deal more moderate than Blessed Pio Nono had wanted).[50]

At the beginning of 1876 Arnold was corresponding with Henry Liddon, leader of the High Church party at Oxford, who was both professor of Exegesis and a canon of St Paul's, and a 'student' (i.e. fellow) of Christ Church. Arnold, who had heard him preach but had never met him, wrote to describe his religious difficulties and his growing sense of the validity of the Catholic position. Liddon's reply, on 9 January (dated '1875' but this is evidently a New Year slip),[51] is long, detailed, and friendly in tone; he draws on Scripture and early church history to deny papal claims and to affirm that the Church of England is the actual Catholic church in England. He hopes to talk to Arnold on his return to London. We do not know how Arnold answered, but Liddon's next letter, dated 16 January, is longer still, in the same vein, taking issue with some of Newman's arguments. In a brief note dated 2 February he invites Arnold to call on him in Christ Church. Liddon evidently saw Arnold as a brand to be plucked from the burning, and regarded an equable, rational, manner as the best means of achieving it. The same could not be said for Tom's dealings with his immediate family. On 13 January he sent Julia a letter from London, which is emotional in tone but not very explicit in content; it hints at a coming change: 'For though, on the whole, it has seemed best to me, everything being very perplexed, to go on as I have done, yet the time while that seemed allowable has pretty well come to an end.'[52] Writing to her again on 12 February, he comes to the point: 'I have made up my mind to resume the practice of the religion which I formerly professed.' It points out there need be no formal readmission to the Church, merely a resumption of the practice from which he had lapsed. Tom makes it sound a simple, straightfoward, business, but Julia was hardly likely to see it that way. What for him was merely a matter of getting back on the right path, looked to her like a second conversion to Rome, as disastrous as the first one twenty years before. Tom adds a postscript: 'With *discretion*, as I said before, I do not think my chance of the Anglo-Saxon chair eventually will be a bit impaired, if the *Beowulf* succeeds.'[53] William S. Peterson, drawing on a diary entry by Mark Pattison, has described the ensuing disturbance in the family:

Without warning, Tom Arnold left one morning in February 1876 for London, where he attended mass and conferred with two Catholic friends, Canon Frederick Oakley and Monsignor Thomas J. Capel, about his wish to change his religious allegiance once again. Julia followed him by train but went instead to see her brother-in-law, William Forster, who joined with Mrs Ward . . . and Julia in attempting to dissuade Tom. For a few days Tom remained in London, still hesitating.[54]

A letter from Mary to her father, dated 16 February, refers to a distressful scene in London. After mentioning a scheme to get him to write for the

Manchester Guardian, which appears to have come to nothing, she continues:

> With regard to my mother your letter did I think bring her some relief, but she is very unhappy mainly I think from the remembrance of your last interview in London. She bids me say that she deeply regrets the bitter things she said and she promises that for the future she will do her very best to abstain from saying wounding or bitter words. She was in a state of frenzy from the feeling of loneliness and lovelessness and hardly knew what she said. And she also bids me to say that if when the children are a little older and your prospects are more assured you decide to become a Roman Catholic she will feel it 'her bounden duty not to oppose you'.[55]

Mary was hoping for a compromise; Tom would make it clear that he wanted to be a Catholic again, but would defer taking the step for some time in the interests of his family. It is the kind of advice that an accommodating Catholic spiritual adviser might have given, since Tom had to consider the good of his family as well as his own pursuit of truth; indeed, there are hints in Mary's letter that this is what Oakley and Capel had proposed. He seems to have been persuaded; writing to Julia the following day, 18 February, he says that he is now reluctant to take any such decisive step at present, having engaged in much anguished consideration about the desolation that would follow from it.[56] This letter crossed with an operatically intense one from Julia, also dated 18 February, which expressed both her undying love for Tom and her detestation of Catholicism. It contains the crucial words, 'And what I went through since last Sunday, was caused by the feeling that by your becoming a member of the Church of Rome, you cut off in our present circumstances the possibility of our living together . . .'.[57] This represented a renewal of the threat to leave him that she made when Tom first became a Catholic in 1856; she did not carry it out on that occasion, but this time she was more in earnest. She explained that it was not because of any changed feelings for him, but because it would be impossible to carry on having live-in students at Laleham if the head of the house was known to be a Roman Catholic. This notion was merely a projection of Julia's prejudice; anti-Catholic feeling was still strong, certainly, but the recent University Tests Act meant that posts in the university were now open to men of any religion or none. Croke Robinson, a fellow of New College, retained his appointment after he converted to Catholicism in 1872.[58] If the holders of university or college posts could be free in their religious convictions, the

same freedom should surely apply to the head of a boarding house frequented by students. Julia's real motive must have been her horror at the
return of the division she had felt during the years in Dublin and
Birmingham.

The next day Julia wrote again, having received Tom's conciliatory
letter: 'Many many thanks for your dear letter. It was with feelings of
bitter shame that I read it. How much more cause my darling I have to feel
dejected and humiliated than you have. Your very errors arise from a too
sensitive conscience. Do believe that I love you very deeply and do help
me to conquer myself.' Anger and abjection were liable to alternate in
Julia's feelings. She says that she is pining to see Tom again but urges him
first to visit Matthew, now living in Surrey: 'there is so much true affection
between you and Matt that I am *always* glad when you meet'.[59] Julia concludes, 'Few families have been blessed with such a home training as
yours, and certainly very few in our rank of life have been cursed with
such as mine.'[60] Tom's extended family did indeed provide support in
this and other crises; not only Matthew, but Jane and William Forster, in
whose London house in Eccleston Square he had been staying. He returned to Oxford and the crisis died down for the time being. In March he
wrote to Josephine, who had visited the Arnolds at Laleham in 1874,
referring to the recent episode:

Whether I have done rightly or wrongly I cannot tell, 'God knoweth', but the net
woven round me, by my own previous acts partly, and partly by the course of
human events, over which an individual has so little power, has proved too strong
for me to break at present. Much depression has been the natural consequence of
all this; still I am well in body, thank God, and can work; and labour blunts the
edge of pain.[61]

His *Beowulf* was delivered to Longman; in May 1876 Joseph Bosworth
finally died at the age of 87, rather early for Tom's plans, and the machinery was set in motion to elect a successor. Tom continued to entertain
high hopes, and in June told Frances that he hoped his *Beowulf* would be
out in September. He gave her an enthusiastic account of his plans, or
dreams, for advancing the subject, such as entering into correspondence
with professors of Anglo-Saxon in other European universities, thoroughly searching the manuscripts in the libraries of Oxford and Cambridge, and publishing a complete catalogue of extant Anglo-Saxon literature, to replace Wanley's ancient one. In the same letter he remarks that
Liddon will shortly be dining with him. If Arnold seemed content to

remain in the Anglican fold, then the professor of Exegesis and canon of St Paul's would have been well pleased, believing that his persuasive apologia for the Church of England had been effective. He assured Arnold of his support in the coming election. Having heard of Tom's hopes, Frances might have been cast down by a letter from Matthew written later in June: 'Mark Pattison told me yesterday that Earle is certain to be elected Anglo Saxon Professor if he stands. Does Tom know this? for the disappointment will be all the greater the longer he is kept without knowing the truth. Pattison thinks Tom would beat Skeat (is it Skeat?) though narrowly; but Earle is *certain* of winning he says, Congregation being what it is.'[62] Earle was a productive Anglo-Saxon scholar who had previously held the Rawlinson chair when it was a five-year appointment, from 1849 to 1854, and in the words of the *Dictionary of National Biography* turned it from 'little more than an elegant sinecure' to a 'position of real usefulness'. Walter Skeat was an active worker in the field of Anglo-Saxon and Middle English studies but he was a Cambridge man, who in 1878 was elected professor of Anglo-Saxon there. John Earle did decide to stand, and immediately became the favourite; it is not hard to see why, given his record. Tom Arnold's *Beowulf* was still in the press, but Earle had already published an edition of two Anglo-Saxon chronicles and some fragments on St Swithin, together with *A Book for the Beginner in Anglo Saxon* and *Philology of the English Tongue*, which ran into several editions. Matthew may have told Tom of this threat to his prospects, or perhaps Frances did. Perhaps no-one did, but Tom, with his professional's interest in the subject, knew what Earle had achieved and the challenge he represented. However, he went on engaging in the sort of discreet campaign that was permitted in the situation, actively supported by Humphry Ward. He received the proofs of *Beowulf* together with the unwelcome news that its publication was likely to be delayed until after the election.

The uncertainties about his future, both in career and belief, caused Tom to engage in some acute self-analysis. Writing to Julia on 3 July he reflected that at times something within him seemed to buoy him up and cause him to feel as if he were treading on air; he became hopeful and adventurous and fancied that all sorts of things were possible. But he knew that between the projecting spirit and the actual execution a gulf was fixed; if he sometimes conceived things with vigour, in performance he was likely to be slow and languid. [63] As T. S. Eliot put it in 'The Hollow Men':

> Between the conception
> And the creation
> Between the emotion
> And the response
> Falls the Shadow
> V. 11–15

The process Tom described repeated itself at intervals throughout his life.

As the election approached his conscience began to trouble him, not necessarily because of the delay in returning to Catholicism but because of the secrecy it involved. The support he had received from Liddon and the High Church party, though encouraging to start with, was troubling. He realized with growing distress that the election was becoming politicized, as was liable to happen in Oxford. Owen Chadwick has pointed out that in a climate of theological controversy elections to chairs 'showed signs that the constituency judged a candidate more by his religious opinions, which they could understand, than by his scholarship, of which they knew nothing'.[64] Liddon and his party were using such elections in a struggle to maintain the essential Anglican identity of the university, in defiance of the Tests Act. Arnold, an Anglican of Catholic sympathies, who had escaped the false embrace of Rome, was their favoured candidate. If he were elected with their support, he would be bound to a cause he ultimately intended to reject. A tougher minded and more politically calculating candidate might have persisted, but Arnold realized with horror that he was, in effect, being set up in an ecclesiastical–political power struggle. He decided to escape from such an intolerable situation by publicly proclaiming his intention of returning to Catholicism forthwith, whatever the consequences for the election, or for his family. He gave George Bradley, the Master of University College, a statement to be made public on 16 October 1876, the day before the election, to the effect that 'any member of Congregation who thinks of voting for me at the election to the chair of Anglo-Saxon, should know that I intend, as soon as may be, to join, or rather to return to, the communion of the Catholic and Roman Church'. He acknowledged that this move might lose him votes, though Bradley assured him he would still get his. He gave the news to Humphry Ward in an emotional letter, sent from his sister Mary's house at Loughborough, to which he had retreated: 'my faith is that God will provide for me, and enable me to provide for those I love. You or Mary will probably show this letter to my wife; it is better than that I should write.'[65]

Liddon wrote to Arnold on the day of the election, 17 October, conveying his pain and disappointment. He felt that Arnold was elevating a scruple to the point of a conviction, and regretted that in the circumstances he could not vote for him without doing violence to his loyalty to the English Church as he understood it, and his hopes for the religious future of Oxford.[66] The election resulted in an overwhelming defeat for Arnold. John Earle received 137 votes, Arnold 31, and Frederick Metcalfe, a fellow of Lincoln and a Scandinavian scholar, 20.[67] The size of Earle's majority shows that Pattison was right in predicting that he was certain to win, an opinion reinforced after the election by Montagu Burrows, Chicele Professor of History, who told Arnold that Earle would in any case have been elected by a large majority. Arnold's announcement of his return to Catholicism forfeited the support of Liddon and his followers, and no doubt of other voters, but Earle had been the likely winner throughout, ending up with 72 per cent of the votes cast; Arnold could have doubled his support at Earle's expense and still lost. He had the qualities to make a very good professor of Anglo-Saxon, but he had no real hope in the contest. The figures disprove the belief which grew up in the family and has been repeated by Janet Trevelyan and John Sutherland in their biographies of Mary Ward, that his announcement cost him the election, and that he wantonly threw away an enviable position because of religious scruples. When the election result was published, Dodgson noted in his diary (giving Arnold 10 votes too many): 'Election to Anglo-Saxon Professorship—*Earle* 137, Arnold 41, Metcalfe 20. Heard the extraordinary news that Arnold has just (for the second time) joined the Church of Rome.'[68]

The double blow of Tom's return to Catholicism and his crushing failure in the professorial election threw the family into consternation. One of Mary Ward's biographers has written, 'Mary, hearing the next day that the Chair was lost, ran round to the T. H. Greens to weep passionately over this action of her honest, beautiful, wholly irrational father.'[69] The idea that he had wilfully destroyed his chances had already caught hold. The day before the election Tom Arnold had visited Newman at Edgbaston, to mark his formal return to the Church. A few days later he wrote from Woodhouse to thank Newman for 'the charity with which you received a wanderer for whom there was so little excuse'. He adds, 'The state of my wife is very sad, and it seems likely that it will be found the best course for me to remain in London for a while.'[70] The news about Tom, reinforced by a sense that he had deceived her, had plunged

Julia into a state of hysteria and uncontrolled distress. Tom communicated via Mary; on 21 October he told her:

> I could not feel with more painful keenness than I do the bitterness of the disap-
> pointment and shock which what I have done has caused your mother. Would to
> heaven that she were linked to some one more capable of satisfying the ambition
> and aspiration of her nature than I am. And yet I must own to you, when I look
> back, the horror of the thought of the mental state into which I must have fallen
> had I let myself be elected through Liddon and his friends, avowing—as he has
> himself avowed to me—that the policy on which they vote in university elections
> is guided by their views and hopes for 'the religious future of Oxford',—the
> horror of this thought, I say, makes me even now tremble and shudder.[71]

Tom was capable of his own flourishes of emotion. His letter continues with expressions of joy at having followed his conscience and returned to the Catholic fold, combined with intense expressions of regret
at the distress he has caused to his family. In her reply Mary refers to her
mother having been not 'really in her right mind' after many sleepless
nights, adding that she is now calmer though still bitter, and looking very
worn and thin. Perhaps as a reaction both to her father's news and her
mother's condition, Mary, who was heavily pregnant, has herself undergone some form of brief breakdown. She conveys her mother's view 'that
it will be best for all parties that you should be away for a time'. She tries
to understand her father's beliefs, as he has urged her to do: 'I think I
understand your step dear one as well as an outsider can. Starting from
your premises all seems natural enough. But as you know the impossibility is to me to see any sufficient ground for granting those premises to
start with.'[72] Mary loved her father dearly, but intellectually she would
not give ground. The perturbation caused by her father's return to
Catholicism was later reflected in her novels; indirectly in *Robert Elsmere*
and directly in *Helbeck of Bannisdale*.

He had already given the news to a more deeply sympathetic recipient.
He told Josephine that he had not been elected to the Anglo-Saxon chair,
and continued, 'but this does not trouble me much, nor will it you, when
you hear that my candidature has been the occasion of my returning to
that sacred shore, from which my feet ought never to have strayed, but to
which, when once a soul has drifted away, and become immersed in the
tides of human respect and worldly care, it is so hard to return'.[73] As on
other occasions, Tom's presentation of a profound existential choice was
touched by Rugbeian priggishness. Joesphine wrote on the envelope,
'Good tidings of great joy'.

In a postscript to his letter to Mary, Tom had written, 'As for the £200 a year from my family, it would be out of the question to propose such a thing until it was certain that I could not myself earn enough to support us.'[74] This sounds like a proposal from the ever-generous Forsters to help Tom and his family in their present straits. Jane Forster wrote to Julia expressing her distress and sympathy, and at the same time her understanding of Tom's move:

With regard to dear Tom himself, one sees now that it is unfortunate we did not all reconcile ourself to the step when he took it in the Spring—for it is evident that the basis of his mind and inclination towards the R. Catholics is too strong for him ever to be settled without joining them—and I can understand the feeling which goaded him into the declaration of his position at the last moment, rather than let the election be made on false pretences. The deep cause of regret and vexation is that he should have let things go on so long. However, it is no use to think of that now—but do not imagine dearest Julia that I do not feel how much this has aggravated the trial for you,—but the question is now, what can be done.

One thing is quite clear, that we must regard this step of Tom's as a permanent one, and sincerely hope it may be so; and that all your plans must be made on that assumption. You have got your boarders with you at present I suppose—so I hope Tom may for the time find something to occupy him elsewhere. *He* has suffered I am sure—he cannot but suffer greatly in knowing all the pain and perplexity he causes you and his children, however much he has gained relief for his own mind and conscience. You must be sure of this, dear Julia—that he too has suffered much—his very vacillations, and the sort of desperateness of his conduct, prove that—and we see how *great* an effort he must have made for your sake and the children's in the spring.[75]

Jane shows great insight into the moral intractability of the situation, and into her brother's temperament and state of mind. Tom responded to the general conviction that he had better remove himself, and took lodgings in London. He and Julia were never again to live together permanently, though the marriage remained very much in being. Newman had hoped and prayed for and perhaps to some extent expected his return to Catholicism, but he seems to have played no active part in Tom's decision. Nevertheless, Julia decided that he was responsible for it and the concomitant disasters. In 1855, when Tom first became a Catholic, she had sent Newman two abusive letters. In November 1876 she sent him a third:

You have now for the second time been the cause of my husband's becoming a member of the Church of Rome and from the bottom of my heart I curse you for it. You know very well how weak and unstable he is, and you also know that he has a wife and eight children. You know well that he did nothing for the Roman Catholic Church in the ten years he belonged to it before, and you know well that he will do nothing for it now, but the temptation of having one of his father's sons under your direction was too much for you, and for the second time you counselled him to ignore every social duty and become a pervert. He has brought utter ruin upon us all, but what is that to you?

Julia was a good hater with an energetically vituperative style, but here, as on other occasions, she gives the impression of being, in Mary's words, 'not really in her right mind'. Newman commented dryly, 'It was fitting, by way of contrast, that so sweet and amiable a fellow as Arnold should have such a yoke fellow—but except as an aesthetic contrast, it is marvellous that such a pair should be.'[76] Newman seems to have been unaware of the psychological attraction of opposites.

Copies of Tom's *Beowulf* finally arrived towards the end of the year. He sent one to Matthew, who thanked him for it warmly, adding, in a reference to the election, 'I much regret, however, that we expended fruitlessly so much of our machinery of praise, before the book was actually before the public.' If the book had appeared in time it might have made a difference to the result, but is unlikely to have much reduced Earle's huge lead; the members of Congregation might have been interested to see it and perhaps turn the pages, but they were not Anglo-Saxon scholars, and there would have been no time for the edition to be professionally discussed and assessed. Matthew ends his letter with a response to Tom's reconversion: 'As to the Catholicism, that is a long story. Catholicism is most interesting, and were I born in a Roman Catholic country I should most certainly never leave the Catholic Church for a Protestant; but neither then or now could I imagine that the Catholic Church possessed "the truth", or anything like it, or that it *could* possess it.'[77]

CHAPTER 8

London Again

In his autobiography, Tom Arnold passes in silence over the family crisis of 1876, his return to Catholicism and his retreat to London. Writing to Josephine on 5 November, he refers to a return to Oxford, though in the event it was only a brief visit:

Not that my wife's resentment is at all appeased; on the contrary she writes that she and I must henceforth live as strangers. Poor thing! I know the blow must have been terrible to her, although she has had abundant warning that this is what I should do some time or other. But her imperious will cannot tolerate in others that which in any way affects herself injuriously, that which runs counter to her plans, or interferes with her own or her children's advancement in the world. She looks upon my conduct as purely 'selfish', and of course finds plenty of so-called friends (not my own brothers and sisters, I think) to support her in this view; forgetting that though we are bound to love our neighbour as ourselves, we are not bound to love him more than ourselves, i.e. to sacrifice our own eternal to his temporal good.[1]

It is evident that Tom is drawing emotionally closer to Josephine, following the crisis and his return to Catholicism, as he tells her about Julia's state of mind. He was soon back at his lodgings in London, to embark on the bleakest and most painful period of his life. Despite the division between them, it would be a mistake to say, in the modern sense, that the Arnolds had 'split up'; they were not even formally separated. Tom always referred to the Oxford house as 'home' and he returned there for varying periods of time. After the crisis, Laleham was sold, as Matthew had long been urging; it was bought by an Anglican evangelical group, enlarged, and turned into a training college, now Wycliffe Hall. Julia and the younger children moved elsewhere in North Oxford to 3 Church Walk, a smaller but still substantial detached house on three floors, built in red and yellow brick, with a suggestion of Gothic about the porch. Tom and Julia corresponded frequently, sometimes daily, exchanging letters about domestic matters and their never-ending troubles with money. Soon after Tom moved to London they were preoccupied with a new family crisis.

The eldest children were now off their hands. Mary, the writer and scholar, was happily married, a young matron whose second child was born late in 1876. William, the eldest son, had been head boy at Rugby, and won a scholarship to his father's college, University, where he followed his uncle rather than his father in taking Second-class honours. But his career was not too badly affected, and he redeemed himself by winning the Arnold Prize, named in honour of his grandfather, for an authoritative essay on Roman provincial administration. In 1877 he married Archbishop Whately's granddaughter, Henrietta, with whose mother, the elder Henrietta, Tom Arnold had once been in love. William went to work on the *Manchester Guardian* and combined journalism with the study of Roman history, and of English Literature, publishing an edition of Keats in 1884.[2] The Arnolds' second son, Theodore, is a shadowy figure, who was an intermittent worry to his parents and to Mary, who gave him financial support; he graduated from Oxford and settled first in Tasmania and then in New Zealand. But the third son, Arthur, who had been born in December 1856, soon after their return from Tasmania, made his presence felt and was regarded as a difficult boy.

In July 1866 Matthew told his mother after a family visit: 'Tom came on Saturday with his boy Arthur, who is by no means as bad as his reputation; at least he got on very well with our children, and though he was said to be restless and to show signs of mischief, he got through his visit without astonishing us. He is much disfigured by the mark of his bite from a dog on his lip.'[3] He adds, with the note of *schadenfreude* that sometimes creeps into his dealings with his younger brother, that he was afraid the need to keep an eye on Arthur made the visit less pleasant for Tom than it might have been. It is not particularly surprising, given the tensions of the Tom Arnolds' household, that one of their offspring should have been troublesome, nor that the reputation might have reinforced the behaviour. It is not clear from Matthew's remark if the disfigurement from a dog-bite was permanent; if it were it might have been a further cause for Arthur's disaffection with the world. As he grew up he took on the role of the black sheep who was to be found in so many large Victorian families. In his late teens he was sent off to Tasmania, in the care of Julia's family, to see if he could make a life there. Writing to Tom on his brother's birthday, 30 November 1875, Matthew remarked, 'It is provoking of Arthur, but are you quite sure that his adventure in New Guinea will not eventually turn out prosperous?'[4] There is no clue as to what this adventure was; if he had got as far as the wild territory of New Guinea, Tasmania was evidently not big enough to hold him. But it is possible that Matthew did not mean it literally; 'New Guinea' might have been a facetious and off-hand way of referring to the Antipodes.

By the beginning of 1877 Arthur was back in England, trailing suspicions of financial sharp practice. He had needed treatment on the voyage from the ship's doctor, but had not paid for it, since he told his father that the doctor supplied his services without charge. His father did not believe him and had to investigate. He found that Arthur had lied to a young man he had met at Hobart and from whom he borrowed money: 'As I told him, he must have lied through thick and thin to Barrett, and that simply because he had not the moral courage to say to him, "I have no funds of my own: the only person through whom you can possibly get your money is my father; I will speak to him when I get on shore."'[5]

Tom pulled as many strings as he could to find a suitable job for Arthur in public service, but in the new professional ethos examinations were becoming important, and Arthur could not pass them. He failed to qualify as a copying clerk in the Civil Service, and as a telegraphist, though he had worked as one for a time in Tasmania. (But, he complained, the systems were different.) Arthur said that he wanted to become an actor, an aspiration that his father could barely comprehend, and in so far as he did, he vehemently rejected it. Other distressing incidents confirmed Arthur as a liar and a sponger. In Wales he called on a friend of the family to ask for a sovereign, saying that he had lost his return railway ticket, an excuse which Tom did not believe, thinking it more likely that his son had taken only a single ticket in the first place. He was not often given to anger, but Arthur provoked a sharp outburst; Tom wrote to Julia from Oxford, when she was in London, saying he was resolved that so worthless a person, so incorrigible a liar, had to leave the house, since he was not fit to associate with his brothers and sisters. Tom decided that if Arthur wanted a theatrical career he might as well go after it, since he could hardly be any worse on the stage than off it. Arthur, though, appears to have made no effort to become an actor, and after he failed to get more conventional work as a clerk his father invoked the familiar option for a black sheep, to be shipped off again to the colonies; Arthur was offered his fare to the Cape and 50 pounds a year for two years.[6] On 8 January 1878 he departed for South Africa; his father, indulgent at the end despite his anger, had opened a bank account in his name in Capetown, with a deposit of 40 pounds.

When he arrived, Arthur became, not an actor but a soldier, joining a unit called the Diamond Fields Horse. He was soon in action against one of the black nations resisting British rule (not the Zulus, whom he had not yet encountered and whom he thought would be a tougher proposition). On 14 May 1878 he sent a Hentyesque account of the fighting, saying how the soldiers had dismounted at 500 yards from the enemy and commenced firing, doing a fair amount of execution at that range. Arthur's basic form had not changed; in this letter he asked if the family could collect together 20 pounds so that he could purchase a commission.[7] Tom, who retained some of his early radicalism, commented: 'The brutal murderous state of mind which can think over with satisfaction and relate with complacency the "execution" which his corps performed on a mob of wretched half-armed Kaffirs, is shocking enough; but such a temper is hardly, for most men, separable from military life, therefore one must not make too much of it.'[8] But the half-armed Kaffirs had the last word: a few weeks later Arthur was killed in action. The death of his son seems to have affected Tom with conventional grief rather than deep sorrow. He acknowledged that Mary was the only one of his offspring with whom he had a close rapport; the younger children he regarded dutifully but with a degree of detachment. There could have been a guilty thought that Arthur's death had resolved a potentially life-long problem.

The sad story of Arthur is like a sub-plot in a Victorian novel. His death closed a chapter in the Arnolds' long engagement with the imperial programme. Dr Arnold was deeply interested in the Australasian colonies and sometimes expressed a wish to end his days in one of them. His pupil J. P. Gell went to work in Van Diemen's Land and wrote to him about it encouragingly, and Arnold bought the land in New Zealand which Tom endeavoured to farm. Rugby School was regarded as providing a perfect preparation for young men who wanted to help run the Empire. At the end of *Tom Brown's Schooldays*, Tom's chum Harry East has gone out to India as an officer. The civilizing influence of Mrs Arnold in her drawing room is fondly recalled: 'Aye, many is the brave heart now doing its work and bearing its load in country curacies, London chambers, under the Indian sun, and in Australian towns and clearings, which looks back with fond and grateful memory to that School-house drawing-room, and dates much of its highest and best training to the lessons learnt there.'[9] At the end of Hughes's novel Dr Arnold is perceived as an emperor, wisely ruling the school: '"What a sight it is," broke in the master, "the Doctor as a ruler. Perhaps ours is the only little corner of the British Empire which is thoroughly wisely and strongly ruled just now. I'm more and

more thankful every day of my life that I came here to be under him".'[10]
East's mission in India recalls that of William Delafield Arnold, who went
there in 1848, fought in the Sikh war and left a disenchanted account of
his experiences in *Oakfield*. In *Tom Brown at Oxford* East returns from
India, having fought in a war rather like Oakfield's; he has been badly
wounded but recovers at home and then goes out to New Zealand as a
settler. East recapitulates the experiences of two of Dr Arnold's sons,
William and Tom, in respectively torrid and temperate portions of the
red-painted map. As Kenneth Allott pointed out, *Oakfield* follows the two
Tom Brown novels in a sequence following the fortunes of the Arnoldian
hero. Arthur's death represented the violent intrusion of real imperial
history into this mythic pattern-making.

Meanwhile, there had been new trouble at home. Julia discovered a
lump in her breast, and was told in homely terms by a consultant in
London that if she were his mother he would have no rest until it was removed, but at the same time he would want a second opinion. Julia was
told by someone else that if the tumour were cancerous—as it was found
to be—then an operation might not cure the disease but would give her a
longer lease of life. This, essentially, proved to be the case. Julia was oper-
ated on in November 1877 and survived the primitive anaesthesia and
surgery of the time. She initially recuperated at 47 Prince's Gardens, the
house of her sister Gussie and her husband James Dunn, who had moved
to England; Tom was in Oxford looking after the younger children. At
the end of November Julia was back there, staying first with Mary in
Bradmore Road, and then at Church Walk. Tom had returned to London,
though on 20 December he wrote that he hoped to go to Oxford for
Christmas Day. This box-and-cox arrangement was to be a feature of
their lives at this period.

In London, Tom was now living in South Street, Thurloe Square, and
trying to earn enough to support himself and Julia and the Oxford household; there were also the expenses of his son Frank, who was training to
be a doctor. Julia took in girl boarders, of whom there were an increasing
number as Oxford reluctantly adapted itself to the higher education of
women, Somerville and Lady Margaret Hall having opened in 1879.
Matthew, though fond of Julia, joked about these boarders in a letter to
Tom: 'My love to Julia; I am glad to hear she keeps tolerably well and
has plenty of novices. I use that word because of her strong R.C. sympathies.'[11] Despite the boarders, Julia always regarded Tom as the
principal earner, and her letters contained frequent demands for more

money. Janet Trevelyan wrote of this period, 'Tom earned what he could by incessant writing', but this appears to be incorrect.[12] In fact, Tom published very little journalism during his years in London, compared with his regular contributions to Acton's magazines in the previous decade. His principal source of income was as an examiner for the Civil Service Commission, work provided by the good offices of Theodore Walrond, the fourth member of the Clougho-Matthean circle, who was now head of the commission. The payment seems to have been adequate, but the arrival of fresh examination scripts was unpredictable, and the commission would not pay in advance, as Tom found out from Walrond at a point when he was particularly hard up. The work, when it did arrive, was tedious, hard on the eyes, and cumulatively tiring. Nevertheless, Tom was dependent on it since, as he acknowledged, he could not make much money from 'literary work'.[13] He was also well aware, as Matthew unhelpfully reminded him, that Walrond might not always be there to send work his way. As is often the case in freelance activity, there was a dependence on *ad hominem* support.

One of the rare bright spots in his life came in 1878 when he received a letter from the government official known as the Master of the Rolls, which told him, 'I have read your very interesting letter with much attention. I agree to your proposition to edit a new edition of Henry of Huntingdon's Historia Anglorum, and I shall have much pleasure in recommending it to the Treasury for publication among the Chronicles and Memorials of Great Britain.'[14] This series had been launched in 1857, under the full title of 'The Chronicles and Memorials of Great Britain and Ireland during the Middle Ages', and provided an interesting example of scholarship employed in the process of deepening a historical sense of national identity. Tom's editions of Wycliffe and *Beowulf* proved his competence for the task. And it would have paid something; as Tom put it to Julia, 'This is good news, is it not?' It was, and there was not a lot of it about. Writing to Julia in February, Tom remarked that the Rector of Lincoln seemed to have been setting her against him again; he reminded Tom of Mephistopheles. It was certainly possible; Pattison was a malicious man, who would have disapproved of Tom's return to Rome just as much as orthodox Anglican Oxford. (And he had lost interest in Mary once she had married.) But Julia was quite capable of turning against Tom without outside influence, and then of turning back towards him with cries of self-reproach.

In the summer of 1878 she and the younger children spent a long holiday in the Isle of Wight, the territory of Dr Arnold's childhood; Tom joined them in August after spending time in Cambridge looking at manuscripts. Then he visited Paris to consult a manuscript of the *Historia Anglorum* in the Bibliothèque Nationale, which occasioned a sardonic comment from Matthew about him 'wallowing' there while Julia was sick.[15] In October Tom was in Oxford while Julia was in London at the Dunns'; she was there again in January 1879.

When he was in Oxford, Tom attended Mass at the new yellow-brick Jesuit church of St Aloysius on the Woodstock Road, which had replaced the little chapel at St Clement's as the Catholic place of worship. In January 1879 he wrote to Newman from Church Walk, thanking him for saying a Mass for Arthur, and referring to the Oxford parish priest, Fr Parkinson SJ, as 'a treasure; I feel sure that the more you saw of him the better you would like him'.[16] He does not say if he had also come across Fr Parkinson's curate at that time, Fr Gerard Hopkins SJ. In the 1860s he might have passed Hopkins as an undergraduate in the quads of Balliol when he visited Jowett; their paths finally converged in Dublin in the 1880s. Tom was sufficiently often in Oxford to have made a lasting impression on a little girl who lived nearby and whose mother was a friend of the family. He had asked this lady, Mrs Hatch, if he could do any errands for her when he was in London. She told him that she had been unsuccessfully trying to buy a pink silk sash in Oxford for her daughter, and he said he would do what he could. The little girl, Ethel, recalled, 'The following week Mr Thomas Arnold . . . tall and grave, with auburn hair turning grey, came to call, carrying a little parcel. He handed it rather shyly to my mother . . . and she found the parcel to contain a sash of a beautiful quality of soft silk . . . He had certainly shown good taste in his selection, but it was difficult to imagine this quiet elderly man in a fashionable London shop, looking at sashes for a little girl . . .'.[17] Tom was always a gentleman, whatever his domestic difficulties.

He wrote to Newman again in October 1879 with a proposal for a 'Catholic Dictionary' he was thinking of compiling; he wrote from London, from 18 Fulham Road, and concluded his letter, 'I am living here because I find living at home impossible.'[18] Number 3 Church Walk was still 'home' even if he could not live there. A letter to Julia in December shows something of Tom's state of mind and of the difficulties in their marriage:

You have spoken of my having been 'disappointed' in you after our marriage, and of the resentment which you felt in consequence. But my own one, supposing I was 'disappointed', it does not follow that there was anything amiss in you; the fault may have been in my own unfounded expectations. That this was so to a great extent, reflexion in later years has shown me. And then as to the 'disappointment'—how far did it extend? I was disappointed in the character of your mind; I had hoped it would be more pliable, plastic and impressionable than it was,—in short more ready to interest itself in those speculations which at that time had an absorbing interest for me. But I was not disappointed in you; you were then and always, in spite of jars and irritations, the delight of my soul, the glory of my life; existence shone for me because it was blest by you, and to this hour Tasmania with its forests and mountains and sparkling sea is as a vision of golden brightness in my memory, because the thought of it is stamped everywhere with your lovely image. How often, looking from many miles away, at the mountain towering above the intervening hills, did I say to myself with fond yearnings, 'There at the foot of that mountain is my Julia, my brilliant beautiful Julia, my wife, my own; there are our dear babes'.

As to my disappointment, it really counts for very little. Had you been as pliable and as plastic as I hoped, you would not have been what God and nature made you. You would not have been the sweet, wilful passionate, original, ambitious Julia whom I married, but something much more tractable, which might have had charms of its own, but not your charms.[19]

Tom's words were hardly likely to make Julia feel better; the combination of dispassionate analysis and sentimental recollection was rather characteristic of him. To have it confirmed that one disappoints one's husband is not reassuring, even if he says that the fault is his (though Julia had her own reasons for being disappointed in Tom).

There was more to Tom than apparent emotional crassness, for he was caught within conflicting ideas about marriage. An older model presented it in terms of duties and responsibilities, where roles are formal, traditional, and authoritative. The later understanding of marriage, now dominant in Western culture, regards it as involving equal persons who negotiate about their various needs and responsibilities. For some of the time Tom attempted to act in the older way. In March 1877 Julia had thoughts of going to live in Cheltenham; Tom told her he did not like the idea and saw no necessity for it, though he added that if it were necessary for her happiness he would not oppose it. But he continued, in a reminder that the older mode was usually tied up with economic necessity, 'After all it is but natural and fitting that the husband not the wife should fix where the home is to be, because it must in most ordinary cases depend on where he can get work.' No more was heard about Cheltenham, but in December of that year, after her operation, Julia was thinking about going to live abroad for a time. Tom's response was reluctantly accepting:

If when it came to the point you really wished to leave England and live abroad for a time, perhaps it might be feasible. As to my 'getting on very well' without you, there is no use in saying that; you know that I am as fond of a settled home and having my children about me, as most men are; but if I thought the change would really be good for you, I could reconcile myself to it . . .[20]

The elder Thomas Arnold was devoted to his wife but it is impossible to imagine him writing in those terms; for him the world ran on duty, not personal inclination. That Tom was disappointed that Julia did not share all his interests indicates the later understanding of marriage; in the older model, a husband would not have expected his wife to. The traditional Victorian paterfamilias would have cut the errant Arthur off with the traditional shilling, because it was the right thing to do, whatever his own feelings about his son. Tom fulminated over Arthur's wrongdoings, but still went to great efforts to try to find work for him, and supplied him with money which he could ill afford.

At times Tom reverted to traditional ideas, as when he told Mary before her marriage that she must now postpone thoughts of 'literature', advice she had no intention of following. Several years later Tom told Julia that the adolescent Judy (the younger Julia) should help her mother in the house, as this was her highest duty, overriding all other concerns. Judy, another intellectual girl, was not inclined that way; she was one of the earliest students at Somerville, took a First, and went on to marry Thomas Huxley's son; their children included Julian and Aldous. Later Julia Huxley set up her own very successful school.

The letters in the Balliol archive that Tom wrote to his wife during the periods of separation (many more than are included in Bertram's edition), and hers to him, have a peculiar and sometimes distressing interest. Much space is given to discussing the state of the weather, as an index, in the mode of the pathetic fallacy, of their respective states of feeling. There is the passing on of amiable gossip: from Julia about events in Oxford; from Tom about people and things in London. They share an interest in the political scene. But these are merely foothills around the looming intensities of the correspondence. Husbands and wives are likely to say harsh and unkind things to each in marital rows; Tom and Julia put them on paper, which made them harder to forget. And yet they remained in love. They were both given to self-pity, and to accompanying expressions of emotion, operatic on her part, sentimental on his. If Tom was disappointed in Julia, she was in him. Dr Arnold's son, the bearer of a distinguished name, had not given the wild colonial girl the entry to the English clerical-professional world that she admired and aspired to; at Oxford she had been, at best, on the fringes of it. The family was always short of money, and now Tom had, for the second time, attached himself to a religion that she detested. But if Julia was ready to blame Tom, she was even more ready to blame herself. She struck dramatic postures of self-reproach and self-abjection. Some years before, when she was staying at Fox How and was unwell and depressed, she had told Tom, 'The feeling grows upon me that I am one of those unhappy people whom *God has abandoned*, and it is the effect of this feeling I am sure which causes me to behave as I often do. Oh! it is an awful thing to *despair* about one's future state.'[21] This sounds like an echo of the ancestral Calvinism that Mary Ward traced in her mother's attitudes, but it is more likely that Julia was using the stern theological doctrine of Reprobation to dramatize her state of mind. Certainly Julia was, as Janet Trevelyan wrote, 'depressed', but such quasi-clinical terminology, like the easy application of 'neurotic', raises more questions than it answers. In everyday terms she had, as Janet puts it (no doubt drawing on her mother Mary's accounts), an 'undisciplined and tempestuous nature, with its strange deeps of feeling ... passionate outbursts of temper'. And she was capable of being, in Mary's words during the crisis of October 1876, 'really not in her right mind'. There was also the question of Julia's health. After the first operation for cancer, there was another early in 1881; it checked the course of the disease for a time, but the wound would not heal and Julia lived in considerable discomfort. Homeopathy helped for a time, or she and Tom thought it did. Her condition, and the perpetual shortage of money, which Mary, living nearby, often had to relieve, sometimes deflecting bailiffs from the house, made Tom feel guilty and ineffectual. Julia said that she missed Tom, but that when he was with her she made him and herself miserable. She took to signing her letters as his loving but sorrowful (or heartbroken) wife. Elements of traditional wifely behaviour remained. She baked and sent him cakes—which he greatly appreciated—and reminded him to put warm clothes on in winter.

Tom affirmed that since they met he had never thought about any other woman. If he entertained more than friendly feelings about Josephine he was suppressing or denying them. He was prepared to admit that Julia should have married someone else, who was better able to fulfil her aspirations. Early in 1880 the question of Tom returning to the Oxford home was raised again. On 23 January Mary wrote to her mother:

For you and Papa to see much of each other just now, seems to me to be running a dangerous risk on your part. Whatever mental worry you may have when he is away, you have double as much when he is at home, mainly from the mere fact that he is there, and that his presence is constantly exciting you to think about topics which if he were not there you might forget, or at any rate not take to heart in such a wearing and painful way. Papa knows that I think this, and I think it more than ever after this last vacation. My earnest wish is that Papa should come down for a short time say a day or two days at fairly short intervals, but that he should not stay in the house for at any rate three or four months to come, that Mr Bamber's treatment may have a really fair trial. I know you find it hard to make up your mind on this, but I am sure dearest that for some little time to come at any rate it is the right course, as much the right course as avoiding any other risk would be. *Short* visits I think would very likely be only good for you, as there would be no *daily rub* to fear . . .[22]

Mary's advice was sensible in the circumstances. In March Julia wrote to Tom telling him of her fresh fears for her health, and repeating what she had told someone else, that although her death would be a shock to him at first he would soon feel it to be a great relief. Tom for his part wrote that he had lived too long to enjoy life and would gladly give his health for her disease. In April he was writing to Julia about the possibility of coming home, though without saying for how long. He sets out some extraordinary conditions: that she should not make things unpleasant for his Catholic acquaintances; that she would not worry herself about the places he thought fit to go to; and that in no circumstance would she destroy any of his books or papers.[23] If they are to be taken at face value, then Julia seems to have been subjecting Tom to anti-Catholic persecution on his last visit; if they are not, his imagination must have been running wild. Julia's reply has not survived, but he shortly complained of what he called an acrid, not to say rancorous, composition he has received from her. A day or so later he wrote again, expressing sorrow for his harsh words, and concern about her state of health.

If Tom did return home, it was only for a brief period. In May Mary wrote to him again, saying that he was 'rather too hard on Mamma about money matters', given the recent fears that her illness was entering a new and worse phase. In the situation, Mary wrote, it was not very wonderful if 18 pounds remained unaccounted for. Her father was no doubt chastened, but bills still had to be paid, and money earned. On 13 June, the thirtieth anniversary of their marriage, Tom sent Julia an affectionate but complacent letter, hoping for a new start in their relations: 'You have fared badly, my Julia, but you might have fared worse; your husband thirty years after marriage might have easily come to hate you, or you him. God knows the first of these is not true, but the very opposite; and I hope the second is not true either. Why should there not be a new departure again?'[24] The following day he wrote again, in a different tone. He had previously written to Julia, telling her that he was considering a return to Dublin. Her reply evidently told him that in no circumstance would she accompany him there. He responded bitterly that she was subject to 'the corrupting breath of the modern world' in her idea of marriage, as she consulted her own comfort and convenience in determining to stay in England.

The correspondence continued until Julia's death several years later; the rapid exchange of letters reflecting equally rapid shifts of mood. What they reveal of the marriage of Tom and Julia shows a sensibility that was moving away from the fixed positions and roles of earlier periods and into the sexual politics enacted in late Victorian fiction and drama. Julia might well have been happy to accept the Pauline injunction that wives should be subject to their husbands, but would have expected Tom to keep his part of the implicit bargain by earning enough to keep his wife and family in the style to which she was accustomed. For her, all might have been different if Tom had remained an Anglican and become an Oxford professor. Not that it would have been plain sailing; Julia would have still delivered passionate outbursts, and Tom would have retreated from difficulty when he could, ideally into a library, if not, into his own thoughts, behind what his brother described as his manner of 'singular placidity'.

By 1879 he found his position was becoming intolerable. His work as an examiner was tedious and uncertain, and hard on the eyes. He felt he was getting too old for it; apart from his own physical and mental resilience, there were always younger men looking for such work. For the third time in his life, he was self-employed and dependent on the vagaries of others for his income, and he did not enjoy it. There had been his short period as a schoolteacher in New Zealand in 1849, and his several years as a freelance tutor in Oxford. Now he was reduced to waiting for the next batch of examination scripts to arrive from the Civil Service Commission. And the continual demands from Julia, backed up by Mary, for more money, meant there was no hope of stepping off the treadmill, unless he could find regular employment with a salary or stipend. In May 1879

Matthew made one of his regular well-meaning but ineffectual attempts at networking on his brother's behalf. He heard that there might be a post coming up at the Bodleian as a sub-librarian, and that the librarian, Henry Coxe, had written to Arthur Stanley in terms which suggested that Tom might have a chance of getting it.[25] Tom by now had learned to ignore his brother's well-meaning suggestions, which, like this one, came to nothing. His thoughts returned to Dublin; he had not been well off when he was there, but he was better off than he was now, with the benefits of regular employment. He began to wonder if there was any prospect of him going back there. Julia told him she would rejoice if he found congenial work in Ireland and that he would be happier there than in England. For her part, she said she would find it easier to have his visits home, which made her feel they were together yet far apart, confined to his vacations.[26]

There may have been external reasons why Tom was thinking about a return to Ireland in 1879. The establishment on St Stephen's Green had been renamed University College Dublin, but the change of name did nothing to affect the institution's deplorable decline. In the words of the historian of its later fortunes:

The Catholic University . . . had a name for failure and inanition. Most of its score or less students were supported by episcopal bursaries, which were to be discontinued in 1880. The only efficient professors, Dr Casey, the mathematician, and Dr Molloy, professor of natural science, devoted their time, respectively, to grinding pupils for London University and other external examinations, and to adult education lectures. Most of the members of staff did not attend or else appeared daily, rang a bell, read their newspapers, and then went home having fulfilled all justice.[27]

The Irish bishops found the Catholic University a great burden; it was supported by the contributions of the faithful, who got no benefit from it, and the bishops, priests, and laity would have been glad to get rid of the place if they knew how.

Its scandalous condition was the result of a long stand-off between the Irish bishops and the British government over higher education. The bishops demanded that the Catholic University should be publicly endowed like the Queen's Colleges, and the distinguished Catholic universities of the Continent, so that it would have a Catholic character just as Oxford and Cambridge had an Anglican character. Indeed, Queen's College, Belfast, was in the process of becoming a separate university with a Presbyterian flavour. The Catholic demand was clearly just, but it was politically inexpedient, given the fanatical anti-Catholicism of much British Protestant opinion. Matthew Arnold published an eloquent and incisive essay, 'Irish Catholicism and British Liberalism', which argued for the Catholic position.[28] Fundamental justice was the primary consideration, and he cited various Continental precedents; but he also believed that the rigid, philistine, and narrow-minded Catholicism of the Irish would be transformed for the better if the Catholic community possessed a properly functioning university which reflected their best traditions and values. This was Newman's ideal, which had foundered between the interests of the Irish bishops and the British state. The Liberal governments that had been in office for a long period were dependent on the strongly anti-Catholic Nonconformist vote. So they left the Catholic University to decline.

In 1874 the Conservatives under Disraeli came into office. They did not have the Nonconformists on their back and they made efforts to resolve the problem of Irish higher education. They were too cautious to do anything directly about the Catholic University, but they introduced structural reforms that would help it indirectly, by providing staff and validated degrees. A body was set up called the Royal University of Ireland, an instance of what Matthew had called, in 'The Function of Criticism at the Present Time', 'the grand name without the grand thing'. Its functions were limited to bestowing degrees and supporting a number of endowed fellows who would provide professors and examiners for the constituent colleges, including both the Queen's Colleges and University College Dublin. By providing, at one remove, a measure of public support to the latter, it attempted to meet Catholic grievances without provoking anti-Catholic opinion at home. The Irish bishops were not enthusiastic about the scheme, but they were prepared to go along with it, and the Royal University was set up in 1879. Tom perhaps felt that it would provide opportunities for him in the future.

In April 1880 Tom wrote to Matthew with an unidentified proposal that astonished his brother: 'You, or I either, might just as well ask Gladstone to make us Chancellor of the Exchequer as to make us Commissioner of Inland Revenue, and I should like to see Coleridge's face when asked to purpose such a thing to him. Who on earth can have put such an idea into your head?'[29] Matthew went on to what he called 'something practical', asking Tom if he would be interested in editing a volume of selections from Burke (which Matthew went on to edit himself). The Liberals were back in government, but the Royal University of Ireland was now launched. In 1880 its senate was appointed; one of the members was Newman's old friend, William Monsell, an Irishman of the Ascendancy but a convert to Catholicism, a Wykhamist, and a Liberal politician who had been ennobled as Lord Emly.

In 1879 Newman had been made a cardinal by the new Pope, Leo XIII, a move which caused pleasure and satisfaction far beyond the Catholic community. Tom Arnold was one of the many people who sent him a letter of congratulation. In his reply Newman, who had been in Rome, remarked, 'It is a strange phenomenon which we heard at the Vatican, that the Pope had been deluged with letters from England by Protestants, stating their satisfaction at his having promoted me.'[30] Newman continued to be concerned at Tom's difficulties, and though he had been disappointed at his performance as a schoolmaster, he believed that there should be a place in academic life for someone of his abilities. Tom himself was interested in the emergence of the Royal University. Writing to Julia in June he told her of his desire for a post in Dublin, even if it paid only two or three hundred pounds a year; he supposed, though, that this was mere castle-building on his part. Her reply, as we have seen, angered Tom by making it plain that if he went to Dublin she would certainly not accompany him. On 12 June, probably following a letter from Tom, Newman wrote to Emly, asking about the new university: 'I am much interested for Thos. Arnold; I won't say more till I know how matters stand and because I think you know him, and because I want your advice how to proceed. His own subject is Anglosaxon and early English literature or history—he does not aspire to a Professorship, but he would make an excellent Reader or Tutor in classics and general knowledge.'[31] Arnold's capabilities and interests were much wider than Newman implied; one gets a depressing sense of him selling himself short, as when he tells Julia that he would be willing to take regular employment for obviously inadequate pay. There is no reason why Arnold should not have aspired to a professorial chair, since he already served as a professor in Dublin, and was now far better qualified, with his *Manual of English Literature*, and his editions of Wycliffe and *Beowulf*. Emly set to work, and in the end achieved more than Arnold had hoped for, but it took time.

Tom made occasional trips to Ireland to visit the Benisons at Slieve Russell. On 19 December 1881 he sent Josephine a 'thank-you' letter, saying how much he had enjoyed his visit. It was written on notepaper headed 'Chief Secretary's Lodge, Phoenix Park, Dublin'. It was the official residence of his brother-in-law William Forster, who held this post in Gladstone's government. Tom refers to a conversation he had had with Dr Molloy, one of the more energetic professors at University College: 'I learnt much from him as to the future which its wellwishers now aim at for the Catholic University, but on this I will write on some other occasion, for my time is now very limited.'[32] In April 1882 the Senate of the new Royal University met to appoint the first batch of fellows; the Catholic bishops were still unhappy about the arrangement and wanted two-thirds of the fellowships to go to Catholics, to reflect the religious balance of the population, without special treatment for the Queen's Colleges. They were unsuccessful in this, and the final division was half Catholic, half Protestant. Tom was appointed a fellow in English, and on 19 April Matthew wrote from the Athenaeum to congratulate him:

I am indeed delighted. From what Lord Emly had told me, I felt pretty sure you were all right; still there is always uncertainty about these things, and I had a horrid moment when I took up the Times and did not find your name among the Classical Fellows; however, I soon came upon it among the English ones. As a question of division of spoil, I don't think the Queen's College professors had any claim at all, since they keep their own grant; but if the new University could not have been so well manned if only Catholics had been taken, it was right to take the Queen's College professors. It is your first really solid post, I consider, since you gave up your post in Van Diemen's Land.[33]

He adds that he had spoken to John Dasent, assistant secretary to the Board of Education, who had assured him that Tom's appointment need not interfere with his work as an examiner. Matthew's belief that Tom's position with the new and untried institution was more solid than his previous jobs in Dublin and Birmingham assumed rather a lot; but in retrospect it appears justified, since Tom remained a fellow of the Royal University for the rest of his life.

To start with, he had no more than a title and a stipend. Fellows had to be given teaching posts in the various colleges of the Royal University, or to have their existing positions confirmed. In several cases the Senate continued the status quo, avoiding the risks of wielding a new broom. A number of the original professors from Newman's time became fellows, notwithstanding their advanced years and tendencies to idleness or absenteeism. It was assumed that Arnold would be taken on by the college, in effect resuming his old job as professor of English, but the run-down state of the institution was an obstacle. The Irish bishops were anxious to get rid of it and were looking for a new manager, preferably a religious order.

In June 1882 Tom Arnold went to Dublin to attend a meeting of the newly appointed fellows of the Royal University. It was not a particularly happy time to be an Englishman in Dublin. Ireland was in a state of unrest because of struggles over Home Rule and the bitter and sometimes violent opposition between tenants and landlords. The violence came close to the Arnolds. William Forster had wanted to impose a more repressive policy than Gladstone and his colleagues would accept, and on 2 May he resigned because of these disagreements. Four days later his successor, Lord Frederick Cavendish, and the permanent secretary, Thomas Burke, were stabbed to death in Phoenix Park by members of a terrorist group called the Invincibles. Forster had been their target: they did not know he had resigned and been replaced. On 7 May Mary wrote to her father expressing horror at her uncle's narrow escape. One result of the murders was that the government imposed the repressive measures which Forster had wanted.

CHAPTER 9

Dublin Again

Dublin, when Tom Arnold returned there, was sinking further into the decline that had been evident in the 1850s. In the words of a modern historian, 'The 1880s were a particularly depressed decade. Unemployment and under-employment were rife. There were numerous appeals to charities, and demonstrations of men seeking work were common. By 1891 the population of Dublin was lower than it had been in 1851. The falling population and decaying properties reflected an impoverished city.'[1] It was also an unhealthy city, with bad drains and high mortality; in 1879 the death-rate in Dublin reached record levels.[2] The poor were most affected but the middle classes were certainly not untouched; the low-lying St Stephen's Green had a particularly bad reputation, and the typhoid which killed Gerard Hopkins in 1889 was endemic. The percentage of Protestants and Unionists was dropping but they were still dominant in the professions. The city administration, though, was now in the hands of aggressive Nationalists. Deep divisions in the society were made worse by the Phoenix Park murders.

Tom Arnold started teaching again in University College, hoping for an improvement in the regime. He would have found the decaying state of the city echoed in the academic buildings. When Hopkins joined the college in 1884 he told Newman, 'These buildings since you knew them have fallen into a deep dilapidation. They were a sort of wreck or ruin when our Fathers some months since came in and the costly last century ornamentation of flutes and festoons and Muses on the walls is still much in contrast with the dinginess and dismantlement all round.'[3] In his reply, Newman sadly remarked, 'I am sorry you can speak of dilapidation.' It was not just the buildings that were decaying; there must have been an element of *temps retrouvé* in Arnold's encounter with his old colleagues. According to Fr Darlingon SJ, Robert Ornsby had to be carried into his classes and propped up in a chair, while James Stewart was averse to doing any work at all; he taught nothing in the first year after the Jesuits took over and very little in the second. Not surprisingly, the students objected.[4]

On 3 September 1882 Tom wrote to Julia from Dublin saying that having come to understand the state of things in the college, he would decline to do any more teaching until the place was reorganized and put on an efficient footing, which he thought would take some time. He would be returning to England in October. (On a personal note, the letter contains one of his *cris de coeur*, begging Julia not to set her heart against him.)[5] It is not clear if by 'any more teaching' he is looking back to his time there in the 1850s, or if he has recently done some teaching in the college, even though it was the vacation. Either way, he changed his mind, or had it changed for him, and he stayed in Dublin. On 25 November Mary wrote to him, expressing the hope that he did not dislike his work in Stephen's Green, and asking if he was teaching a class in literature, and if so, of what period.[6] Early in 1883 Tom enjoyed dining with Edward Dowden, professor of English at Trinity, a critic and biographer, author of *Shakspere, His Mind and Art*. It was one of his rare contacts with the social world of Ascendancy Dublin.

Meanwhile, Cardinal McCabe, Archbishop of Dublin, was looking round for someone to take over the college. The Jesuits were certainly interested; indeed, despairing of Newman's old foundation, they had attempted to launch a university college of their own, to be staffed by academically qualified Jesuits from all over Europe. That scheme had not taken off, but its prime mover, Fr William Delany SJ, set his sights on the establishment in Stephen's Green once the Royal University was in existence, which assured it of endowed professors and validated degrees. He was an energetic and far-sighted man who had been a successful headmaster; the Society of Jesus could make out a good case for running the College; the Jesuits' Catholic fervour was manifest, and so was their commitment to high intellectual achievement; and they had long experience of directing educational institutions. Fr Delany, like Newman thirty years earlier, wanted a first-class university, and was prepared to appoint the best people to teach in it, even Englishmen. This was not a popular policy in Dublin in the 1880s. Delany encountered opposition, not only from the bishops but from his fellow Irish Jesuits, who were suspicious of English importations. But he was a skilful manipulator, with contacts in Rome; he went over the head of the Irish Provincial to the General of the Jesuits and had his policy upheld. Fr Delany comes across as the archetypal Jesuit, with useful friends everywhere, including some in the upper reaches of the British political and social establishment.

The bishops wanted the college off their hands, but they did not altogether trust Fr Delany and the Jesuits. Tom Arnold was not informed of the way the discussions were going, and on 4 October 1883 he wrote to his sister Frances:

The future of this place, the Cath. University College, is uncertain. Cardinal McCabe is said to intend handing it back again to the Bishops, finding he can make nothing of it. The poor C.U. is being walked about from one master to the other like a White elephant, or like the 'tall horse' of the Pickwickians, which they could not let go, but would have given anything to be quit of. I have ceased to hope for anything good, because the Principal of the College, though a good and kindly man, is quite unfit for the post. With his ponderous and sluggish personality he is crushing it out of existence. The Cardinal knows nothing about universities, and is a man of small mental power; were it otherwise he would at once appoint a head of a different stamp; and then, if he would, or could, spend money on the place it might soon prosper; for there is really a great opening.[7]

But even as Tom wrote, tough negotiations were drawing to a conclusion; on 26 October 1883, Fr Delany, on behalf of the Society of Jesus, signed an agreement with the episcopal trustees of the Catholic University. It had been a narrow victory for the society; some of the bishops had wanted the college to be run by the Holy Ghost Fathers of Blackrock. In November the Jesuits took over the college, with Fr Delany as president; he was the 'head of a different stamp' whom Arnold had hoped for and whom he came to admire immensely. For Delany, the professorial fellowships from the Royal University, then worth 400 pounds a year, were the heart of the matter; in T. J. Morrissey's words, 'The fastening of the fellowships to the college in St Stephen's Green was to be the decisive factor in the Jesuits agreeing to run it . . .'[8]

Delany's aim was to replace the lay professors, once they had left the scene, with Jesuits. He was prepared to wait, since the professorial fellowships appear to have been for life, without provision for retirement. Delany's long-term plan made practical sense, since the number of academically qualified Catholic laymen in Ireland was small, and it was becoming politically difficult to import English converts. But the principal consideration was financial; the Jesuit fathers surrendered their stipends to the order, thus providing the college with financial resources, first to pull it out of its decayed state and then, as Delany wanted, to establish it as a first-class place of learning. In order to do this it was essential for all the Catholic fellowships provided by the Royal University to be concentrated at St Stephen's Green. Delany was opposed by some at least of the bishops, who wanted the fellowships to be distributed among the other establishments loosely associated with the college. Delany got his way, but there was harsh episcopal revenge; just before the Jesuits took over, the entire library, apart from medical volumes, was removed to the archdiocesan college. The books were never returned, despite many requests; a library in exchange for fellowships seems to have been the bishops' idea of a deal. Delany set himself to collecting replacement volumes, and the college made an arrangement with the National Library to borrow books, but it was a disabling start.

Delany's policy of appointing Jesuits to professorial posts was launched when he proposed Fr Robert Curtis, an Irish mathematician, for a fellowship in Natural Philosophy, and Fr Gerard Hopkins for a fellowship in Classics. He had first heard about Hopkins when he was making enquiries among the English Jesuits on behalf of the proposed Jesuit University College; he had received mixed reports. Fr Hopkins was said to be a brilliant man and a fine Classical scholar, but he was eccentric and liable to be a square peg in a round hole. Nevertheless, Delany decided to appoint him after receiving particularly warm reports from Hopkins's tutors at Balliol, Jowett and R. L. Nettleship. There was no problem about Fr Curtis, but Hopkins, as an English convert and an Oxonian, provoked all the old objections. Dr William Walsh, the president of St Patrick's College, Maynooth, proposed instead one of the Holy Ghost Fathers from Blackrock; Fr Delany regarded this man as deficient in Classical learning—there was also the financial consideration that he was not a Jesuit—and insisted on Hopkins. The episcopal committee were against appointing him; the archbishop, Cardinal McCabe, vacillated and then very late in the day agreed with the committee. Fr Delany somehow got round the adverse decision, in a stroke of 'jesuitical' manœuvering (the details are recorded in the biographies of Hopkins by Norman White and Robert Bernard Martin), and the election went forward to the Senate of the Royal University. There Hopkins was supported by the 'Catholic Whigs', Lord O'Hagan and Lord Emly, and despite the expressed opposition of the episcopal senators, Dr Walsh and Cardinal McCabe, he was elected by a majority of 21 to 3. As Hopkins put it, 'there was an Irish row at my election'.

Dr Walsh took defeat very badly, and though he and Delany had formerly been friends they became alienated. Walsh's opposition to the college caused problems after he was appointed Archbishop of Dublin, following McCabe's death in 1885. Tom Arnold, as a survivor of Newman's original establishment, took it upon himself to raise the question of the sequestered library with Dr Walsh. 'The archbishop informed him that, the practical difficulty about restoring the library was that University College had, from the beginning, established a tendency to identify itself with the Catholic University and to virtually ignore the other colleges.'[9] (That is to say, the lesser Catholic colleges.)

Arnold's dealings with Hopkins were, on the face of it, collegial rather than close. Hopkins seems to have shared the opinion of the other Jesuits that Arnold, like the other survivals from Newman's day, was a venerable relic, though he had a lot more life in him than Ornsby and Stewart. Hopkins was the fourth considerable poet he had known, after Wordsworth, Matthew, and Clough, but he probably did not know about his colleague's poetry. The only people with whom Hopkins was prepared to share his secret and show his work were other poets: Robert Bridges, Coventry Patmore, and Richard Watson Dixon. Hopkins and Arnold evidently had literary discussions, and Hopkins lent him a copy of Bridges's *Prometheus the Firegiver*. Arnold was responsible for one of the few elements of the Hopkins canon to appear in his lifetime, and for his only published piece of literary criticism. Arnold's *Manual of English Literature* had been regularly reprinted since the first edition of 1862; it was the work which kept his name before the wider public. In 1884 he was preparing a new edition, the fifth, and decided it was time to revise and update the book. Arnold commissioned his son William to write an entry on Blake; keeping matters within the family, he also acknowledged the help of his daughters Julia and Ethel, but their contributions are unidentified.

Hopkins had probably told Arnold about his friend Dixon (their friendship was almost entirely epistolary) and his poetry; Arnold invited him to write a short entry on this minor contemporary poet for the new edition. Hopkins was happy to accept, though complaining, in the familiar manner of academics, that it had come 'at this most inopportune time'.[10] He wrote the entry, though regretting that a few cuts had to be made before it was published. It is a competent piece of writing, about 400 words long, outlining Dixon's career, listing his works, and engaging in a mainly appreciative discussion of the poetry. It duly appeared in the fifth edition of Arnold's *Manual*. (It is reprinted as Note K of Hopkins's letters to Dixon.) But it did not remain in that form for long. The copy of the fifth edition in the Bodleian was evidently Arnold's own, and contains his annotations and markings, and some intercalated items. Hopkins's piece on Dixon is a lot longer than the other entries in the section on lesser Victorians, and it has been crossed through and marked with a deletion sign. Despite the cuts he had asked for, it was evidently still longer than Arnold wanted; perhaps he was embarrassed because he had not properly briefed Hopkins about what was needed, or was reluctant to offend him by rejecting it. At all events, when the sixth edition appeared in 1888, Hopkins's entry had been brought in line with the others. It is cut down to a few lines of factual material, plus a sentence of appreciative comment on Dixon's poetry from the earlier entry. Hopkins would hardly have been pleased about this act of truncation, but perhaps he never knew about it.

The *Manual* was a popular work, steadily in demand, but the Rolls editions on which Arnold worked from 1878 were directed at an audience which may have been fit, in Milton's phrase, but was certainly very few in numbers. These books were Latin historical records from the Middle Ages, edited from the manuscripts in various libraries. If, in Pattison's scheme of things, the *Manual* represented the suspect ideal of 'teaching', the Rolls editions were works of scholarship at its purest and most disinterested, though arguably the purity was a little tarnished by the implicitly nationalistic intent of the series. The first title, the *Historia Anglorum*, by Henry, Archdeacon of Huntingdon, written *c.*1130, was published in 1879. Arnold then took on successively longer editions. The next of them, the *Opera Omnia* of the eleventh-century Northumbrian monk Symeon, came out in two volumes in 1882. At one point the Latin text is diversified by a poem in Anglo-Saxon. The final Rolls edition is *Memorials of St Edmund's Abbey*, published in three volumes between 1890 and 1896. Literary readers had been reminded of the abbey by Carlyle's account of it in *Past and Present*. Arnold refers to Carlyle in the introduction and says that though a lesser figure he offers his work in the same spirit. The memorials were indeed diverse; volume 2 contains a poem of 4,000 lines in Old French on the life of St Edmund. In his introduction to the first volume Arnold refers to the magnitude of the task: 'a work so arduous and encumbered with detail that I must confess it ought to have been undertaken by a man of fewer years and greater leisure than myself'. In the modern academy, probably a transatlantic one, the editor of such an enterprise would have several research asistants, or have been part of a team. Arnold was probably foolhardy to have taken on the Rolls project, but he was heroic to have completed it. However, it was an age of energetic single-minded and single-handed editors.

From 1880 onwards Arnold made occasional ventures into higher journalism, but in contrast to his widely ranging work for Acton's magazines in the 1860s, these essays were mostly on Catholic subjects and had an apologetic or propagandist intent. In 1880 he published in the *Contemporary Review* a lengthy demolition of a book by a Dr Littledale called *Plain Reasons Against Joining the Church of Rome*. Anti-Catholic polemic called forth an anti-Protestant counterblast. Arnold is particularly severe on Littledale because he is an Irish Protestant; he is prepared to respect Anglicans in England because they follow the religion of the majority of the people, but he has little time for Protestants in a Catholic nation like Ireland, finding their dominant position offensive and anomalous. Here, and in other writings of this period, Arnold adopts the offensive–defensive rhetoric which characterized the public discourse of English Catholicism at least until the Second Vatican Council (reinforced in the early twentieth century by the polemical Anglo-Frenchman Hilaire Belloc). Arnold resumed a connection with the *Dublin Review*, to which he had contributed an essay in the 1850s. It had been founded by Cardinal Wiseman and was still under clerical direction. In 1880 it published a note on Spenser by Arnold, questioning whether the poet was suitable for study in Catholic schools, given his anti-Catholic bias and his hostility to the Irish; he was also 'an author whose mind was so deeply tainted by licentiousness, and whose moral sense in some directions was so perverted'. Here Arnold's defence of Catholicism merges with what the present-day reader would regard as Victorian puritanism; but an energetic resistance to 'indecency' united Catholics and Protestants and unbelievers.

Arnold later published 'Church Extension and Anglican Expansion', which makes a stern defence of the Roman position against Anglican Latitudinarianism.[11] The charge of 'Latitudinarianism' was a sensitive one for Arnold, since it had been levelled at his father, though Dr Arnold denied it; Tom continued to revere his father, despite their differences in religious attitude. In this essay he makes a stern, Torquemada-like call for the severe, uncompromising assertion of doctrine, without too much tolerance. He also stresses the importance of miracles. Arnold gives the impression of writing from his head rather than his heart, which remained kind and indulgent. His tone may have been affected by his long difference of religion with Julia, whom he blamed for turning their children away from Catholicism; and, indeed, his differences with Mary, though their mutual affection remained strong. His emphasis on miracles reflects this possibility, since Mary looked, like her Uncle Matthew, for a religion which was theistic but not supernatural, focused on the human figure of

Christ. 'Miracles do not happen', Matthew had asserted. Another essay, on the Catholic University, fudges the early history of that institution; Arnold refers to Newman setting it up with the warm support of Cardinal Cullen. Though Cullen had invited Newman to Dublin, he frequently obstructed him as rector and tried to block Arnold's own appointment in 1856. Arnold's remark looks like a Soviet-style rewriting of history, but it may represent what he had genuinely come to believe thirty years after the event. As he grew older he showed a marked capacity to misremember or rearrange the past, even in his own family history. He had developed a retrospective admiration for Cullen as a strong leader, just as in his Tasmanian days he had admired Sir William Denison.

Arnold's Catholic interests and enthusiasms were given a coherent and useful outlet in the *Catholic Dictionary*, which he compiled with Fr William Addis. He had first written to Newman about this project in 1880 and had elicited Acton's support. The book appeared in 1884; it sets out information on Catholic doctrine, history, and practice in an accessible form. Arnold supplied the entries on medieval and modern history, the religious orders and canon law; Fr Addis wrote those on dogma, ritual, and the ancient church. Addis was a theologian of some reputation, who played a part in the life of Hopkins; they were close friends as Balliol undergraduates; under Newman's influence they entered the Catholic Church within a few days of each other. Hopkins continued to like and admire him. Addis became an Oratorian priest, but at the time Arnold collaborated with him he had reverted to the ordinary clergy, and was parish priest of Sydenham, on the southern fringe of London. Like Arnold, Fr Addis proved to be a religious wanderer, but of a more startling and adventurous kind. Four years after the *Dictionary* came out he abandoned Catholicism and the priesthood; he married one of his parishioners and went to Australia, where he became a Presbyterian minister. After some years he returned to England and adopted Unitarianism; he was for a time professor of Old Testament Criticism at Manchester College, Oxford. He finally returned to the Church of England in which he had grown up and was vicar of All Saints, Knightsbridge, from 1910 to 1917. Hopkins was distressed by Addis's abandonment of Catholicism and angrily rebuked Robert Bridges, who had made a tactless reference to it in a letter. Notwithstanding the defection of half the team, 'Addis and Arnold', as it was known, became a standard work of reference and was regularly reprinted, the last time in 1951.

Arnold sent copies to Newman and to Mary, who responded graciously, 'I am delighted to hear of the success of the Dictionary—in spite of its doctrines.'[12] In a later letter she thanked him again, mainly praising the book's appearance, though she said she would enjoy dipping into it. It is in fact likely that Mary made quite a close study of the book several years later, when she was writing the novel in which she closely engaged with Catholicism, *Helbeck of Bannisdale*. Catholics, naturally, were more enthusiastic about the dictionary. Writing to Mary on 6 February 1884, Tom thanked her for the limited sympathy that she had been able to muster for the work: 'Alas! it is only from those who are not of my blood and name that full and hearty sympathy comes. The President of the College in Stephen's Green, Fr Delany, stopped me today in the street, and said some pleasant things. He said it was exactly the sort of book that had long been wanted.'[13]

Arnold's sense of alienation is close to that expressed by Hopkins in his sonnet 'To seem the stranger':

> To seem the stranger lies my lot, my life
> Among strangers. Father and mother dear,
> Brothers and sisters are in Christ not near . . .
> ll. 1–3

For Arnold and Hopkins, as for Newman a generation earlier, to be an English Catholic in Dublin was to be an anomaly, a walking category mistake, mistrusted by both Nationalists and Unionists. Hopkins was acutely miserable in that situation, though out of his misery he made the great poetry of the 'terrible sonnets'. Arnold characteristically made the best of things and was not too perturbed for much of the time. Mandell Creighton, ecclesiastical historian and future Bishop of London, who was acquainted with several of the characters in this narrative, wrote to Hopkins in April 1885, 'I am glad to hear that you are settled in Dublin about which I hear sometimes from Tom Arnold, who seems to enjoy his work on the whole.'[14] That was an adequate summary of his feelings.

Matthew made a final attempt to find a better post for Tom. The University of Oxford had come to terms with the rise of English studies by seeking to appoint a professor. The Merton Chair of English Language and Literature had been launched, and from the start it was an ambiguous position, as its title indicated. A literary scholar would be needed for one part, a philologist for the other. Those who emphasized 'literature' were sufficiently well placed for informal representations to be made to Matthew, to see if he would be interested in the post, as a reader if not as a professor. He did not take long to decide that he was not interested, but wondered if it could be directed towards Tom. On 29 April 1884 he wrote to Frances, after a visit to Oxford, 'I saw Jowett, who was very kind. I told him I had quite made up my mind not to accept either Professorship or Readership; and then I made an effort to do something for Tom as to the Readership—the Professorhip I knew was impossible; but Jowett after a little reflexion said decidedly that it was out of the question.'[15] In some respects Tom was well suited for the post; he had been one of the first professors of English in the British Isles and had a long experience in the field. His interests were both linguistic and literary, as shown in his edition of *Beowulf,* the *Manual of English Literature,* and his editions of medieval and later texts. But he was already over 60, and relative youth was in demand; the accommodating days when Joseph Bosworth could be appointed for life to the Rawlinsonian Chair of Anglo-Saxon at the age of 69 were no more. Furthermore, Tom Arnold's academic career and religious progress had been so untidy and irregular that his return to Oxford was, in Jowett's words, 'out of the question'. The successful candidate, A. S. Napier, was only 32 when he was appointed, and was very much a language man; after reading science at Oxford he turned to philology and Old English, which he studied in Berlin; he was an academic networker of a recognizable modern kind, whose application was supported by testimonials from eighteen professors, mostly Continental.[16]

Mary proposed a different initiative to her father; not for a job but at least for recognition from the English intellectual establishment. In October 1886 she wrote to him:

> I have had an idea in my head for a while past which I have just been discussing with Uncle Matt and Humphry. It is that you ought to be elected a member of the Athenaeum by the Committee. It is due to you, it is one of the few honours open to literary men in this country, and I should like it so much. Uncle Matt thinks it could be arranged so does Humphry. What do you think dearest?[17]

The Athenaeum was an élite institution, which provided its members with both distinction and convenience. Matthew had for years used it as a study, a library, an office and a mail-box; and Humphry, who was now working on the *Times,* had recently been made a member. In Stefan Collini's words:

> The Athenaeum was (and to some extent still is) distinguished among London clubs by the fact that whereas most of these institutions primarily catered to those who inherited their wealth and social position, the membership of the Athen-

aeum included a far higher proportion of writers, bishops, judges, senior public servants, and such like. Ordinary members of the club were elected by the whole membership after having been nominated by existing members of their acquaintance, and the process was subject to the familiar clubland hazards of snobbery, 'blackballing', and waiting lists. Under Rule II, however, the committee could elect each year to immediate membership a certain number of men who were considered as being 'of distinguished eminence in Science, Literature or the Arts, or for Public Service'.[18]

Tom did not join the Athenaeum, though he was certainly worthy of election by the committee. As he lived in Dublin for most of the year he would have been able to make only limited use of its resources, and it would have involved him in expense (Mary proposed that her uncle and husband would raise the initial entrance fee). Mary wanted her mother to move to the capital to be near the Wards, and if Tom had the Athenaeum as an attraction and a base it would encourage him to spend more time in London.

Julia, though, had no intention of leaving Oxford; since Tom went to Dublin he appears to have been spending part at least of his vacations with Julia. In a bitter letter she complained that he was giving too much of his time and effort to the college, unlike the notorious absentee Professor Stewart. It is characteristic of the relationship that after a sarcastic outburst Julia concluded her letter by asking Tom if he would like another cake sent. He had evidently been entertaining thoughts of the Merton Chair at Oxford, perhaps encouraged by Matthew. Julia's response was harshly discouraging, revealing her sense of Tom's castle-building temperament: 'What you say about a Chair at Oxford is so visionary that it is not worth discussing. I do not think that any one in your circumstances would have the slightest chance of being elected here to any such post. And for *myself* the time is past when to see you in that position would give me the slightest gratification.'[19] He may have been again suggesting that she consider moving to Dublin, but the idea provoked an angry response:

Once for all I will not leave England and go to live in Ireland. I should loathe it, if things were not as they are, but as things are *I will not do it. You have pleased yourself* and as you have made your bed so you must lie on it, but while I live I will never know one of your R.C. friends. Your whole life is outside mine and this is of your own making.[20]

Despite this, Julia still signed her letter 'Yr affecte wife'. Tom may have felt that Julia was selfish in not joining him in Dublin, as he had implied in the past; she had no doubt that he was selfish for being there, and for being a Catholic at all.

Julia's anger was part of her temperament, but it would have been exacerbated by her ill health. It is not easy to trace the progress of her cancer; it seems to have been checked by the two operations, but they had left her with a wound which would not heal and considerable discomfort. By the later 1880s the disease had reappeared, though she made efforts to live as normal a life as possible. Her younger daughters were leaving home; Lucy had married a clergyman, E. C. Selwyn, and in 1885 'Judy'— the younger Julia—married Leonard Huxley, at that time a master at Charterhouse and later editor of the *Cornhill Magazine*. Julia had expected Ethel, the youngest child to marry before long, but she never did so. Ethel was therefore left in the role of the dutiful youngest daughter who remains at home to look after her ailing mother; it was not one she particularly welcomed or felt at home in, for like Mary and Judy she was an intellectual girl. She had literary ambitions and a certain amount of talent; in later years she took up photography with some success. Despite the reduced household Julia's money troubles continued; she ran up bills she could not settle and Tom warned Oxford tradesmen not to give her more credit. In March 1885 Mary wrote to her father protesting against his apparent hard-heartedness: 'I don't think you in the least realise the perpetual malaise and discomfort of Mamma's life, or you would surely try to make things easier for her.'[21] Mary begged him to try to spare Julia some more money for housekeeping, implying that in financial terms he was now not doing so badly. She may well have been right; the original stipend from the Royal University had been 400 pounds; J. E. Axon states that after some years Tom was earning 700 pounds, perhaps because he continued to take on examining for the Civil Service Commission. Knowing Julia's incapacities as a housekeeper he may have been reluctant to go on throwing good money after bad, though as Mary said it was a cruel response to someone in her condition. Tom was selfish in some respects, it must be conceded, though he spent little money on himself. But he wanted a quiet, untroubled life, in which he could devote himself to scholarly pursuits, and he tried to avoid unpleasant facts for as long as he could. Even though he was earning more money, he still had the expense of keeping up two homes; and the intermittent journeys from Dublin to Oxford and back would have cost much more than his visits when he was living in London. Their lives would have been easier, at least financially, if Julia had been prepared to share a home with him.

Writing to Tom Julia was inclined to emphasize the extremity of her condition; she told him in one of her letters of March 1884, 'It is not so easy to look "all eventualities in the face" when you have a deadly disease knawing [*sic*] at your vitals . . .'.[22] But with other people Julia tried to appear as normal as possible. In February 1885 Charles Dodgson remarked in a letter to his friend Ethel Arnold, 'I was very glad to see your mother looking so well and so much up to joining in the dissipations of the day.'[23] Julia was still able to get out and about at that time. In October Matthew, who had spent some days in Oxford, told Frances: 'On Thursday afternoon I paid a long visit to Julia; her house is very nice, far the nicest they have ever had, though not large. She did not give a good account of Tom or of Frank, but was herself on the way to an afternoon tea, and Ethel with her.'[24] Number 2 Bradmore Road, the semi-detached house where Julia was now living, would seem large enough to modern eyes, though it was certainly smaller than the imposing yellow-brick pile a few doors away where Mary and Humphry had lived when they were first married. The house was slightly untypical of North Oxford, since it was built entirely of red brick, without any of the prevailing yellow, and its steeply pitched roofs with ornamental woodwork along the eaves gave it a vaguely Continental appearance. It may have been this that appealed to Matthew.

Two years later Dodgson visited the house and reported, 'I called on Mrs Arnold, and am sorry to say she looks *very* ill: though she reported herself as convalescent.'[25] By 1887 it was evident that Julia's cancer was advancing again, and she had given up taking on boarders. Tom's letters from Dublin express, after some reluctance to face the facts, his distress and concern at the news: 'I am as it were torn in pieces by the feeling that you are prostrated by these attacks of pain, and that I am so far from you.'[26] After marking a great many examination papers he returned to Oxford at the end of July.

Tom wrote from Bradmore Road to Josephine, who was visiting England, on 28 September 1887:

I have to leave Oxford for Dublin next Monday. But could you not, either before or after that, come down for three or four days? Mrs Arnold seldom leaves her bedroom now, so you would not see much of her, but Ethel would do all she could. I have got leave to return here after the examinations are finished, that is probably about the 26th October. If at Christmas my wife is about in the same state, I shall think, as I said to the President, that the doctors were mistaken in thinking her case had a character of urgency, and shall apply for no more special leave of absence.[27]

Tom took his leave and spent the autumn term in Oxford. He had to pay a substitute to cover his teaching; Hopkins mentions lending a book to 'a young man who teaches English for the Royal University curriculum and in Mr Tom Arnold's absence takes his class'.[28] Tom did not spend all his time in Oxford, for he took the opportunity to visit Cambridge and Bury St Edmunds to work on the *Memorials of St Edmund's Abbey*. The matter-of-fact tone of his comments about Julia in his letter to Josephine reflects his disconcerting tendency to alternate strong expressions of feelings with dry detachment. Julia was in the care of her son Frank, who had recently qualified as a doctor, and of a more experienced practitioner, a Dr Symonds. They were not mistaken in thinking her case was urgent, but although Julia had no strong desire to live she proved remarkably tenacious of life. She was in considerable pain and needed frequent injections of morphia. But her decline was arrested from time to time, and between 28 December and 18 January 1888 there was little change in her condition; on the latter date, Tom, not having applied for any further leave, returned to Dublin; whatever his concern for Julia, he needed to hold on to his job. And perhaps he may have been guiltily relieved to be away from the small house so overshadowed by death. Once he was back in Ireland, Julia, ill as she was, wrote him frequent letters. She was living longer than she, or anyone else, had expected. Charles Dodgson records in his diary how he called at the Arnold house on 7 February, 'and was asked to go upstairs and see Mrs Arnold, who seems to be near her end, and with whom Ethel and I had a long talk, on more serious topics than we have ever before discussed'.[29]

Julia hung on for precisely two more months. Tom was back in Oxford for the Easter vacation and was due to return to Dublin when the final crisis came. On 6 April he wrote to Frances:

On the Wednesday morning—the day, as I told you, on the evening of which I was to have crossed to Dublin—Symonds came to see her, and told me that he thought it likely that she might not outlive the day. I asked him if I was warranted in saying, in telegraphing to Dublin, 'my wife is dying'; and he said I was. She then wished to see everyone in the house; and first to have five minutes alone with me. In that five minutes she spoke of herself in a very lovely and humble way; then she wished to have all her children round her, and they came; all but poor old Theodore [who was in the Antipodes]; and she talked to them out of her loving heart for some little time, and sent affectionate messages to Humphry and her other sons-in-law.

Julia was still not quite ready to die; later in the day Tom added some more sentences to the letter: 'She has spoken very little this morning; once she said, "Don't let anybody leave me". Last night, before I left her, she asked me to read to her; I read part of 119th and one or two other psalms, and a collect or two; read her to sleep in fact.'[30] Religion, which had so divided Tom and Mary, now united them.

The end came the next day, when some of their offspring had left. On 7 April Tom wrote again to Frances:

My beloved Julia died at five minutes to 7 this morning... When I came down, the breathing was short and quick, the eyelids half closed and the eyes almost without expression. She evidently knew no-one. The breathing gradually subsided; there was a slight rattle in the throat; the features fixed; and she was gone from us. Of her children only Mary Judy and Ethel were present, for Frank was necessarily at the Infirmary.[31]

Julia, who felt a close affinity with the larger Arnold family, had asked to be buried in the vicinity of Fox How, and this was accomplished in the churchyard at Ambleside, with Frances making the arrangements. Julia's clerical son-in-law, the Reverend Carus Selwyn, gave an address at the funeral. Later in the day Mary wrote, 'This morning we laid my dear Mother to rest in her grave among the mountains, and this afternoon I am free to think a little over what has befallen me personally and separately during this past week.'[32] She was referring to the discussions she had been having, immediately after her mother's death, with William Gladstone about the recently published *Robert Elsmere*.

Tom and Julia had been married for almost thirty-eight years. It could hardly be called a happy marriage, after their early life together in Van Diemen's Land, but to describe it as unhappy is to simplify a complex and ultimately opaque relationship. In their letters, amidst the mutual reproaches and the rancour, there are expressions of continuing love, and there is no reason to disbelieve them. Love does not necessarily ensure harmony or happiness. In fact, the Arnolds' situation might have been more tolerable if their love had dwindled into a minimally affectionate companionship, or even a loveless *modus vivendi*. As it was they loved and angered and frustrated each other, like Meredith's modern lovers:

> Their hearts held cravings for the buried day.
> Then each applied to each that fatal knife,
> Deep questioning, which probes to endless dole.
> Ah, what a dusty answer gets the soul
> When hot for certainties in this our life!
>
> *Modern Love*, L, 8–12

CHAPTER 10

Golden Autumn

Two weeks after Julia's death Tom Arnold wrote to Thomas Collinson, now a retired general of engineers. Collinson had known Julia in Van Diemen's Land, and Tom recalls that he had advised against the marriage:

Your advice was quite sound, for in many ways we were quite unsuited to one another; and yet not only was it *impossible* for me to take it, for she had subjugated me by her beauty to that degree that I belonged much more to her than to myself—but now I thank God with all my heart for having given us to one another, and hope, and believe, that I shall see and know my darling again on the other side of the grave.[1]

On 29 April Tom told Frances:

This living in Dublin without the hope of returning to my Julia is far more dreadful than I had ever imagined. How was I bound up in her! my spirit and being linked and interwoven in hers! I never knew how much, and now she is gone. I have written some rough verses upon her, of which I send you a copy. I seem to have an intense desire that all the world should know how beautiful, how original, how valiant she was; so little prepared by education to meet what she had to suffer, yet meeting it on the whole so nobly, so victoriously.[2]

As James Bertram remarks, Tom was no poet; the verses he sent Frances are not so much rough as stylistically indecorous in their attempt to express a sense of loss and longing in a jaunty metre. One stanza reads:

> Sometimes, after days of hard riding
> On my rounds to the schools of the land,
> As I paused on some hill-top dividing
> Two glens sloping down to the strand,
> Sublime, without equal or brother,
> The Mountain far off I could see,
> And I thought how the beautiful mother
> At its foot there, sat waiting for me.[3]

Tom's posthumous feelings about Julia were set out at length in the memoir of her that he wrote in 1889 for his children, now among his papers at Balliol. He gives a vivid account of his first meeting with her and their early years together, but he plays down the subsequent rifts and bitterness and the years of separation, presenting them merely as the kinds of minor quarrels that will occur in any marriage. His descriptions of life in New Zealand and Tasmania are sharp and lively, and contribute to the history of those territories.

There were other deaths. His sister Mary's third husband, Robert Hayes, died on 7 April, the same day as Julia. On 9 April Matthew wrote to Tom, thanking him for 'your touching and beautiful letter, which I shall always keep'. He is in a difficulty because Julia's memorial service in Oxford, before her body was taken to Westmorland, was on the same day as Robert Hayes's in Leicestershire; he has decided to go to the latter because his sister had so few people around her.[4] Shocking news was to follow: on 15 April Matthew himself died of a heart-attack. He had gone to Liverpool with his wife to meet his daughter Lucy, who had married an American and settled in the United States, and was returning on a visit. On his way to the dock Matthew collapsed in the street and died soon afterwards. The congenital heart weakness that had claimed his father and paternal grandfather in middle age, and his own son William at the age of 18, had now carried off Matthew at the age of 65. Tom had to postpone his grief; as he put it to Collinson on 24 April, in his account of Julia's death:

This terrible and overpowering loss has so absorbed my faculties, so taxed every source and possibility of feeling that is in me, that the death of my dear brother, coming eight days afterwards, did not stun me as it otherwise would. The time of weeping over his memory too will come to me; but it has hardly come yet; the other blow is too fresh.[5]

Within a few days, though, he was able to focus on Matthew's death. In his letter to Frances of 29 April he says that he had been re-reading a wide range of his brother's work: 'The "Scholar Gipsy" seems to me the most perfectly beautiful poem of modern times. And in another key, how supremely felicitous is "Culture and Anarchy", in which his gift of banter, rallying, persiflage, whatever one may call it appears in its full force and bloom. I am writing something about him for Willy: you shall have it.'[6] The brothers, nearly twins from the proximity of their ages, were always close, and fraternal affection deepened with the years. Matthew, the more forceful character, had sometimes adopted an impatient, condescending, and occasionally hectoring tone in his dealings with Tom. But his concern for him was always apparent, as was evident in his frequent but unsuccessful attempts to find him a better job. Though close, the brothers had followed very different courses in life. Matthew was never wealthy but earned enough to live on and bring up his family. He had a literary reputation and a place in society; the regularity of his life, centred on the Education Office and the Athenaeum, with regular visits to Oxford, professional excursions to France and Germany, vacations in Switzerland, and in later years lecture tours of the United States, contrasted with Tom's wanderings, his penury, and his Irish exile. Tom might have envied Matthew, but there was never any trace of it on his part, only steady admiration and affection.

The article which had been commissioned by his son William appeared anonymously in the *Manchester Guardian* for 18 May 1888 as 'Matthew Arnold by one who knew him well'. It is an adroit and comprehensive piece of writing, and shows that Tom had not lost his journalistic facility. He traces the course of Matthew's life and career, and has something to say about his successive phases of literary and intellectual activity. There are some precise and revealing observations:

For though it is probable that he could have become a formidable satirist if he had chosen, he never did choose; he was too good-natured for that role; he did not go beyond banter, but in that no-one ever surpassed him. Things which said by anyone else would have produced a deadly quarrel, were said by him with such a bright playfulness, such a humorous masterfulness, that the victim laughed before he had time to feel hurt. As an undergraduate he seemed bent on accumulating various experiences; he read a little with the reading men, hunted a little with the fast men, and dressed a little with the dressy men.

Quoting a despairing passage from Matthew's poetry, Tom remarks, 'It might have been thought that this mood would grow upon him; that he would diverge more and more from his father and draw nearer to Schopenhauer and Leopardi. But there was nothing more remarkable in Matthew Arnold's personality than his power of recovery and self-correction.' Though he admires the poetry, Tom comments discriminatingly on the limited place that it occupied in his brother's career:

Between 1849 and 1860 all that is really great in Matthew Arnold's poetry was written—parts of 'Empedocles on Etna', the first 'Stanzas on Obermann', 'Self Dependency', 'Morality', 'A Wish', 'Rugby Chapel', the 'Scholar Gipsy' and 'Stanzas from the Grande Chartreuse'. 'Thyrsis', written in 1861, although it is usually rated so high, shows that the tide of inspiration had already begun to ebb;

read, as it always should be, in connection with the Scholar Gipsy, it betrays its inferiority to this last in a thousand ways.

This is attentive criticism, in Matthew's own spirit. Tom writes warmly about the critical writings, but as an orthodox Catholic he has to dissent from Matthew's ventures into theology: 'Matthew Arnold was, in truth, not furnished either with that kind of learning or those forms of spiritual experience which enable a man to write on religious subjects with profit.' He complains of Matthew writing on Isaiah without knowing any Hebrew, but in fact his brother had been studying the language. Despite these reservations, Tom ends his article with a paean of deeply felt praise:

When we survey the wide field over which ranged the powerful mind of him whom we have lost—the poetry of every age, classical literature, the philosophy of the Graeco-Roman and Christian worlds, all that is best in modern literature, beside the special knowledge of education and its methods which his calling required, and then consider that more than forty years ago, when he was but twenty-four years old, this man knew that he was in a certain sense doomed—an eminent physician having told him that the action of his heart was not regular, and that he must take great care of himself—the spectacle of his unflagging energy all these years, his cheerfulness, his hopefulness, his unselfish helpfulness, his tender sympathy with all the honest weak and all the struggling good, seems to bring before us one of the most pathetic and beautiful pictures that modern life affords.

Back in Dublin Tom had to pick up the threads of everyday life. There were Civil Service papers to mark, and proofs to correct of the first volume of the *Memorials of St Edmund's Abbey*. Friends invited him to lunch, and he dined with Dowden.

Mary was deeply affected by the death of her mother, and of her uncle, to whose ideas she was much closer than to her father's. But these occasions of grief were balanced by a great and sudden change in her fortunes, following the runaway success of her novel, *Robert Elsmere*. It was published in February 1888, her second novel for adult readers. The critics were very slow to respond, though in March the Wards' friend Walter Pater wrote warmly of it in the *Manchester Guardian*, in a review which Mary had arranged. Janet Trevelyan writes of the dying Julia, 'the last pleasure which she enjoyed on earth was the news that reached her of the growing success of her daughter's book'.[7] This, alas, is a pious fiction; Julia might have read Pater's review, but the one in the *Times* was published on the day she died. *Robert Elsmere* did indeed enjoy a growing success, but not in Julia's lifetime. Its popularity was not based on the late, sparse, and sometimes unenthusiastic response of reviewers, but on word-of-mouth recommendations. Somehow this over-long novel of ideas, exploring distinctly old-fashioned religious controversies, caught the enthusiastic attention of the readers who borrowed novels from circulating libraries (priced at a guinea and a half for three volumes, novels were rarely bought by private purchasers). Orders followed on orders, and the novel was steadily reprinted. One of its most attentive readers was W. E. Gladstone, who was out of office as prime minister and had time for such reading; he disapproved of *Robert Elsmere* for what he saw as its bias against orthodox Christianity, but he was fascinated by it, and soon after her mother's death he met Mary in Oxford for a long conversation about it. Gladstone published a substantial review-article on the novel in the *Nineteenth Century*, which gave a further boost to its reputation. The book became a bestseller and remained so. It sold very widely in America, though these sales were of little financial benefit to Mary, since there was as yet no international agreement on copyright. Nevertheless, she was on the way to becoming a wealthy woman.

Robert Elsmere's success remains inexplicable. It is a monster of a book; long even for a three-decker novel, and much longer still in the manuscript which Mary Ward had delivered to her disconcerted publisher. It had to be cut radically to be published at all, and the cuts adversely affected the form of the book.[8] Its essential story is straightforward: a sincere but conventional clergyman loses his faith in traditional Christianity; not, indeed, to become an atheist, but to adopt a non-institutional form of belief, without supernatural elements—where 'miracles do not happen'—but with a firm belief in God and a strong devotion to the person and lessons of Christ. This would describe the position of many people who at the present time regard themselves as Christians, but in the 1880s it was heresy, and the author's sympathy with the eponymous hero provoked many attacks, which nevertheless helped along the novel's success. Mary Ward is evidently drawing on her own spiritual progress away from the Evangelical intensities of her teens. There are many echoes of the Oxford of the 1850s, when she had listened with troubled fascination and ultimate assent to Mark Pattison's iconoclastic discourses. Leading characters are based, in part at least, on her friends from those days: Pattison himself, T. H. Green, Pater. But where the book comes closest to Mary's own experience is in the state of Robert's marriage, when his wife, the narrowly devout and Evangelical Catherine, realizes that he is losing his faith, and reacts with pain and distress whilst trying to continue acting as a loving wife. Here Mary seems to be presenting, in a different key, her memory of how deep religious divisions affected her parents' marriage. In novelistic terms it seems to me the most accomplished part of her lengthy narrative.

Mary had always been generous, and even when the Wards were not well off she had contributed towards Frank's medical training, and made regular payments to Theodore, who was finding it hard to make ends meet in Tasmania. With her newly acquired wealth she offered to settle her father's debts in Oxford, at least up to a total of 100 pounds, which Tom was happy to accept. Mary had plans for him. The insecure, ardent girl who had sat at the feet of Mark Pattison was becoming a *grande dame*, and a fixer and manipulator, whether she was organizing favourable book-reviews or the lives of her family. She wanted Tom to be looked after by Ethel, and in July 1889 the sisters went to see him in Dublin. Mary was appalled by his living conditions, as she told Humphry: 'never swept and never dusted. The dirt of everything is oppressive—and this with a payment of £2.18.0 a week!'[9] Mary sorted Tom out by finding him better lodgings. Ethel was supposed to act as his housekeeper, and apparently did so for a time, but she was not enthusiastic. She had not greatly enjoyed looking after her invalid mother, and did not now want to take on her sexagenarian father with his abstracted, bachelor ways. And as a Protestant she was not at home in a Roman Catholic city, any more than her mother had been. In the event, Tom had other plans for himself. Sometime in 1888 or early 1889 he asked Josephine to marry him and was accepted. A letter from Josephine to Tom, dated 4 May 1889, thirteen months after Julia's death, suggests, given the conventions of the time, that they are already engaged. In contrast to her former reticent openings, it begins, 'My own dearest'. After giving news of her family, she continues:

And now for your dear letter, it was good in my best sense, my heart is so moved by your tenderness, & your letting me into your wishes & affairs—we agree in thinking a move likely to prove permanent, the only prudent one,—a change of apartments might turn out a mere frittering away of money, for I feel poor Ethel is not likely to sit down contentedly in such surroundings, your present ones must seem impossible to her just now—yet I think all Mary describes, is most difficult of attainment . . .

Your past is dear to me as belonging to your life, I would not, if I could take away, or dull one memory you prize. When you anticipate any change which brings us nearer, it is simply a feeling of awe which comes over me,—of one thing alone I am certain, the fulness of my affection for you.[10]

Josephine was looking forward to a permanent life together with Tom, but Mary was not yet informed of their plans, so she had her own way in finding another set of lodgings for him. Widowers are expected to re-marry, and Josephine had probably been quietly in love with Tom for many years. Julia's long illness is likely to have prompted some contradic-tory responses in her: distress at the ordeal of a woman she had known and liked, and the hope, perhaps never fully acknowledged, that she might marry Tom after Julia's death. The mutual affection and concern in their correspondence indicate a great fondness, which would be a good foundation for the union of these two mature spirits. It was important that Josephine was a Catholic; Tom had found solace in discussing his religious crises with her. They deserved their happiness.

A letter from Tom to Josephine, dated 20 August 1889, begins 'My sweet beloved Josephine'. He refers to her brother Joe being told of the engagement:

It was a great happiness, my own darling, to receive your letter this morning and to learn how Joe had taken the announcement. Your brother's affection and kind-ness to you are as if they were shown to myself. I have been working hard at my Rolls book, and now it is nearly post time. It is an indescribable relief to know that Joe takes the prospect so well; it seems to send everything forward by a long stage. As to Mary, I do not apprehend difficulty either.[11]

Mary did not in fact learn the news until late October; her response was positive but stiff:

I was not altogether unprepared for your announcement and certainly dearest I have nothing but sympathy and affection to give you with regard to it. To all grown-up children I suppose a father's second marriage must always carry with it something infinitely sad and moving. But at the same time I recognise that you have owing to our family circumstances many needs your children cannot supply, however much they might wish; and I rejoice that you will find in Miss Benison that fundamental sympathy which is and ought to be precious to all who hold their faith strongly.[12]

Mary had known of Josephine's existence for many years—in 1872, be-fore her marriage, she had written thanking her for a present—and they had occasionally met. But she may not have fully understood the state of feeling between Miss Benison and her father. She wrote crossly to Tom when at the last minute he told her that he would not be spending the Christmas of 1889 with the Wards in London as they had expected, but would be going to Fox How to stay with his sister. Mary did not like having her plans changed; she told Tom that she had hoped to see him before his forthcoming marriage.

Josephine, though, was happy in feeling accepted by the Arnolds. In December she told her sister-in-law, 'Every member of his family wrote to him on his birthday, and associated me with him in the kindliest way. Mrs Forster says he must bring me to visit her when we first go to England, that she wants to know me. Mary's little girls sent him their photos with such pretty letters.' She was not too old to want to be turned out properly for her wedding: 'Mrs Macky told me of the trousseaux she made for Lord Massey's daughter, she went to Limerick to fit on her wares—I think she will turn me out right & not too costly. I find I must have my things very nice, I enter such a wide circle.'[13]

Tom and Josephine married on 9 January 1890—it is not certain where, but it was probably at Slieve Russell—and moved into a house in Leinster Road, Dublin. Josephine appears to have taken to marriage easily after her long spinsterhood; she was used to looking after men, since she had acted as housekeeper for her widowed father and her brother. She was a devoted and much-loved aunt to the young offspring of her brother Joe and her sister Thomasina, both of whose spouses died. Soon after her marriage, the newly wed of 58 sent her sister-in-law a matter-of-fact account of her life with Tom:

My days pass in busy quiet, so my letters cannot have much interest, still I want you and Joe to know exactly what my life is. We breakfast at quarter to 9oc, and dawdle over it, Tom dealing out the news to me, when the breakfast things are cleared he always reads the Introit, Collects, Epistles etc. from the Mass of the day. That over he goes out, I settle luncheon & dinner, or, in point of fact agree to what the Cook proposes . . . We dine at ½ past 6 or 7oc—for it, I come down in my red Tea-gown, it is so easy and comfortable—while Tom takes his pipe, I read to him out of whatever book he chances to have in hand, last night I was so sleepy & as the book was not lively, I made such a hash of it towards the end. Indeed the reading does not last long, though I try to be industrious and knit while he reads. There will be lots of work for me in various ways I see, I have just collected his shirts & stockings which need seeing to . . . Tom has not to resume his lectures till Feb 2nd, altogether my life is very perfect just now, such is my conceit, I hope to grow necessary to Tom, & life must be always easy & happy if he cares for me as does now.[14]

It is a charming record of a kind of domestic and religious harmony that Tom had not known before; the last years of his life were a golden autumn. He was, for a time, still possessed by memories of Julia; he had once described his love for her as 'a kind of enchantment'. Some months after his marriage he told Frances, 'I sometimes feel so little changed in heart and inner consciousness by the forty years that have passed since I first saw Julia that I can imagine myself falling in love again with the beautiful darling were the chance given me at this moment.'[15] But he was content in his new marriage. On 10 January 1891 he wrote to Josephine, who was at Slieve Russell: 'Yes, yesterday was the anniversary of our wedding day, and it does me good to think that you do not wish the past undone and are ready to put up with all my faults and shortcomings. You have been all to me that I ever counted on, nor were my expectations low pitched.'[16]

In June 1892 Tom and Josephine were at Rugby for a great commemoration of the fiftieth anniversary of Dr Arnold's death. Tom wrote to Frances, 'Here I am, and here, this same day of the week and of the month, fifty years ago, dear Papa passed into the unknown. I remember sitting on the sofa in the study that morning in much distress, little imagining that I should be alive in the flesh fifty years after, and that he, in memory reverence and honour, would be yet more alive.'[17] Some of Tom's children and grandchildren were there, but many of his Rugby contemporaries had not survived. However, Thomas Hughes was much in evidence; he made himself generally agreeable, but gave an address to the assembled company and school which went down badly. In that year the Arnolds moved to Adelaide Road, which was nearer the college in St Stephen's Green. A memorialist of the college has noted, 'In his later life he found great happiness in his second marriage with Miss Benison, an Irish lady of a family well known in Co. Cavan. Together they gave pleasant lunch parties, generally of a Sunday, in a smallish house in Adelaide Road. The hostess was indeed charming, but Arnold in his shyness was more like one of the guests than the chief entertainer.'[18] Tom Arnold was now finally and in every sense at home in Dublin. As one of a Catholic couple, with an Irish wife, he could be accepted in the way that the anomalous figure of an English Catholic convert without local attachments could not be. Although he had been reluctantly in favour of Home Rule his Nationalist sentiments now strengthened under Josephine's influence. He was at ease with the members of her extended family, as they were with him; there were regular visits back to Slieve Russell, and

Josephine's relations stayed with the Arnolds when they were in Dublin. One of them wrote of him, 'He is such a nice kind man. I get fonder of him every time I see him. It is a lesson to see him take such a keen delight in all he sees, & turn his travels to account the way he does. He never allows little things to worry him which I wish I could imitate him in.'[19]

Tom and Josephine crossed to England during the summer vacations, but he no longer had the expense of maintaining a second home there. Josephine knew how to manage money—a new experience for Tom. After his death Frances complimented her on 'your admirable management of your affairs, and the splendid way in which while helping our dearest Tom to the utmost in discharging old obligations you have enabled him to know an ease of mind & comfort as to money matters which he had never known before'.[20] There were no more debts and the couple were even able to save a little.

At the college Tom Arnold appears to have been regarded by Fr Delany's keen young Jesuits as a has-been, a survivor of the remote Newman epoch: 'What they could see of his exterior was that he was very shy, slow of speech, far from bright in conversation, rather, to tell the whole truth, a dull-seeming person. He was, however, tall and intellectual looking, and carried himself with a distinguished bearing like a courtier . . . it must be allowed that he did not count for much in the *entourage* of St Stephen's Green.'[21] Tom had a certain mythicized reputation; he was believed, in rather too literal a fashion, to have been the dashing radical, Philip Hewison, in Clough's *Bothie*, in striking contrast to the dim impression he now made. Some of his students, though, thought a good deal better of him. One later wrote, 'I well remember Mr Thomas Arnold and the charm which he could impart to a lecture on early English.' Another, the Revd Professor P. M. McSweeney, remembered him warmly: 'My attitude towards Mr Arnold was one of reverence. He was in manner not donnish but shy. A slight impediment in speech accentuated this impression. When, however, you came to know him intimately this disappeared and he was quite outspoken and, when stirred, enthusiastic or passionate . . . I felt it was a unique privilege to read, say, Wordsworth with one who belonged to the most intimate Wordsworth circle.'[22]

Arnold had last seen Newman in Birmingham in 1888:

I noticed then, and not for the first time, how much more distinguished his features had become, for regularity, dignity, and even beauty, since he had become a very old man. There was not the least sign in his talk of the infirmities of age. When I rose to go, I spoke of the pleasure it had given me to find him in such comparatively good health and strength. He replied with a smile, 'But you know, Arnold, I am so *very* old.'[23]

On 11 August 1890 Newman died of pneumonia, the first English Catholic since the Reformation to be nationally admired. Arnold attended his requiem in the Brompton Oratory; he noted that a large number of Protestants were present. Yet his attitude to Newman had become ambivalent; perhaps had always been so to some extent. On 28 August he wrote to Collinson, 'I was at Newman's funeral last week. A fine and honourable consistency marked his long career, but there was a lack of the saint's self-immolation, the missioner's fire; hence his service to the Church was hardly what might have been expected, considering his extraordinary powers.'[24] Arnold felt that Newman had been reclusive and inactive and had not done enough for the Catholic Church after he had joined it; as he put it in a letter to his sister, 'He was borne along as on a mighty tide-wave; but in 1845 he was stranded on the beach,—the tide receded—and he was left high and dry.'[25] This comment underestimates and misrepresents Newman, but at that time his thought was not widely grasped or understood in the Catholic Church; indeed, it would not be so until the Second Vatican Council, which has been described as 'Newman's Council'. Tom Arnold's objections to Newman may also reflect the way in which his own Catholicism had become rather narrow and convergent. There was also his admiration for heroes and men of action, such as Sir William Denison, whom he felt had all the qualities Newman lacked. In retrospect he had come to see Newman's opponent, Archbishop Cullen, in that light. On 29 January 1892 he responded to a letter of enquiry about Newman from Acton: 'Cullen was a strong man and not hostile to learning and culture on principle; and if Newman had been less shrinkingly sensitive, less English, less Oxonian, in short something different from what he was, the two might have worked together to some profitable account.'[26] Arnold had in a sense gone native in Dublin, and begun to see Newman through Irish eyes; the result is a caricature. (The strongly Ultramontane Manning had made a similar criticism: 'I see much danger of an English Catholicism of which Newman is the highest type. It is the old Anglican, patristic, literary Oxford tone transplanted into the Church.'[27] Manning, like Newman and Tom Arnold, was himself an ex-Anglican Oxonian.) References to Newman in his autobiography are more admiring. In July 1890 Tom and Josephine entertained Newman's future biographer, Wilfrid Ward, to lunch; he was in Dublin as an examiner in Catholic philosophy at the college. He was the son of the Ultramontane W. G. Ward, whose degradation Tom had witnessed at Oxford; Wilfrid, though entirely orthodox, was more moderate in his Catholic opinions.

Just as Tom was accepted by Josephine's extended family, so was she by the Arnold clan. Mary, after her initial coolness, sent Tom and Josephine some furnishings for their new home on their marriage. She warmed to her new stepmother, though there is back-handed praise in her remark to Humphry: 'She is really a good sort—if only Nature had made her a little fairer to look upon.'[28] In their summer visits the Arnolds would stay with the Wards at Stocks, the Hertfordshire mansion which Mary at first rented and then—being now a high earner and a big spender—bought. Then they would move on to Fox How, where Frances was the hospitable chatelaine. In August 1895 Tom's daughter Julia Huxley was also there with her family. Josephine remarked of the youngest Huxley child, 'Aldous is a dear little man, so sweet-tempered— he is just a year old but does not try to get on his feet, I fear he is not strong, he looks so white.'[29]

The passing years brought more deaths to note and sometimes mourn. William Forster had died in 1886, and in 1888, a few months after Julia and Matthew and her own husband, so did Tom's thrice-married sister, Mary. His colleague Fr Hopkins died in 1889, and in 1894 his daughter Lucy Selwyn died suddenly of a clot on the brain; she was 36 and left seven children. She was buried alongside her mother in Ambleside churchyard. Mary was much affected by her sister's death, but we do not know how Tom responded, as there is no surviving correspondence from him for that year.

In 1896, much to Tom's relief, the third and final volume of the *Memorials of St Edmund's Abbey* was published. It was followed in 1897 by *Notes on the Sacrifice of the Altar*, a slender work in the format of a prayer book brought out by the Catholic publisher Burns and Oates. Here Arnold returns to the expository vein of the *Catholic Dictionary* and writes a lucid, descriptive analysis of the Mass, seeing it as exemplifying four different modes of worship: praise, prayer, good works and sacrifice. He points out that the Church of England cannot offer the true sacrifice of the Mass, following on the recent Roman pronouncement that Anglican orders are invalid.

Matthew had once urged him to keep up the Anglo-Saxon, and he now returned to *Beowulf*. He prepared a series of lectures on the poem in its historical, geographical, and cultural contexts and delivered them at St Mary's University College, Merrion Square, a branch of the St Stephen's Green establishment attended by women students. A historian of the college recalled, 'It was said that for a course of lectures upon early English which he wished to publish as having been delivered in the College, he had had to count upon the kindness of a friend to supply him with even a shadow of an audience.'[30] One picks up a sense of malicious Dublin gossip here, but Tom acknowledged that the lectures were not well attended and were possibly over the heads of his audience. He wrote to Frances, 'This afternoon I resumed my Beowulf lectures at St Mary's College to a very small audience indeed, but I do not care much about that, for my object has been always the reading, not the listening world.'[31] He was still following Pattison's rather than Jowett's model of higher education; in the present-day university he would have emerged badly from a 'teaching assessment exercise'. The lectures were published by Longman in 1898, as *Notes on Beowulf*. Another Anglo-Saxonist, Wentworth Huyshe, in the notes to his own translation of the poem, described it as a 'small but valuable volume'.

With advancing years Arnold's ideas on education were growing steadily more conservative, though he remained politically a Liberal. On 17 February 1894 he published a letter in the *Spectator* lamenting the decline of standards at Oxford. He dismisses the University Extension movement as doing no more than spread a 'thin film of learning', though back in the 1850s he had been enthusiastic about a similar movement in Dublin. He adopts the tone of a *laudator temporis acti*, comparing the poor quality of present-day dons with the great men he had known in his youth, such as Keble, Newman, Pusey, Liddon, and Stanley; he concludes with a gloomy septagenarian blast at the modern world:

It is true that for all these changes, it is not so much Oxford itself, as the ever-rising tide of ignorant democracy, that is responsible. But whoever may be at fault, the result is the same, and what I marvel at and protest against is the disposition to glorify the moral laxity and indifference to truth that have produced a state of affairs which the University may find, in the course of a few years, pregnant with disintegration and decay.

Thinking about those early days had brought Clough back to his mind. He had failed to provide Mrs Clough with a memorial article soon after his death, but now he wanted to set down his memories of him. He wrote to Blanche Clough asking her to return Clough's letters to him, which he had sent her when she was preparing the *Letters and Remains*: 'I am hoping to print before long an article on your dear husband, to whose friendship I have always looked back as to one of the chief honours and blessings of my life, and whose equal—taking all the gifts and qualities together—I have never yet met with.'[32] Tom's article, 'Arthur Hugh Clough: A Sketch' appeared in the January 1898 issue of the *Nineteenth Century*. It is pervaded by his enduring love for the poet he had first known as a schoolboy a few years his senior; he gives a clear sense of the remarkable personality that so impressed everyone who came across him, and his recollections of Oxford days and the 'Clougho-Matthean circle' are clear and precise. Tom included some extracts from the article in *Passages in a Wandering Life*; it may be that the opening up of memory involved in the essay on Clough prompted him to write his autobiography.

It was not only present-day Oxford that he was feeling doubtful about; he was showing signs of disaffection with his own employer, the Royal University of Ireland. On 29 June 1892 he wrote a cross letter to the Secretaries of the University, pointing out that that day was the Feast of Sts Peter and Paul, and was for Catholics a Holiday (i.e. 'holy day') of Obligation, when they were required to hear Mass and, if possible, abstain from 'servile work'. Instead of which, Arnold complained, he had been obliged to give up the day to the oral examination of degree candidates; examining, he remarked, may not be precisely 'servile work', but is drudgery none the less. He continued, 'Because the Protestant side of the Royal University has no respect for Catholic holidays, that is no reason why the Catholic side of the University should let itself be coerced into holding the same attitude. Rather the contrary is the case.'[33] In his article 'The Catholic University of Ireland', published in the *Dublin Review* in 1887, Arnold had stated that the system whereby the Royal University funded the University College in Dublin, though far from ideal, was a reasonable compromise and worth supporting. Ten years later, in a pamphlet called *Catholic Higher Education in Ireland*, which he described as a *balon d'essai*, he had changed his mind. He goes so far as to say that there were two Protestant universities in Dublin: Trinity, which was avowedly so; and the Royal University, which had become so by default, by not being clearly Catholic. The Jesuits running University College might have disagreed with their elderly colleague. Arnold calls for a new and specifically Catholic university in Ireland, and, like everyone who had engaged in this discussion from Newman's time onwards, looks to Louvain as the ideal. He refers, against the historical evidence, to Newman's original venture as having been 'supported by the zealous and substantial aid of Cardinal Cullen'.

In 1896 Mary Ward started thinking about a new novel, in which she would directly confront the subject which had so profoundly affected the lives of her parents and their children—Catholicism. In the chilly spring of the following year she rented an Elizabethan mansion in Westmorland, Levens Hall, which lay between the mountains of the Lake District and Morecambe Bay. Here she entertained a succession of visitors, Henry James among them, and Tom and Josephine. At Levens, and at the neighbouring Sizergh Castle, Mary found a physical setting which enabled her to start work on the book. Sizergh, the home of an old Catholic family, provided Mary with a particular inspiration, as her daughter recalls:

There the talk turned one day on the fortunes of an old Catholic family (the Stricklands), who had owned Sizergh Castle, near Sedgwick, for more than three centuries, steadfastly enduring the persecutions of earlier days, and, now that persecutions had ceased, fighting a sad and losing battle against poverty and mortgages. 'The vision of the old squire and the old house—of all the long vicissitudes of obscure suffering, and dumb clinging to the faith, of obstinate, half-conscious resistance to a modern world that in the end had stripped them of all their gear and possessions, save only this "I will not" of the soul—haunted me when the conversation was done'.[34]

The novel became *Helbeck of Bannisdale*; Bannisdale is a combination of Sizergh and Levens, in the same setting. As Janet Trevelyan puts it:

The theme of the book was, as all Mrs Ward's readers know, the eternal clash between the medieval and the modern mind in the persons of Alan Helbeck, the Catholic squire, and Laura Fountain, the child of science and negation; while beyond and behind their tragic loves stands the 'army of unalterable law' in the austere northern hills, the bog-lands of the estuary, the river in gentleness and flood. Almost, indeed, can it be said that there are but three characters in *Helbeck*—Alan himself, Laura, and the river, which in the end takes her tormented spirit.[35]

Helbeck of Bannisdale is a compelling story, and, as a novel dealing with large intellectual and moral questions, much superior to *Robert Elsmere*. Helbeck is an impressive creation, a bleak, austere figure who continually strives to repress his emotions. He is an embodiment of brooding unhappy maleness, akin to Charlotte Brontë's Mr Rochester. The *donnée* of the story is the arrival at the crumbling Bannisdale Hall of Laura Fountain, a fatherless girl who is the stepdaughter of Alan's sister. He has offered her a home there. Laura is an agnostic who has been brought up among advanced thinkers in Cambridge. Mary Ward insisted that Laura was 'not myself', and one can treat the claim with the respect and reserve that such statements warrant. She did, though, admit that she had given Laura her mother's intense anti-Catholicism. Despite their overwhelming differences in ideas and attitudes, Alan and Laura fall in love, and the novel moves to a predictably tragic conclusion. It has a markedly Gothic dimension in the stern, powerful character of Helsbeck and his crumbling mansion, but also in the larger consideration that Catholicism itself had a Gothic aspect for the English Protestant imagination. It was Italianate, exotic, given to strange rituals and cruel austerities, where nuns were immured in convents and priests repressed human freedoms. It was threatening but strangely fascinating.

In Mary Ward's novel Helbeck is a tormented, appealing figure; it is Laura who is 'on the side of life'. She contrasts the fresh beauty of the surrounding countryside with the gloom of Bannisdale Hall. She is shattered when Alan sells the one remaining beautiful object in the house, a portrait by Romney which she loves, to aid a Catholic charity. He persuades her to overcome some of her prejudice against Catholicism, but the most she can concede is that it is a good religion to die in but not to live in. Mary Ward wants to be fair to her father's religion, but her own prejudices prompt her to include what John Sutherland has called 'a gallery of gullible, ignorant, and sinister Catholics in her cast'. Acknowledging that, it is nevertheless true that in *Helbeck of Bannisdale* she caught something of the mode of Catholicism that was common in Northern Europe and North America at that time, and indeed up to the Second Vatican Council (and is still far from extinct), which, influenced by Jansenism, was austere, rigorous, and joyless.

Since her mother's death, Mary's relations with her father had become close and very loving. She wanted him to like the book, and when she was planning it asked him, 'Would you mind my dearest, if I chose a certain Catholic background for my next story?' It was hardly a question expecting the answer 'yes'. She also consulted the eminent Catholic, Lord Acton, with whom she had become friendly, 'who cordially encouraged me to work it out'.[36] Janet Trevelyan recalls:

She loved to discuss these matters with her father, from whom she had no secrets, is spite of their divergencies of view; when he came to visit us at Levens—still a tall and beautiful figure in spite of his seventy-three years—they talked of them endlessly, and when he returned to Dublin she wrote him such letters as the following: 'One of the main impressions of this Catholic literature upon me is to make me perceive the enormous intellectual pre-eminence of Newman. Another impression—I know you will forgive me for saying quite frankly what I feel—has been to fill me with a perfect horror of asceticism, or rather of the austerities—or most of them—which are indispensable to the Catholic idea of a saint.'[37]

When Mary had finished the book she engaged in some extensive rewriting which she hoped would make it more acceptable to her father. But he was silent when sent a set of proofs, and she concluded, probably rightly, that he still did not like it very much. Josephine made some cryptic remarks about it in a letter to her brother on 4 April 1898: 'she is to send Tom a proof copy, she gave me the opening chapters to read when we were at Levens—it promises to be a very striking work, & one to make a sensation, though not in the usual acceptation of the word—however not the keenest critic can predict how the public may take it'.[38] *Helbeck of Bannisdale* was published in June 1898 to good but not wildly enthusiastic reviews; Mary hoped that Catholics would like it, and she was agreeably surprised by the review in the *Tablet*. Two priests were reported to have spoken favourably of it: Tom's Jesuit colleague Fr Darlington (though he had the reputation of speaking well of everything); and Fr Ignatius Ryder, Newman's successor as superior of the Birmingham Oratory. Mary eagerly reported these responses to Tom, but he never commented.

In the summer of 1898 Tom and Josephine took separate holidays. On the afternoon of 30 July he set sail from Hull for Sweden. It was a country he had long wanted to visit as the home of St Brigid, and he hoped to see her shrine. He also wanted to go to Röskilde in Denmark, which was reputed to be the setting of *Beowulf*. Mary was rather anxious about him undertaking this solitary journey at his age, but Josephine was quite relaxed. She told her brother, 'I believe that 99 men out of 100 like "an out" to themselves occasionally—Tom says "a man's inclination is to fling apart for a while"—he was quite willing to bring me with him, but truly, I do not believe he was sorry to go alone—it has always been his way—he will DV return to me quickened in his love and tenderness by our little absence.'[39] Josephine meanwhile was in France with her cousin Lottie Geary, another female companion, a niece, and an assortment of nephews for a seaside holiday at Veules-les-Roses, near Dieppe.

From Göteborg Tom travelled across southern Sweden on water, by lakes and canals. He broke his journey at Vadestena, where St Brigid was said to be buried in a medieval church that was full of tombs. A sexton showed him a collection of bones, contained with two chests, that were said to be those of St Brigid and her daughter; but when Tom got to Stockholm he was told by an authority that these relics were almost certainly inauthentic and that no-one knew for certain where the saint was buried. He continued his journey to the east coast and his first sight of the Baltic, and then sailed on to Stockholm. He got as far as Uppsala, where he was shown St Brigid's apron in the treasury of the cathedral, and was struck by a modern painted window, presented by the king of Sweden, showing the saint life-sized, in the habit of her order. The Lutheran Swedes venerated Brigid as a great national figure. Tom commented, 'It is impossible to imagine Queen Victoria similarly presenting Canterbury Cathedral with a window representing St Thomas à Becket in full canonicals; the shock which such an act would inflict on the Protestant feeling of the country could not safely be disregarded.'[40] Tom was kindly received by the scholars and academics to whom he had introductions; he appreciated Sweden but was clearly not enthusiastic about it. He travelled back via Copenhagen, Kiel, Hamburg, and Rotterdam.

By 20 August Tom had joined Josephine in France; 'he looks well', she reported, 'still I think he will be glad of a rest here'. At the beginning of September they were back in England and spending a few days in London, enjoying the social and cultural life of the city, and each other's company; Josephine told her brother, 'Tom and I were just "daundering about" all day—did the National Gallery—had an early dinner at a Restaurant—visited Mrs Dunne [Julia's sister], who always gives us a most cordial welcome—we had afternoon Tea there, & dine with her on Sunday.'[41] Then they were at Stocks and at Fox How, before returning to Dublin.

In the spring of 1899 Tom made another trip abroad, this time with Josephine. Mary, still spending lavishly, was renting an apartment in the Villa Barberini at Castel Gandolfo, outside Rome, and she invited them to a holiday there at her expense. Tom was never averse to accepting hospitality and he readily took up her offer. Mary recorded with complacent but understandable pride her father's first visit to Rome:

My dear father, with his second wife, arrived to spend a week with us [three weeks, according to Tom]. Never before, throughout all his ardent Catholic life, had it been possible to tread the streets of Rome, or kneel in St Peter's. At last, the year before his death, he was to climb the Janiculum, and to look out over the city and the plain whence Europe derived her civilization and the vast system of the Catholic Church. He felt as a Catholic; but hardly less as a scholar, one to whom Horace and Virgil had been familiar from his boyhood, the greater portion of them known by heart, to a degree which is not common now. I remember well that one bright May morning at Castel Gandolfo, he vanished from the Villa, and presently after some hours reappeared with shining eyes.

'I have been on the Appian Way—I have walked where Horace walked!'[42]

In *Passages in a Wandering Life* Tom gives a detailed account of the things he had seen and the places he had visited in Rome; his pleasure in the experience is evident, but his descriptions are dry and impersonal. There is no mention of Mary, to whose generosity he owed the visit, and nothing about Josephine and how she spent the time. He does, however, engage in some interesting reflections about the contemporary political situation in Rome. After the kingdom of Italy, now finally united, took over the papal lands in 1870 the papacy refused to recognize it and adopted a rejectionist stance. Tom Arnold, writing as a loyal Catholic, felt that this situation could not continue indefinitely, and that church and state would have to come to some kind of compromise. Eventually they did, but not for another thirty years.

In October 1899 the Boer War (more precisely, the Second Anglo-Boer War) broke out and found Mary and Tom on different sides. She had become jingoistic over the years and was strongly in favour of the British cause. Tom, despite the growing conservatism of his social and intellectual attitudes, retained some of his early radicalism, and this, combined with the moderate Irish nationalism of the milieu in which he now lived, made him firmly opposed to the war. He described it as 'an unjust and abominable war' in a draft letter to a magazine protesting against an attempt to make French-Canadian students celebrate the relief of Ladysmith, saying that these students 'naturally object to becoming Jingoes under compulsion'.[43] Despite these differences, Mary and Tom were used to agreeing to disagree, as they did about religion, and John Sutherland's claim that 'Tom and Mary quarrelled bitterly about the Boer War ... a final rift between them that haunted her after his death'[44] is very wide of the mark. There is no trace of a 'final rift' in the gentle, affectionate letters that she sent him in the last year of his life, which was also the first year of the war.[45] In April 1900 he was staying with her in London, and referring to the 'dear child' and her solicitude for his cold (Mary was nearly 50).[46] The previous November Tom and Mary had been together at a large, melancholy family gathering at Wharfeside in Yorkshire, for the funeral of Jane Forster, Dr Arnold's first child, the beloved 'K'.

Tom Arnold kept up a connection with University College Dublin until his death, at least to the extent of giving occasional lectures. They were not all on literary subjects; in February 1899 he was lecturing on German history, and wrote to Acton asking for information on a disputed point. If Arnold's fellowship at the Royal University of Ireland, which provided his income, was for life, he might have felt that he should go on doing something to earn it. Constantine Curran, who was a first-year student during Arnold's last year of life, 1899–1900, wrote an engaging account of him in 1954:

In reviving the memory of Father Delany's first staff, I must necessarily rely on tradition, but curiously enough, my own recollection goes back to one who was in the original group appointed by Newman himself, and yet was one of my own examiners. I mean, of course, Thomas Arnold. Tommy Arnold, as we all called him, was Matthew Arnold's brother and held the first chair in English Literature. He was a man of seventy-six or seven when I knew him and had for some years given up regular class work, but I heard him once in the Aula Maxima and, though I have forgotten what he said of Beowulf and Cynewulf, I am not alone in re-membering his clear but thin utterance with its slight stammer, his tall figure stooped at the reading desk, clear-cut features with wide mouth and the fringe of the side whiskers which he wore in the fashion of men of his generation like the old Chief Baron. Looking down on the Green from the windows of our English Literature class we used to see him pass every Saturday morning coming from his house in Leeson Street [the adjacent Adelaide Road, in fact] to the University Church, and we watched with affectionate respect this old gentleman of varied religious experience who, at Grasmere, had seen Wordsworth called to order at a meeting held in protest against the introduction of railways to the Lake District, and in the poet's own house had heard him read a sonnet he had just written.[47]

Curran was a close friend of his fellow-student James Joyce, who drew on his own experiences at the college in *Stephen Hero* and *A Portrait of the Artist as a Young Man*. In his book *James Joyce Remembered* (written when he was well into his eighties) Curran refers more briefly and coolly to Arnold: 'In our time he took no part in the day-by-day teaching. Joyce, like myself, may have attended some of the formal public course of lectures . . . to which Tommy Arnold contributed, but our only real contact with him was at the University Orals, over which, as the oldest Fellow, he presided.'[48] Though Arnold was not involved in everyday undergraduate teaching, there was at least one occasion when he had direct contact with Joyce. Stanislaus Joyce, in his memoir of his brother, recalls, 'He had at-tacked *Macbeth* vigorously for its formal deficiencies in an essay to which Thomas Arnold had assigned a high classification . . .'.[49] The encounter between Arnold and Joyce, however fleeting, is symbolically resonant.

On the outside wall of the old college in St Stephen's Green, now Newman House, there is a plaque recording the three great writers who had passed through its doors: Newman as rector, Hopkins as a professor, and Joyce as an undergraduate. Arnold had dealings with all three.

This brief contact with one who was to become a transforming literary force of the twentieth century shows the temporal range of Arnold's acquaintance; in his youth he was familiar with Wordsworth, who was born in 1770, and he had seen at close quarters the Duke of Wellington, born a year earlier. In other respects, too, he had witnessed the prodigious cultural and technological changes of the nineteenth century, and, before he died, had a glimpse of further innovations. He had experienced the passing of stage coaches and the arrival of the railway, and at the very end of his life he encountered an early version of the cinema. On 13 April 1900 he wrote to Josephine from London, where he was staying with Mary, about his visit to the Biograph in Regent Street: 'The "biograph",—another name for the "cinematograph", is very well worth seeing. To see a squadron of cavalry galloping straight down upon you, and then, bearing slightly to the right, pass outside the field of vision, is an astonishing and incomprehensible sight.' [50] This may be the first account of a film by an English writer, even earlier than Kipling's 'Mrs Bathurst'.

Tom Arnold's last book, *Passages in a Wandering Life*, was published in 1900, under the imprint of his nephew, the younger Edward Arnold. It is a relaxed, good-natured narrative if read as an account of people and places, and is at its best in the detailed recall of his early life and his experiences in New Zealand and Tasmania. It is a book that gives away very little of his feelings and which avoids emotionally difficult situations, to the extent of being evasive. Although Tom was in the house at the time of his father's death, in 1842, he declines to say anything about it, referring readers to the account by Arthur Stanley, who got it at second-hand. He says nothing about Julia's hostile reactions to his successive conversions to Catholicism. Indeed, he passes over in silence the six difficult years he spent in London, between his departure from Oxford and his move to Dublin, when his relations with his wife were often at crisis point. He refers to himself as being resident in Oxford from 1865 to 1888, though spending the university terms during the last six years in Dublin; this is true only in the technical and misleading sense that he remained an Oxford householder during that time. There is no mention of Josephine and his second marriage. Tom's offspring Mary and Frank read a draft of the book and commented on the omissions, but he does not seem to have made material changes as a result, though his remarks about Thomas Hughes and *Tom Brown's Schooldays* may have been inserted in response to a suggestion of Frank's.

It is only in the rather bleak Preface, dated 'Dublin, February 1900', that he suggests depths and complexities of feeling. He refers to his father's influence on Matthew and himself, and his belief in their future:

> In my case, it must be confessed, his confidence was somewhat rash; and there is no telling whether difficulties which I escaped, or was helped through, simply because I bore an honoured name, might not have overwhelmed me under other circumstances.
>
> Through Oxford I passed according to my father's wish and disposal; and what is said in the narrative as to the early unsettlement of my opinions must not be taken for an admission that I had lost all power of self-control. I held on to the Oxford life, though it had become distasteful to me, till I had taken my degree; knowing that an Oxford degree, and a good place in the class-list, were an insurance against future embarrassment and want, which who ever had the power to provide himself with, was inexcusable if he did not do so.
>
> Whether or not I acted foolishly in going out to New Zealand, I declare on my conscience I do not know; those who shall do me the favour to read the following chapters will be in as good a position to form a judgment on that point as I am myself.[51]

Readers of the autobiography are no more likely than Tom himself to be able to decide the matter. Going to New Zealand was a way of distancing himself from the family and his father's memory, and of following a different path from his brother. In 1847 both Matthew and Tom were in government employment, with the patronage of Whig ministers. Leaving his poetry out of account, Matthew went on from there to a useful if unglamorous life in public service, and eventually to renown as a public moralist. If Tom had stayed in London he might have followed a similar course, but given his temperament it was probably not feasible for him. In his last years he occasionally engaged in troubled, counter-factual reflections about how different things might have been. In 1896, after telling Frances about his lecture on *Beowulf* to 'a very small audience indeed', he remarked on the fact that he had read it without being at all troubled by his stammer. 'This sets me thinking. If I could have had the same command of my voice 40 years ago, many things might have happened differently. Lord Carlisle might not then have found it so impossible to induct me into some government employment, and the terrible word, "*Inefficiency*"! would not then have burnt itself in upon my brain.'[52]

Nothing else is known about this possible attempt to enter public service in Dublin in the 1850s, nor the source of the charge of 'inefficiency'. Such soul-searching is absent from the rest of the autobiography; it is characteristic of Tom's devout and generally sunny temperament that by the end of the letter he is expressing his trust in the goodness of God and his hope to serve him better.

To read Victorian correspondence is to encounter a people who enjoyed ill-health. Tom's letters, and those of the other principal figures in this narrative, are full of accounts of coughs, colds, rheumatism, eyestrain, and other disorders, with careful notes of whether they seemed to be getting better or worse. It is easy to dismiss them as background noise (the progress of Julia's cancer was a different matter, of course, though one still gets the sense that she enjoyed describing it). Despite all this, Tom seemed healthy enough and managed to lead a cheerfully active life. In April 1900, when he was staying with Mary, he had suffered from a bad cold but had shaken it off. In the autumn he succumbed to another, combined with a fresh attack of what he described as rheumatism. On 21 October he wrote to Frances:

I have been troubled during the last week with a severer form of rheumatism than I am used to; the pain of it not flying but fixed, and the result incapacitating. The day after my return here from Fox How, the first attack came; severe pain in the chest, causing faintness and a sense of weakness; several nights since then the pain, though less severe, has returned; so yesterday, as Josephine wished it, I saw Cox, and he has prescribed no end of medicine. Today, though the sun is bright, the north west wind is bitterly cold, and I feel quite unable to brave it.[53]

Tom was not to recover, and died on 12 November; the cause of death was stated as congestion of the lungs and heart failure. After his death, Josephine described his last days to General Collinson:

His illness ran its course quickly, at first it seemed a simple cold—the 26 Oct his doctor saw him, it was not till four days later that he kept his room; the 3rd Novr. I was anxious, for nothing relieved his cough, and his nights were restless, the 5th Novr. his daughter Mrs H Ward came, and that night his son Dr Frank Arnold arrived from Manchester, then the 7th his daughter Mrs Huxley, and Ethel Arnold also came, so he had the comfort of four of his children beside him. There was no acute suffering, and the cough lessened, the bronchitis was slight from the first, it was his weakness which baffled all remedies. God called him, and we could not keep him. Sunday, Novr. 4th, he received the last Sacraments with a faith and reverence, it was an example to witness. All through his illness he was so sweet and patient, though there was much to try him in the constant taking of medicines, and of nourishment, he was not inclined for.[54]

The last Sacraments had been administered by Fr Darlington, the original of the Dean of Studies in Joyce's *Portrait of the Artist*. Mary, who was, as Sutherland remarks, a connoisseur of deathbed scenes, described the situation to her brother Will, himself a very sick man at that time: 'He knew me quite well—when I arrived between six and seven—said "Mary!" with a look of pleasure, opened his arms, and said God bless you.' Later she asked him if he loved her and forgave her everything: 'He made a motion as though to put up his hand to my cheek, with a sweet faint smile.'[55] In her letter to General Collinson Josephine wrote, 'It was a great privilege to have shared his companionship for ten years, life beside him was so beautiful only those who came into close contact could realize the tenderness and unselfishness of his character.'[56] Josephine's sentiments were echoed in the *Times* obituary published on 13 November: 'his steadfast pursuit of high aims, his gentle nature and his exquisite old-fashioned courtesy made him greatly beloved'.

Tom's children were happy for him to be buried in Dublin, and Josephine remarked, 'it is a comfort to me that he rests in the land he loved, and served so well'. In a letter to Mandell Creighton on 15 November, Mary wrote, 'My father's was a rare and *hidden* nature.' She described the requiem Mass and the burial at Glasnevin cemetery: 'The service yesterday in Newman's beautiful little University Church, the early mass, the bright morning light on the procession of friends and clergy through the cypress-lined paths of Glasnevin, the last "requiescat in pace" answered by the Amen of the little crowd—all made a fitting close to his gentle and laborious life.'[57] Tom Arnold is commemorated in the University Church by a plaque showing him in handsome profile; it was said by the family to be a good likeness.

Tom had made a will, but it was not properly executed, so he was regarded as intestate. A Letter of Administration was granted to Josephine by the Probate Divison of the High Court, dated 19 December 1900. It showed that his gross estate was 1,256 pounds 3 shillings 6 pence, on which duty of 35 pounds 19 shillings 3 pence had been paid.[58] It was a respectable sum for someone whose earlier life had been so entangled in debt. Various sums were distributed to his children, in accordance with the wishes he had expressed in his will.

Josephine returned to Slieve Russell and was active in caring for members of her family and carrying out other good works; she died in 1919. Tom had outlived all his brothers and two of his four sisters. Two of his adult children had predeceased him, Arthur and Lucy. William was already very ill when his father died, suffering from the long-term effects of syphilis, which the respectable scholar and journalist had picked up at some stage of his life; a troubling manifestation of the large dark side of Victorian sexuality. When he could no longer work, Mary supported him financially until his death, in 1904. Before he died he collaborated with her in an admiring and informative memorial article on his father, which was published in the *Century Magazine* in New York in 1903; at Mary's insistence it appeared with only his name on it. Of Tom's other children, Theodore was in New Zealand and had been lost sight of. Julia died in 1908, when she was only 46; her death deeply affected her young son Aldous Huxley and is reflected in his writings. Mary died in 1920, Frank in 1927, and Ethel in 1930. Mary was outlived by Dr Arnold's youngest child, Frances, Aunt Fan of Fox How, who died in 1923 at the age of 90.

The elder Thomas Arnold had been in every sense a character, to be summarized in the words Matthew used in 'Rugby Chapel': 'O strong soul … that force … that strength'. Duty was his ideal; one might, after examination of conscience, find one had been on the wrong path. In which case one took to the right path and did not look back. Life was too short for much self-questioning. The younger Thomas was more of a personality than a character. As a personality he was attractive but sometimes awkward, never sure of himself in the way his father was, but always curious about the world. His encounters with people, places, and ideas made him a remarkable witness to his times. He was an immensely likeable man, dogged by a sense of failure, of false steps and missed opportunities. He may have been right about the failure, at least as the world saw it. But stories of human failure can be as interesting, moving, and enlightening as success stories.

Appendix: A letter from Matthew Arnold

This previously unpublished letter is in the Benison family papers, and is now printed by kind permission of Harriet Bennett and Frederick Whitridge. It continues Matthew's practice of sending his brother a letter of greetings on his birthday; it bears no year, but internal evidence shows it was written in 1881. Matthew refers to Lord Emly's efforts to find a position for Tom in the new Royal University in Ireland, which were successful the following year when he became a professorial fellow and returned to Dublin. The poem Matthew describes is 'Westminster Abbey', written in memory of Arthur Stanley, Dean of the Abbey, who had died in July. The poem draws on a legend that St Peter had appeared to an Anglo-Saxon fisherman on the Thames and shown him a vision of the abbey in all its future glory. It is one of the last of Matthew's poems of any substance, and was published in the January 1882 number of the *Nineteenth Century*, edited by A. S. Knowles. Matthew's reference to a post at the Bodleian that he had been considering is puzzling; there is no reference to it in his published correspondence or in Honan's biography. Two years before Matthew had looked into the possibility of Tom's taking up a sub-librarianship at the Bodleian, which had come to nothing. On this occasion, with Tom offering advice to Matthew, their customary relationship was reversed.

Athenaeum Club,   Nov. 29th
Pall Mall, S.W.

My dear old boy. One word of cordial and affectionate good wishes on your birthday. It will be cheered by your nomination to this examinership—a nomination which Lord Emly tells me will probably be followed by your appointment as professor and fellow. Jane comes over today, and will be in London till Friday, when Lucy returns with her. Hutton, the bonesetter, has certainly done the foot great good, but it will be a while before she can move it like the other. When are you going over to Dublin? I wish you would give us a night first. I have been writing a poem on dear A.P.S., which I am rather pleased with. It is for Knowles, of the

XIXth Century. You will learn from it who consecrated the original Westminster Abbey. It is just the sort of poem that dear A.P.S. himself would have liked, I think, and that is a source of great satisfaction to me.

As to the Bodleian, I have heard nothing more from Jowett, but I have seen Mark Pattison, who says the post would be intolerable to me, and that I should not retain it for six months. This was rather your view, though you did not put it so strongly. But I think you clearly leaned to the opinion that I should be bothered in the post—and probably you were right. It will not now be offered to me, I imagine; but I like the thought of it even less than I did when I talked to you. Let me have one line to Cobham; I hope Julia is well and prospering.

Ever your most affectionate brother, M.A.

I was glad to hear of Theodore's having got a Schoolmastership.

Bibliography

MANUSCRIPT SOURCES

Balliol College, Oxford: Thomas Arnold papers
Harriet Bennett, Felixstowe: Benison family papers
Brotherton Library, Leeds: Arnold family papers
Cambridge University Library: Acton papers
Pusey House, Oxford: Ward papers
Wordsworth Trust, Grasmere: Arnold family papers

PUBLISHED WRITINGS BY THOMAS ARNOLD THE YOUNGER

'The Filibusters in Nicaragua', *Dublin Review*, Dec. 1857.
'Genius of Alcibiades', *Atlantis*, July 1858.
'Mill, *On Liberty*', Pts 1 and 2, *Rambler*, Nov. 1859 and March 1860.
'The Catholic University of Ireland', *Rambler*, May 1860.
'Sir Walter Scott', *Rambler*, May 1860.
'The Negro Race and its Destiny', Pts 1 and 2, *Rambler*, July and Sept. 1860.
'The Irish Church', *Rambler*, March 1861.
'Reminiscences of New Zealand', *Fraser's Magazine*, August 1861.
A Manual of English Literature, Historical and Critical: With an Appendix on English Metres (London, 1862; further rev. edns in 1867, 1873, 1877, 1885, 1888, 1897).
'Hayti', *Home and Foreign Review*, Oct. 1862.
'Venn's *Life of St Francis Xavier*', *Home and Foreign Review*, Jan. 1863.
'Albania', *Home and Foreign Review*, July 1863.
'The Formation of the English Counties', *Home and Foreign Review*, Oct. 1863.
'The Colonization of Northumbria', *Home and Foreign Review*, April 1864.
'Bristol Churches', *Fraser's Magazine*, Feb. 1865.
'Recent Novel Writing', *Macmillan's Magazine*, Jan. 1866.
Select English Works of John Wiclif, edited from Original Mss, ed., 3 vols. (Oxford, 1869–71).
Chaucer to Wordsworth. A Short History of English Literature from the Earliest Times to the Present Day (London, 1870).
The Revival of the Faculties at Oxford (Oxford, 1872).
Selections from Addison's Spectator Papers, ed. (London, 1875).
Pope: Selected Poems, ed. (London, 1876).

Beowulf: A Heroic Poem of the 8th Century, With a Translation, Notes and Appendix
(London, 1876).

Henrici, Archdiaconi Huntendunensis, Historia Anglorum, ed. (Rolls series, London,
1879).

'Dr Littledale's *Plain Reasons Against Joining the Church of Rome*', *Contemporary Review*,
May 1880.

'Spenser as a Textbook', *Dublin Review*, October 1880.

Symeonis Monachi opera omnia, ed., 2 vols. (Rolls series, London, 1882–5).

*English Poetry and Prose. A Collection of Illustrative Passages from the Writings of English
Authors*, ed. (London, 1882).

Catholic Dictionary (with W. E. Addis), (London, 1884; rev. edns., 1893, 1897, 1903,
1917, 1928, 1951).

Clarendon. History of the Rebellion, Book V, ed. (London, 1886; 2nd edn., 1894).

'Church Extension and Anglican Expansion', *Dublin Review*, April 1887.

'The Catholic University of Ireland', *Dublin Review*, Oct. 1887.

Sketches from the Carte Papers, Including Several Unpublished Letters of Oliver Cromwell,
ed. (Oxford, 1888).

'Matthew Arnold, by One who Knew him Well', *Manchester Guardian*, 18 May
1888.

'Louvain and Dublin', *Dublin Review*, Oct. 1888.

Dryden's Essay of Dramatic Poesy, ed. (London, 1889).

Memorials of St Edmund's Abbey, ed., 3 vols. (Rolls series, London, 1890–6).

'King John and the Abbot of Bury', *Contemporary Review*, June 1893.

Notes on the Sacrifice of the Altar (London, 1897).

Catholic Higher Education in Ireland (Dublin, 1897).

Notes on Beowulf (London, 1898).

'Arthur Hugh Clough: A Sketch', *Nineteenth Century*, Jan. 1898.

Passages in a Wandering Life (London, 1900).

The New Zealand Letters of Thomas Arnold the Younger, ed. J. Bertram (Auckland and
Oxford, 1966).

The Letters of Thomas Arnold the Younger, ed., J. Bertram (Auckland and Oxford,
1980).

OTHER SOURCES

Acton, Lord and Simpson, Richard, *Correspondence*, ed. J. L. Altholz, D. McElrath,
and J. C. Holland, 3 vols. (Cambridge, 1973).

Altholz, Josef L., *The Liberal Catholic Movement in England: The Rambler and its
Contributors 1848–1864* (London, 1962).

Arnold, Matthew, *Complete Prose Works*, ed. R. H. Super, 11 vols. (Ann Arbor,
1960–77).

—— *The Poems*, ed. Kenneth Allott (London, 1965).

Arnold, Matthew, *Letters*, ed. C. Y. Lang, 6 vols. (Charlottesville and London, 1996–2001).

Arnold, W. T., 'Thomas Arnold the Younger', *Century Magazine*, May 1903.

Arnold, William Delafield, *Oakfield; or, Fellowship in the East* (London, 1853; new edn., ed. Kenneth Allott, Leicester, 1973).

Askwith, Betty, *Lady Dilke: A Biography* (London, 1969).

Axon, J. E., 'The Life of Thomas Arnold the Younger', Ph.D. thesis, University of Leeds, 1975.

Bagehot, Walter, *Literary Studies*, 2 vols. (London, 1911).

Carroll, Lewis (C. L. Dodgson), *Diaries*, ed. R. L. Green (London, 1953).

—— *Letters*, ed. M. N. Cohen (London, 1979).

Carlyle, Thomas, *Wilhelm Meister's Apprenticeship and Travels, Translated from the German of Goethe*, 2 vols. (London, 1907).

Chadwick, Owen, *The Victorian Church*, 2 parts (London, 1966 and 1970).

—— *A History of the Popes 1830–1914* (Oxford, 1998).

Chorley, Katharine, *Arthur Hugh Clough: The Uncommitted Mind* (Oxford, 1962).

Clough, Arthur Hugh, *Correspondence*, ed. F. L. Mulhauser, 2 vols. (Oxford, 1957).

—— *The Poems*, 2nd edn., ed. F. L. Mulhauser (Oxford, 1974).

—— *Oxford Diaries*, ed. Anthony Kenny (Oxford, 1990).

Cockshut, A. O. J., *Truth to Life: The Art of Biography in the Nineteenth Century* (London, 1974).

Collini, Stefan, *Public Moralists: Political Thought and Intellectual Life in Britain 1850–1930* (Oxford, 1991).

Coventry, John (ed.), *Bishops and Writers: Aspects of the Evolution of Modern English Catholicism* (Wheathampton, 1977).

Curran, C. P., *James Joyce Remembered* (London, 1968).

Daly, Mary, 'Dublin in the 1880s', in *Hopkins and Dublin: The Man and the City*; special issue of the *Hopkins Quarterly*, 14, 1–4 (1987–8).

Dodds, J. W., *The Age of Paradox* (London, 1953).

Engels, Friedrich, *The Condition of the Working Class in England* (1845; London, 1986).

Faber, Geoffrey, *Jowett: A Portrait with Background* (London, 1957).

Gill, Stephen, *William Wordsworth: A Life* (Oxford, 1989).

Hill, Roland, *Lord Acton* (New Haven and London, 2000).

Hinchcliffe, Tanis, *North Oxford* (New Haven and London, 1992).

The History of the University of Oxford, Vol. 5, *The Eighteenth Century*, ed. L. S. Sutherland and M. G. Mitchell (Oxford, 1986).

—— Vol. 7, *The Nineteenth Century*, pt 2, ed. M. C. Brock and M. C. Curthoys (Oxford, 2000).

Honan, Park, *Matthew Arnold: A Life* (London, 1981).

Hopkins, Gerard Manley, *Letters to Robert Bridges*, ed. C. C. Abbott, 2nd edn. (London, 1955).

—— *Correspondence with Richard Watson Dixon*, ed. C. C. Abbott, 2nd edn. (London, 1955).

—— *Further Letters*, ed. C. C. Abbott, 2nd edn. (London, 1956).

Howell, P. A., *Thomas Arnold the Younger in Van Diemen's Land* (Hobart, 1964).

Hughes, Thomas, *Tom Brown's Schooldays* (London, 1857).

—— *Tom Brown at Oxford* (London, 1861).

Huxley, Julian, *Memories* (London, 1970).

Huyshe, Wentworth, *Beowulf: An Old English Epic* (London, 1905).

James, Henry, *Letters*, ed. Leon Edel, 4 vols. (London, 1974), i.

Jones, E. W., *Mrs Humphry Ward* (London, 1973).

Ker, Ian, *John Henry Newman: A Biography* (Oxford, 1988).

Kneale, Matthew, *English Passengers* (London, 2000).

McGrath, Fergal, *Newman's University: Idea and Reality* (London, 1951).

Martin, R. B., *Gerard Manley Hopkins: A Very Private Life* (London, 1991).

Matthew, David, *Lord Acton and his Times* (London, 1968).

Morrissey, T. J., *Towards a National University* (Dublin, 1983).

Newman, J. H., *Loss and Gain* (London, 1848).

—— *The Idea of a University* (London, 1873).

—— *A Letter addressed to His Grace the Duke of Norfolk* (London, 1875).

—— *Letters and Diaries*, ed. C. S. Dessain *et al.*, Vols. 16–29 (London and Oxford, 1965–76).

A Page of Irish History: The Story of University College, Dublin 1883–1909, compiled by Fathers of the Society of Jesus (Dublin, 1930).

Pattison, Mark, *Memoirs* (London, 1885).

Peterson, William S., *Victorian Heretic: Mrs Humphry Ward's Robert Elsmere* (Leicester, 1976).

Sand, George, *Jacques* (Paris, 1834).

Sinclair, Keith, *A History of New Zealand* (London, 1961).

Stanley, A. P., *The Life of Thomas Arnold, D.D.* (London, 1844; 1903).

Strachey, Lytton, *Eminent Victorians* (London, 1918).

Sutherland, John, *Mrs Humphry Ward: Eminent Victorian, Pre-eminent Edwardian* (Oxford, 1990).

Tierney, Michael (ed.), *Struggle with Fortune* (Dublin, 1954).

Trevor, Meriol, *The Arnolds: Thomas Arnold and His Family* (London, 1973).

Trevelyan, Janet Penrose, *The Life of Mrs Humphry Ward* (London, 1923).

Ward, Mrs Humphry (Mary), *Robert Elsmere* (London, 1888).

—— *Helbeck of Bannisdale* (London, 1898).

—— *A Writer's Recollections* (London, 1918).

Ward, Mrs Humphry and Montague, C. E., *William Thomas Arnold: Journalist and Historian* (Manchester, 1907).

Ward, Wilfrid, *The Life of John Henry Cardinal Newman*, 2 vols. (London, 1912).

West, John, *The History of Tasmania*, 2 vols. (Launceston, 1852; facsimile reprint, Adelaide, 1966).

Wilde, Oscar, *Complete Works* (London, 1948).

Wilson, A. N., *God's Funeral* (London, 1999).

Woodward, F. J., *The Doctor's Disciples: A Study of Four Pupils of Arnold of Rugby* (London, 1954).

Wordsworth, Mary, *Letters 1800–1855*, ed. M. E. Burton (Oxford, 1958).

Wordsworth, William and Wordswoth, Dorothy, *Letters*, ed. A. G. Hill, Vols. 6 and 8 (Oxford, 1982, 1993).

Wymer, Norman, *Dr Arnold of Rugby* (London, 1953).

Young, G. M., *Victorian England: Portait of an Age*, 2nd edn. (London, 1960).

Notes

CHAPTER I

1. Norman Wymer, *Dr Arnold of Rugby* (London, 1953), 70.
2. Ibid., 88.
3. Ibid., 137.
4. MW, 9.
5. MW, 9.
6. MW, 10.
7. MW, 8 n.
8. G. M. Young, *Victorian England: Portrait of an Age*, 2nd edn. (London, 1960), 70 n.
9. A. P. Stanley, *The Life of Thomas Arnold D.D.* (London, 1844; 1903 edn.), 197–8.
10. *Letters of William and Dorothy Wordsworth*, ed. A. G. Hill, 8 vols. (Oxford, 1993), viii. 215.
11. *Letters of Mary Wordsworth 1800–1855*, ed. M. E. Burton (Oxford, 1958), 137.
12. TA, 12–13.
13. TA, 38–9.
14. 'Fox How Magazine', 1838, Arnold Papers, Wordsworth Trust, Grasmere.
15. 'Fox How Magazine', 1838.
16. TA, 16.
17. Stanley, 217.
18. Stephen Gill, *William Wordsworth: A Life* (Oxford, 1989), 406.
19. 'Arthur Hugh Clough: A Sketch', *Nineteenth Century*, January 1898, 105–16.
20. Katharine Chorley, *Arthur Hugh Clough: The Uncommitted Mind* (Oxford, 1962), 37.
21. 'Arthur Hugh Clough', 105–16.
22. Walter Bagehot, *Literary Studies*, 2 (London, 1911), 275–6.
23. Park Honan, *Matthew Arnold: A Life* (London, 1981), 46.
24. Wordsworth, *Letters*, vi. 709.
25. MA, i. 39.
26. Dr Thomas Arnold, Journal-Notebook, Arnold Papers, Box 2, Brotherton Library, Leeds.
27. Arthur Hugh Clough, *Correspondence*, ed. F. L. Mulhauser, 2 vols. (Oxford, 1957), i. 114.
28. TA, 55.
29. L, 226–7.
30. Stanley, 317.
31. A. O. J. Cockshut, *Truth to Life: The Art of Biography in the Nineteenth Century* (London, 1974).

CHAPTER 2

1. MA, i. 53 n.
2. TA, p. vi.
3. Arthur Hugh Clough, *Oxford Diaries*, ed. A. Kenny (Oxford, 1990), lxii; NZL, 233.
4. TA, 58.
5. MA, i. 359.
6. TA, 58.
7. L, 157.
8. MA, i. 135 n.
9. TA, 59.
10. MA, i. 63.
11. MA, i. 155.
12. MA, i. 446.
13. W. T. Arnold, 'Thomas Arnold the Younger', *Century Magazine*, May 1903, 115–28.
14. Quoted by A. N. Wilson, *God's Funeral* (London, 1999), 406.
15. MW, 40.
16. 'Emerson', *Complete Prose Works*, ed. R. H. Super, vol. 10 (Ann Arbor, 1974).
17. TA, 150.
18. TA, 57.
19. Owen Chadwick, *The Victorian Church*, Part One (London, 1966), 210.
20. MW, 12.
21. NZL, 210–11.
22. Frances J. Woodward, *The Doctor's Disciples: A Study of Four Pupils of Arnold of Rugby* (London, 1954), 44.
23. TA, 41–2.
24. MA, i. 69.
25. Clough, *Correspondence*, i. 150.
26. Clough, *Correspondence*, i. 159.
27. NZL, 210.
28. NZL, xxviii.
29. Friedrich Engels, *The Condition of the Working Class in England* (London, 1986), 57.
30. NZL, 215.
31. NZL, 1.
32. TA, 58.
33. Clough, *Correspondence*, i. 181.
34. NZL, 7–8.
35. MA, i. 71.
36. TA, 150.
37. 'Arthur Hugh Clough', 105–16.
38. NZL, xxx.
39. NZL, 217.

40. L, 38.
41. J. W. Dodds, *The Age of Paradox* (London, 1953), 306.
42. Clough, *Correspondence*, i. 181.
43. NZL, 2.
44. Clough, *Correspondence*, i. 243.
45. MA, i. 97.
46. MA, i. 109.
47. NZL, 4.
48. NZL, 5.
49. MA, i. 16.
50. NZL, 6.
51. TA, 64.
52. NZL, 11.
53. NZL, 12.
54. NZL, 7.
55. Chorley, 132.
56. MA, i. 72.
57. MA, i. 73–4.
58. 'Reminiscences of New Zealand', *Fraser's Magazine*, August (1861), 246–56.

CHAPTER 3

1. TA, 68.
2. NZL, 217.
3. TA, 69.
4. NZL, 27.
5. NZL, 27.
6. NZL, 29.
7. Keith Sinclair, *A History of New Zealand* (London, 1961), 22.
8. L, 8–9.
9. TA, 85.
10. NZL, 54.
11. NZL, 54.
12. NZL, 58.
13. NZL, 62.
14. TA, 91.
15. NZL, 82.
16. Sinclair, 79.
17. TA, 97.
18. TA, 106.
19. NZL, 105.
20. NZL, 116.
21. See the account of Gell in Woodward, *The Doctor's Disciples*.

22. Quoted by Chorley, 226.
23. NZL, 124.
24. Sinclair, 88.
25. NZL, 118.
26. NZL, 127.
27. NZL, 127.
28. NZL, 131.
29. MA, i. 167.
30. L, 1.

CHAPTER 4

1. NZL, 173.
2. NZL, 174.
3. John West, *The History of Tasmania* (Launceston, 1852; Adelaide, 1966), ii. 368.
4. NZL, 175.
5. BC, 1.
6. NZL, 163.
7. West, i. 89.
8. MW, 4–5.
9. Janet Penrose Trevelyan, *The Life of Mrs Humphry Ward* (London, 1923), 6.
10. Trevelyan, 2.
11. NZL, 184–5.
12. NZL, 187.
13. L, 5–6.
14. MA, i. 207.
15. MW, 65.
16. BC, 1.
17. NZL, 133–4.
18. NZL, 142.
19. L, 42.
20. L, 45.
21. L, 24.
22. L, 56.
23. TA, 143.
24. NZL, 196.
25. TA, 127.
26. P. A. Howell, *Thomas Arnold the Younger in Van Diemen's Land* (Hobart, 1964), 18.
27. NZL, 193.
28. NZL, 137–8.
29. TA, 136.
30. L, 28.
31. L, 57.

32. L, 88.
33. L, 53.
34. L, 54.
35. Meriol Trevor, *The Arnolds: Thomas Arnold and His Family* (London, 1973), 10.
36. NZL, 153.
37. NZL, 153, 167.
38. TA, 153.
39. JHN, xvi. 500.
40. L, 60–1.
41. L, 56.
42. MW, 7.
43. L, 62–3.
44. L, 67.
45. TA, 155.
46. Information from *Australian Dictionary of Biography.*
47. Julian Huxley, *Memories* (London, 1970), 16.
48. JHN, xxiv, 34.
49. L, 69.

CHAPTER 5

1. MW, 4.
2. L, 75.
3. MW, 4.
4. L, 80.
5. MW, 24.
6. L, 80.
7. Trevelyan, 7.
8. L, 83.
9. MA, i. 349.
10. L, 80–1.
11. JHN, xvii. 417.
12. JHN, xvii. 424.
13. TA, 160.
14. In the following account I am much indebted to Fergal McGrath SJ, *Newman's University: Idea and Reality* (London, 1951).
15. Wilfrid Ward, *The Life of John Henry Cardinal Newman* (London, 1912), i. 355.
16. L, 81.
17. L, 84.
18. L, 85.
19. L, 85.
20. J. E. Axon, 'The Life of Thomas Arnold the Younger', Ph.D. thesis, University of Leeds (1975), 224.

21. TA, 165.
22. Mrs Humphry Ward and C. E. Montague, *William Thomas Arnold* (Manchester, 1907), 5–6.
23. BP for this and subsequent extracts.
24. JHN, xvii. 485.
25. L, 86.
26. BC, 8, 23 July 1858.
27. Howell, 52.
28. JHN, xviii. 188.
29. MA, i. 369.
30. MA, i. 379.
31. *Manchester Guardian* (18 May 1888).
32. L, 92.
33. L, 89.
34. MW, 87–8.
35. Clough, *Correspondence*, ii.555.
36. Ibid., ii. 560.
37. L, 93.
38. JHN, xix. 10.
39. L, 93.
40. L, 100.
41. JHN, xviii. 360.
42. MA, ii. 61.
43. L, 101.
44. BC, 5, 26 August 1859.
45. *The Correspondence of Lord Acton and Richard Simpson*, ed. J. L. Altholz, D. McElrath and J. C. Holland (Cambridge, 1973), i. 212.
46. BC, 5, 5 December 1859.
47. L, 105.
48. Acton–Simpson, ii. 49.
49. L, 109.
50. Acton–Simpson, ii. 120.
51. L, 116.
52. L, 111.
53. Clough, *Correspondence*, ii. 573.
54. L, 107.
55. Acton–Simpson, ii. 57.
56. L, 112.
57. L, 115.
58. L, 113.
59. MA, ii. 20–1.
60. L, 114.
61. MA, ii. 73.
62. JHN, xx. 62–3.

63. W. Ward, ii. 456.
64. MA, ii. 117.

CHAPTER 6

1. L, 118.
2. TA, 167.
3. JHN, xx. 132.
4. JHN, xx. 136.
5. JHN, xx. 164.
6. L, 122.
7. JHN, xx. 268.
8. MA, ii. 125.
9. L, 126.
10. TA, 171.
11. JHN, xx. 268.
12. MA, ii. 155.
13. L, 127.
14. MA, ii. 184.
15. MA, ii. 167, 198.
16. JHN, xx. 480.
17. MA, ii. 118.
18. John Sutherland, *Mrs Humphry Ward: Eminent Victorian, Pre-eminent Edwardian* (Oxford, 1990), 17–19.
19. Sutherland, 13.
20. MA, ii. 222.
21. MW, 95.
22. MW, 99, 136.
23. Trevelyan, 13.
24. Ibid., 8.
25. Ibid., 8.
26. Axon, 305.
27. J. L. Altholz, *The Liberal Catholic Movement in England: The Rambler and its Contributors 1848–1864* (London, 1962), 200.
28. Roland Hill, *Lord Acton* (New Haven and London, 2000), 136.
29. L, 125.
30. L, 126.
31. TA to Acton, 23 December 1862, Acton Papers, Cambridge University Library.
32. L, 132–3.
33. Acton–Simpson, iii. 130.
34. MA, ii. 312.
35. Hill, 137.
36. Ibid., 138.

37. JHN, xx. 294–7.
38. JHN, xx. 291.
39. L, 127.
40. Acton–Simpson, iii. 46.
41. JHN, xx. 352.
42. L, 130.
43. JHN, xxi. 83–4.
44. In 'The Function of Criticism at the Present Time', first published in the *National Review* (November 1864).
45. Owen Chadwick, *A History of the Popes 1830–1914* (Oxford, 1998), 176.
46. L, 142.
47. Acton–Simpson, iii. 189.
48. TA, 176.
49. TA, 173–4.
50. JHN, xxi. 4.
51. L, 138.
52. JHN, xxi. 5.
53. L, 140.
54. TA, 175.
55. TA to Acton, 5 February 1864, Acton Papers, Cambridge University Library.
56. BP, 30 April 1864.
57. MA, ii. 335.
58. MA, ii. 337.
59. JHN, xxi. 205.
60. JHN, xxi. 254.
61. L, 144.
62. JHN, xxi. 284.
63. L, 145.
64. MA, ii. 373.
65. MA, ii. 383.
66. MA, ii. 385.
67. MA, ii. 386.
68. MA, ii. 376.
69. MA, ii. 373.
70. L, 146.
71. Stanley, 35–6.
72. JHN, xxi. 450.
73. L, 151.
74. JHN, xxi. 484.
75. L, 155.
76. L, 160.
77. JHN, 22, 60.
78. L, 220.
79. TA, 179.

80. JHN, xxi. 486.
81. JHN, xx. 480.
82. Acton–Simpson, ii. 250.
83. JHN, xxi. 48.
84. JHN, xxi. 494.
85. JHN, xxii. 19.
86. JHN, xxiv. 34.

CHAPTER 7

1. L, 153–4.
2. Sutherland, 26.
3. MW, 101.
4. BP.
5. BP.
6. BP.
7. L, 158.
8. TA, 204.
9. L, 157.
10. MW, 100.
11. Stefan Collini, *Public Moralists: Political Thought and Intellectual Life in Britain 1850–1930* (Oxford, 1991), 43.
12. TA, 191.
13. M. C. Brock and M. C. Curthoys (eds.), *The History of the University of Oxford*, vol. 7, *The Nineteenth Century*, Part 2 (Oxford, 2000), 120.
14. Tanis Hinchcliffe, *North Oxford* (New Haven and London, 1992), 103–4.
15. MA, iii. 141.
16. L, 162.
17. L, 161.
18. BC, 1.
19. MA, ii. 377.
20. '. . . a man's children are not really *sent*, any more than the pictures on his wall or his horses are *sent* . . .': ch. 6, Pt 4.
21. MW, 102.
22. Henry James, *Letters*, ed. L. Edel, vol. 1 (London, 1974), 111.
23. L, 167.
24. MA, iii. 4.
25. L, 164.
26. MW, 100.
27. Acton–Simpson, iii. 210.
28. Wentworth Huyshe, *Beowulf: An Old English Epic* (London, 1905), 214.
29. BC, 9.
30. MA, iii. 271.

31. MA, iii. 58.
32. MA, iii. 325.
33. Sutherland, 30.
34. L, 168–9.
35. MA, iv. 17.
36. MA, iv. 245.
37. Lewis Carroll, *Letters*, ed. M. N. Cohen (London, 1979), i. 221–2.
38. MA, iv. 304.
39. W. T. Arnold, 126.
40. JHN, xxiv. 34.
41. *Selected English Works of John Wiclif*, vol. 3 (Oxford, 1871), x.
42. L, 163–4.
43. L, 176.
44. BP, Jan.–Feb. 1866.
45. BP.
46. Trevelyan, xvi. 26.
47. Julian Huxley, *Memories* (London, 1970), 17.
48. MW, 100.
49. BP, 30 Nov 1868.
50. Trevor, 183.
51. BC, 10.
52. L, 176.
53. L, 177.
54. W. S. Peterson, *Victorian Heretic: Mrs Humphry Ward's Robert Elsmere* (Leicester, 1976), 39.
55. L, 178.
56. BC, 3.
57. L, 179.
58. Brock and Curthoys, 57.
59. L, 179.
60. Trevelyan, 1–2.
61. BP, 14 March 1876.
62. MA, iv. 330.
63. BC, 3.
64. Chadwick, *The Victorian Church*, Part 2 (London, 1970), 441.
65. L, 182.
66. BC, 10.
67. *Oxford University Gazette*, October 1876.
68. Lewis Carroll, *Diaries*, ed. R. L. Green (London, 1953), ii. 356.
69. Enid Huws Jones, *Mrs Humphry Ward* (London, 1973), 51.
70. L, 183.
71. L, 184.
72. L, 185.
73. BP, 19 October 1876.

74. L, 185.
75. L, 182–3.
76. JHN, xxviii. 157.
77. MA, iv. 352.

CHAPTER 8

1. BP.
2. See Mrs Humphry Ward and C. E. Montague, *William Thomas Arnold* (Manchester, 1907).
3. MA, iii. 34.
4. MA, iv. 290.
5. L, 189.
6. L, 191.
7. BC, 5.
8. L, 209.
9. Part II: Ch. I.
10. Part II: Ch. VIII.
11. MA, iv. 90.
12. Trevelyan, 27.
13. BC, 4, 12 June 1880.
14. L, 194.
15. MA, iv. 436.
16. L, 198.
17. Exon, 320.
18. L, 199.
19. L, 199–200.
20. L, 190–2.
21. Trevelyan, 8.
22. L, 201.
23. BC, 4, 22 April 1880.
24. L, 202.
25. MA, v. 28.
26. BC, 6, 26 June 1879.
27. T. J. Morrissey SJ, *Towards a National University* (Dublin, 1983), 57.
28. Collected in his *Mixed Essays* in 1879.
29. MA, v. 89.
30. TA, 205.
31. JHN, xxx. 282.
32. BP.
33. MA, v. 201.

CHAPTER 9

1. Mary Daly, 'Dublin in the 1880s', in *Hopkins and Dublin: The Man & the City*, special issue of the *Hopkins Quarterly*, 14, 1–4 (1987–8), 97.
2. Daly, 98.
3. Gerard Manley Hopkins, *Further Letters*, ed. C. C. Abbott, 2nd edn. (London, 1970), 63, 413.
4. Norman White, *Hopkins: A Literary Biography* (Oxford, 1992), 369.
5. BC, 4.
6. Ward Papers, Pusey House, Oxford.
7. L, 205.
8. Morrissey, 60.
9. Ibid. 138.
10. *The Correspondence of Gerard Manley Hopkins with Richard Watson Dixon*, ed. C. C. Abbott, 2nd edn. (London, 1970), 123.
11. *Dublin Review*, April 1887, 243–65.
12. L, 207.
13. L, 207.
14. Hopkins, *Further Letters*, 424.
15. MA, iv. 422–3.
16. Brock and Curthoys, 398.
17. Sutherland, 113.
18. Collini, 15–16.
19. BC, 6, 8 March 1884.
20. L, 211.
21. L, 213.
22. L, 211.
23. Lewis Carroll, *Letters*, ed. M. N. Cohen (London, 1979), i. 560.
24. MA, vi. 67.
25. Carroll, ii. 663.
26. L, 214.
27. BP.
28. Hopkins, *Letters to Robert Bridges*, ed. C. C. Abbott, 2nd edn. (London, 1970), 269.
29. Carroll, ii. 696 n.
30. L, 216–17.
31. L, 217.
32. MW, 239.

CHAPTER 10

1. L, 219.
2. L, 221.
3. L, p. xxxii.

4. MA, vi. 361.
5. L, 219.
6. L, 221–2.
7. Trevelyan, 54.
8. See Peterson for a detailed account of the novel's genesis, composition, and reputation.
9. Sutherland, 170.
10. BP; transcribed by Susan Ward, original missing.
11. BP.
12. Sutherland, 170.
13. BP.
14. BP, January 1890.
15. L, 226.
16. BP.
17. L, 229.
18. *A Page of Irish History: Story of University College, Dublin 1883–1909*, compiled by Fathers of the Society of Jesus (Dublin, 1930), 90.
19. BP, Lottie Geary to James Benison, 11 September 1895.
20. BP, 17 November 1900.
21. *Page of Irish History*, 89.
22. *Page of Irish History*, 124, 241.
23. TA, 205–6.
24. L, 225.
25. L, 224.
26. L, 229.
27. Quoted in *Bishops and Writers: Aspects of the Evolution of Modern English Catholicism*, ed. J. Coventry (Wheathampstead, 1977), 25.
28. Sutherland, 171.
29. BP, to Joe Benison.
30. *Page of Irish History*, 89.
31. L, 236.
32. L, 237.
33. BC, 5.
34. Trevelyan, 144.
35. Ibid., 143–4.
36. Sutherland, 154.
37. Trevelyan, 146.
38. BP.
39. BP, 6 August 1898.
40. TA, 225.
41. BP, September 1898.
42. MW, 343.
43. BC, 5, 9 March 1900.
44. Sutherland, 235.

45. In the Ward Papers, Pusey House, Oxford.
46. BP.
47. In Michael Tierney (ed.), *Struggle with Fortune* (Dublin, 1954), 222–3.
48. C. P. Curran, *James Joyce Remembered* (London, 1968), 8.
49. Stanislaus Joyce, *My Brother's Keeper* (London, 1958), 113.
50. BP.
51. TA, p. vi.
52. L, 236.
53. L, 245.
54. L, 243–4.
55. Sutherland, 236–7.
56. L, 246.
57. Quotations from Mary Ward in Trevelyan, 174.
58. BP.

Index